Pitman Business Correspondence

Geoffrey Whitehead BSc (Econ)
and David H Whitehead MA BEd

D1665831

Pitman

PITMAN PUBLISHING LIMITED
128 Long Acre, London WC2E 9AN

Associated Companies
Pitman Publishing Pty Ltd, Melbourne
Pitman Publishing New Zealand Ltd, Wellington
Copp Clark Pitman, Toronto

Text set in IBM Press Roman by Morgan-Westley, Bristol
Printed and bound in Great Britain
at The Bath Press, Avon

ISBN 0 273 01797 7

Contents

Preface

The role of the business letter has changed in recent years, for we live in an age of instantaneous communication around the world. Much routine correspondence has been replaced by quick telephone calls to make inquiries, answer queries, discuss proposals, make complaints and deal with many other business problems. This has not lessened the importance of correspondence: instead its effect has been to increase the importance of the average letter. Written correspondence is now reserved for the serious matters of business life: the formal proposal, the offer and acceptance which make a legally binding contract, the letter of appointment, claims and counter-claims, etc.

This book seeks to place business correspondence in its proper position as a central feature of formal business communication: that point where business people are in contact with one another to fix prices, arrange supplies and agree terms for services to be rendered. Each of these major areas is explained and discussed. Offer, acknowledgment of the offer, acceptance of the offer, fulfilment of orders, payment of the price, imports, exports, carriage, insurance, banking, agency and other areas are fully covered.

It is hoped the book will be helpful to students in many subjects: office practice, commerce, secretarial studies, business administration, etc. The general field of business communication, both 'in house' and between firms and companies, is covered, and a short English appendix in each chapter covers many of the problem areas for those whose English is weak. It is hoped that the practical activity of letter-writing will assist the vocabulary and the self-expression of students and young executives alike.

In writing this book we have been greatly helped by the cooperative attitude of many firms and organisations who have kindly agreed to supply typical letters, and to sanction the use of their letterheads and house styles. Their names are listed in the Acknowledgments pages. It has been impossible to name all the individuals who have answered questions for us on particular aspects of the subject-matter, but their unfailing courtesy and forbearance is much appreciated. We should particularly like to express our thanks to Margaret Berriman for her encouragement of the project, and to David's wife, Anne, not only for her indefatigable typing, but also for her criticism and appraisal of the text.

GEOFFREY M WHITEHEAD
DAVID H WHITEHEAD

Acknowledgments

This book contains many specimen letters. Some of these letters are from genuine firms who have given permission for letters to be reproduced. Their courtesy is acknowledged below. All other firms are entirely imaginary and no reference to an existing firm is intended or implied in any way whatsoever. Every attempt has been made to check that names do not conflict with real names of real people.

The following organisations have kindly permitted the use of letters in this textbook, and have gone to considerable trouble to provide them, and to permit the use of letterheads, etc. The authors are most appreciative of their courtesy and cooperation.

Agovox Answering Ltd, 4 Sydenham Road, London SE26 5QY

Automobile Association Insurance Services Ltd, Monmouth Road, Cheadle Hulme, Cheadle, Cheshire SK8 7BT

T D Bailey Dairy Products Ltd, 28 Brighton Road, Crawley, West Sussex RH10 6AE

Barbican Centre for Arts and Conferences, 11 Cromwell Tower, Barbican, London EC2Y 8DD

Barclays Bank International Ltd, 168 Fenchurch Street, London EC3P 3HP

A & C Black Ltd, 35 Bedford Row, London WC1R 4JH (for permission to refer to *Titles and Forms of Address — A Guide to Their Correct Use*)

Josiah Brown Ltd, West Gate, Long Eaton, Nottingham NG10 1EG

Chewton Glen Hotel, New Milton, Hampshire BH25 6QS

Collins (William), Sons and Co, Ltd, 14 St James's Place, London SW1A 1PS (for permission to use extracts from *Roget's International Thesaurus,* 3rd edition, and *Collins New World Thesaurus*)

Croner Publications Ltd, Croner House, 173 Kingston Road, New Malden, Surrey KT3 3SS

Easibind Ltd, Eardley House, 4 Uxbridge Street, Kensington, London W8 7SZ

Esso Petroleum Co Ltd, Esso House, Victoria Street, London SW1E 5JW

Executemps Ltd, Atlantic House, 351 Oxford Street, London W1R 1FA

Formecon Services Ltd, Gateway, Crewe CW1 1YN (for permission to reproduce documents of various sorts)

Gray Cook and Partners, 27 St Andrews Street, Cambridge CB2 3BS

GKN Sankey Ltd, Marketing Department, St John's House, St John's Square, Wolverhampton WV2 4BH

International Federation of Freight Forwarders Association, 29 Brauerstrasse, POB 177, Ch 8026, Zurich, Switzerland

Office of Fair Trading, Field House, Bream's Buildings, London EC4A 1PR

Park Air Services Ltd, Room 1129, Building 521, Stansted Road, Heathrow Airport London, Hounslow, Middlesex TW6 3LX

Pitman Examinations Institute, Godalming, Surrey GU7 1UU

R G Reis and Co Ltd, 10 Jesus Lane, Cambridge CB5 8BA

Stadt Solingen, Der Oberstadtdirektor, Postfach 10 01 65, D5650, Solingen 1, West Germany

Tyzack and Partners Ltd, 10 Hallam Street, London W1N 6DJ

George Vyner Ltd, PO Box 1, Holmfirth, Huddersfield HD7 2RP

1 Correspondence and the pattern of business communication today

1.1 The changing pattern of business communication

We live in a world of instantaneous communication. Telex machines rattle away in the dark offices of Australia receiving the messages tapped out by operators in the day-lit offices of the United Kingdom. Our evening news bulletins show us the waves actually breaking in some tornado-hit town in the Gulf of Mexico. Facsimile documents transmitted in four minutes from London to Singapore arrive before the air freighter carrying the cargo has asked for clearance for take-off at London Airport. In such a world of electronic miracles traditional business correspondence seems out of place. One firm estimated recently that every letter it produced cost at least £5, even though it placed enormous emphasis on secretarial efficiency. Barclays Bank, through its Visa-Barclaycard system, can check the credit card of an American tourist, including searching a computer file of stolen cards in the computer centre in America, in less than eight seconds. Even at peak charges for transatlantic calls this only costs fourteen pence, and that precious few seconds when the bank, the retailer, the customer and the American computer are all in contact with one another cements their business relationship. A few seconds later a satisfied customer departs with a gift-wrapped parcel; a satisfied retailer has a signed payment voucher for the price and a confirmation number from Barclaycard to prove its reliability; the bank has the prospect of earning some interest on the funds it has made available, and the computer is busy with someone else. In such a world, who needs correspondence?

1.2 The enduring nature of the business letter

The answer to the question 'Who needs correspondence?' is that we all do. Of course traditional business correspondence must yield pride of place in many situations to the telephone, the telex, the facsimile copier and transmitter. Where there is an emergency, or where time is money, and instantaneous communication is cost-effective, we shall use the facilities available. Where there is plenty of time, or the matter will not particularly benefit from the personal link which the telephone establishes, the traditional method may be cheaper, more certain and more deliberate than the electronic method. It is unlikely that correspondence will ever be entirely replaced as a means of communication between businesses. We may list the following reasons, among others:

a Business correspondence is a permanent, tangible record of a business relationship.

b It is admissible as evidence in the courts, and will often prove the existence of a contract to the satisfaction of the court. The vast majority of business activities result in contracts of one sort or another. Written evidence that a contract was being negotiated, or that certain representations had been made, and in what exact circumstances, etc. may be invaluable at a later date. It is of fundamental importance in business correspondence that the legal implications of what is being written or dictated should be borne in mind.

c Correspondence is a more formal and deliberate method of communication than conversation, discussion and debate. In speech we may rely on conveying a meaning by the tone of the voice, or the words used may be chosen on the spur of the moment and not be the best for the purpose. With correspondence it is possible to polish and improve the letter until it says exactly what we intend; a precise, clear, unambiguous statement of our point of view. We can deal with the most complex subject-matter in logical order, building from a basic presentation of our case to a detailed analysis of any part that requires amplification or elucidation.

1.3 Functions of the business letter

Business letters provide a channel for communication between business houses and a permanent record of that communication from the standpoint of the writer. Whether the record is an accurate one is quite another matter, but it is clearly wise for the recipient of a letter which appears to include some mis-statement or misunderstanding to rebut the incorrect statement without delay.

We must choose the form of a letter to suit the particular circumstances. Factors entering into the choice include the following:

2

a Economy. Since all letters cost money, we must keep communication costs down by using the most economical method possible. Quick-reply letters and standard-form letters will frequently serve the purpose just as well as conventional letters.

b Speed. Certain correspondence may justify the employment of courier services or express or special delivery services.

c Distribution. Certain items of correspondence are of interest to individuals only; others require circulation or distribution. Circulars may have a very wide distribution, other letters may be circulated to named individuals or copied to all those interested.

d Secrecy. It may be necessary to ensure reasonable secrecy, or even absolute secrecy, about a matter under consideration. There may even be a duty of care to ensure that information does not become common knowledge. This would be true in many legal matters, in medical correspondence, in personnel matters, in arrangements about mergers, takeovers, patents, etc.

e Special clauses. Frequently legal safeguards require standard clauses to be adopted in certain types of letters, and serious consequences might follow a failure to include them. Examples are exclusionary clauses in contracts of carriage; service and maintenance clauses in contracts for hire or supply of capital equipment; restrictive covenants in leases, etc.

While all these requirements are only incidental to the objective of correspondence as a channel of communication between business houses, they can be crucial in ensuring that the firm's viewpoint is properly expressed, carefully worded and with the desired legal effect should litigation ever arise.

1.4   How to write effective letters

Business correspondence will only be effective if the writer knows exactly what he wishes to say, and expresses himself/herself clearly. For important letters it is advisable to write down the main points on a note pad first, so that the subject-matter for the letter has been carefully considered and the points numbered in a logical sequence. The task is then reduced to one where we have to express ourselves crisply and clearly about each particular point.

The concept of the paragraph is important. A sentence is a set of words which express a complete thought. A paragraph is a set of sentences which deal with a complete topic. Just occasionally a single sentence may deal adequately with a whole topic, but this would be exceptional. Paragraphs of only one sentence give a staccato effect which can be abrupt and irritating. If points have been arranged in a logical sequence, they will fall into paragraphs fairly easily. Some will group together into a single paragraph; others may form the basis for a complete paragraph of several sentences. In general long paragraphs should be avoided, unless a particular theme takes time to develop and maintains the reader's interest because of the sequence within the paragraph. The danger with long paragraphs is that the reader will lose the thread of the argument, or become bored with the topic.

The content of the paragraph should be crisp. Crispness comes from the use of exactly the right words. The reader is strongly recommended to buy a good medium-size dictionary and a *Roget's Thesaurus* at once. A dictionary helps us to spell, and also to know the exact meaning of a word we were proposing to use. If in doubt, check the dictionary meaning before you actually use the word in your letter.

A thesaurus (the word means 'treasury') is a treasury of words. With a dictionary we know a word and we look up its meaning. With a thesaurus we know the idea we are trying to convey, but we cannot think of the best word. One part of the thesaurus is an index of ideas. Let us use the idea 'exact' to illustrate the use of a thesaurus. In the index of ideas under the word 'exact' we have:

verbs		*adjectives*	
	extract		detailed
	require		faithful
	demand		limited
	oblige		precise
	wrest from		meticulous
	assess		literal
	levy		formal

There are obviously many ideas suggested by the one word 'exact', but I am thinking about the choice of the 'exact word' to express my thoughts in a letter. Of the words listed 'precise' is closest to the idea I have in mind. The index shows:

precise 515.15

Turning to section 515.15 I find:

exact, precise, express, direct, just, even, square, definite, positive, absolute, absolutely, definitely or positively right, distinct, clear-cut, clean-cut, well-defined; faithful, servile; unerring, undeviating; strict, stern, severe, rigorous, rigid, mathematically exact, mathematical; scientifically exact, scientific; religiously exact, religious, nice, delicate, subtle, fine, refined; pinpoint.

Our letter-writing will improve considerably if we develop the habit of using a thesaurus to find the exact, precise, absolutely right word for every occasion.

Some words are 'slang'; words in popular usage but not considered to be part of formal English. The use of slang is not advisable in business correspondence. The meaning may not be understood by the recipient of the letter, or the use of slang may lower the writer in the estimation of the addressee. The best rule is 'formal English for all business correspondence'. Remember that if litigation arises and correspondence is produced in court a judge may feel that the use of informal expressions detracts from the certainty of the statements made.

To use formal English is one thing; to be excessively formal, cold and impersonal is another. We must remember that our correspondent is a human being with his/her own personal attitudes to almost every subject under the sun. To fail to take these personal points of view into account may result in a lost order or an indifferent attitude to our needs on the part of the correspondent. Everyone knows that a contract has to be mutually satisfactory or it will never be made.

The writer of effective letters will usually make good use of the power of suggestion. When we wish our correspondent to believe something we suggest that he will. It is easy to suggest that the quality of goods is excellent, that their price is low, that a commission to be paid is generous, that an arrangement for payment is reasonable or a concession given is valuable. Often these ideas are better implied than actually expressed.

Most people are susceptible to compliments. Such phrases as 'You will remember' or 'You will appreciate' imply that the writer believes the correspondent to be a person of affairs, with a balanced understanding of both the matter in hand and business in general. It conveys the writer's own appreciation of, and respect for, the correspondent, without making any direct statement to that effect.

Courtesy is essential in business correspondence. However crisp the content, however brief the letter, we should not be so brief that we are discourteous. We cannot succeed in business on the strength of a single transaction; we need the continuing goodwill both of our customers and our suppliers. The salutation and the close of a letter give an opportunity to express the usual courtesies of correspondence, and promote the goodwill that is essential between business houses.

1.5   The impact of technology on correspondence

Many matters which are of a complex nature cannot be brought into their final form at once, and it is quite common for important letters and reports to be produced in 'draft' form. A draft is a preliminary copy, for subsequent improvement. The resulting retyping can be tedious. Fortunately the latest secretarial technology removes much of this labour. The cost of word processing systems is reducing all the time, and they are now within the reach of almost all offices.

The essential feature of a word processing system is that the draft of any letter is recorded on a memory device at the same time as the draft is typed. The 'memory' may be magnetic card, or a tape cassette, or the floppy-disk memory of a mini-computer. At any future time the 'memory' can be recalled to retype the letter at high speed, stopping at each point where a correction, alteration or insertion is to be made. Mini-computers may display the letter on a visual display unit (VDU) so that the corrections or insertions can be made and the subsequent rearrangements, moving the original text to make room, etc. can be seen.

Clearly word processing systems have much to recommend them and should assist both executives and secretarial staff to produce the impeccable correspondence which is the hallmark of an efficient organisation.

1.6   About this book

The good business correspondent is made, not born. Practice makes perfect, and in serving an apprenticeship we can learn much from considering good examples of the work of established craftsmen. Many of the letters in this book have been written by experienced managers who agreed to co-operate in providing specimen letters. They have their own personal style, and very often have written the letters in the 'house style' laid down by their particular companies. They thus exercise a personal choice of phrase and content within a 'house style' of presentation designed to give uniformity to the correspondence leaving a particular business house.

The specimen letters thus assembled in each chapter are recommended for close study, but readers are advised not to learn them by heart. You cannot pass examinations merely by repeating someone else's letters which your photographic memory, or sheer hard work, has enabled you to learn by heart. What you have to do is take in the layout and the style of the letters, and then to develop a style of your own which makes use of the knowledge you have acquired. You must practise writing your own letters in a similar style to the specimen letters, but about different subject-matter and using phrases which seem to you to be appropriate in the quite different situation that you are considering.

The practice material which is provided at the end of each chapter should help you to improve your letter-writing over a period. You should not be satisfied with the work you have done until you have written a letter for every question in every chapter. Clearly that is not the work of a week, or a month, but a solid year's work of conscientious effort. It will be impossible for any teacher to mark every exercise you attempt, so you will have to rely on self-criticism for much of what you write. This is exactly what happens in real life: an executive writes or dictates a letter, and revises it until it satisfies him/her. You must develop your own critical faculty, and set your own high standard of what is acceptable.

At the end of each chapter there is a short 'English' section which it is hoped will help you to develop your own use of the English language. Gradually, by repetition of words and phrases and the extension of your vocabulary, you will produce good business correspondence. Return regularly to these earlier sections as you progress through the book, and revise the points covered in them. The secret is the conscientious application of knowledge acquired earlier, to new circumstances.

At the end of this book there is a 'Glossary of Terms' which defines the technical words and phrases printed in **bold** in the text.

The Romans had a phrase *festina lente*; it means 'hasten slowly'. We all want to qualify as quickly as possible, but there are no short cuts in education, and conscientious work over a long period is the best way to ensure success. It is no good starting work one month before the examinations. The vital months of any course of study are the first few months when you establish a system of study which breaks the new ground with determination, improves it with steady and patient effort over a long period and prepares it for the intensive cultivation of the months ahead. Get down to hard work as soon as your course begins, not three weeks before the end.

1.7 Appendix on the English language: sentences and clauses

A sentence is a group of words which expresses a complete thought, and has meaning. In order to be meaningful, two elements are necessary, a *subject* (a person or thing to be considered) and a *predicate* (something to be said about the person or thing under consideration). Occasionally the subject is left out, because it is understood, as when a sentry shouts 'Halt!'. The subject of that sentence, which is understood, is the person approaching, for the sentry might have shouted:

'(You) halt!'

Sentences may be classified in two ways, according to use or according to structure. Classified by use there are four types:

a Sentences which make statements or declarations about the subject, called **declarative sentences**:
  i 'Economics is the study of mankind in the everyday business of life.'
  ii This machine has an operating speed of 5000 revolutions per minute.
b Sentences which ask questions, called **interrogative sentences**:
  i Can you deliver the machine by September?
  ii Are you a qualified accountant?
c Sentences which give commands, called **imperative sentences**, because they have to be obeyed:
  i Halt at the major road ahead.
  ii Use the red channel if you have anything to declare.
d Sentences which give expression to strong feelings, called **exclamatory sentences**:
  i Impossible!
  ii Enough, it's time for a decision!

Clearly we do not make much use of exclamatory sentences in business correspondence.

Classified by structure, we have four different kinds again: **simple** sentences, **compound** sentences, **complex** sentences and **compound-complex** sentences. **Simple sentences** have one subject and one predicate:

a Harrods is a famous London store.
b Manama is the capital of Bahrain.

The other types, which are not simple, consist of a number of **clauses**. A clause is a part of a sentence which has its own subject and predicate. In each of the three types described below we have a sentence which has more than one subject and predicate, because it has more than one clause.

Compound sentences have two or more main clauses, which are of equal importance and independent of one another:

a Production engineering is a science, but management is an art.
b Man proposes; God disposes.

Complex sentences contain one main clause and one or more subordinate (dependent) clauses:

a The microprocessor is the most brilliant technological development *that has ever been achieved.* (The subordinate clause is in *italics*.)
b Professor Einstein was the most gifted mathematician *who ever came to live in this country.*

Compound-complex sentences contain two or more main clauses and one or more subordinate clauses:

a *However much money we spend on it* dispatch department will never be more than a dreary shed; export department will always be a more exciting department. (There are two main clauses separated by a semi-colon. The subordinate clause is in *italics*.)
b Foreign trade is of crucial importance, *which explains its inclusion in the statistics*; home trade does not affect the roll-on roll-off ferries, *and consequently can be omitted from the tables.*

In developing your ability to write business letters, you should return again and again to this analysis of sentences. Business correspondence written entirely in simple sentences would be disjointed and tedious to read. You should gradually develop your ability to write compound, complex and compound-complex sentences.

1.8 Exercises on the use of sentences

Special note: In this book the instructions given in the exercise sections require the student to 'write' answers to the questions. You are asked to treat this instruction as meaning 'type' whenever you have a typewriter available. Not all readers may have their own typewriter, and correspondence can be practised long-hand just as easily, but the authors believe that everyone should learn to type if possible, and the normal form of business correspondence would be the typewritten letter.

1 Copy out the following sentences and say in brackets at the end whether they are declarative, interrogative, imperative or exclamatory sentences.
   a Danger, keep out!
   b The price of this filing cabinet is £85.
   c How beautiful you are!
   d Have you obtained an export licence for this equipment.

2 Write a simple sentence about each of the following:
   a Energy.
   b Agriculture.
   c Foreign currency.
   d New Year's Day.

3 Write a complex sentence about each of the following:
   a A recent natural disaster somewhere in the world.
   b Air transport.
   c The typewriter you use, or the one you would like to own.
   d A public figure you admire in your own country.

4 Choose two of the following topics. Write five sentences about each. They may be simple, compound, complex or compound-complex sentences:
   a The importance of family life.
   b The role of business in the life of your own country.
   c The protection of the environment from the business point of view.
   d Space exploration.
   e The importance of transport.

2 The layout of a business letter

2.1 The component parts of a letter

A letter consists of a number of parts, each of which is essential to the letter, or contributes in some way to its impact on the recipient. We may list them as follows:

a the letterhead
b the references
c the date
d the inside name and address
e the salutation
f the subject heading
g the opening paragraph
h the body of the letter
i the closing paragraph
j the complimentary close
k the signature
l enclosures and copies.

A detailed explanation of the importance of each of these parts is given later in this chapter. Every file of correspondence begins with an introductory letter, often an offer of goods or services by a supplier, or a request for goods or services from a customer. The layout of such a letter may be crucial. A slovenly, badly set out letter may create a poor impression on the recipient who will consequently fail to respond to the invitation to do business. As a business correspondent you should remember that in the early stages of any transaction the only link between you and your customer or supplier is the letter which you are drafting. By using an acceptable style of correspondence, which includes the essential elements listed above, you will ensure that all the necessary information for establishing a sound business relationship is included. Imagine a situation where your chief supplier of a vital component is taken over by another firm and well-established relationships with sales staff are broken. The new owners must be made aware of the reliance you place upon their supplies, so that they can read the files and make themselves familiar with your requirements and the terms and conditions which have been established over the years. Therefore, while the first letter is vital, every letter has an enduring importance as part of the file of correspondence in each business.

It is essential that copies are taken of all business correspondence, for human memory is fallible and a complete file is the only certain way of ensuring that a proper account of a business relationship is available. At times when memos, telex messages or 'standard form' letters are sent there may be a tendency not to keep copies, but it is very undesirable that files should be incomplete in this way.

In business correspondence the style of a letter is important and firms frequently lay down a 'house style'. In this book the style is usually as recommended in Pitman's *Universal Typing*, by Edith Mackay. Students who are combining a study of business correspondence with typing training are recommended to buy a copy.

2.2 The recipient: to whom shall we write?

Many firms embody in their letterheads a requirement to address correspondence to a particular individual. Thus 'Please address all correspondence to the managing director' gives a tight system of control on correspondence inwards, while an 'in-house' requirement to staff to have all letters signed by the same individual gives an equally effective control on correspondence outwards. Clearly there will be occasions when the managing director is not available and someone else must act on his/her behalf, while in large organisations it will be quite impracticable and there must be delegation of authority in this respect. Often the idea is preserved that top management is entitled to see all correspondence inwards, while all outwards correspondence is written in its name. Thus even junior members of staff may answer routine inquiries but will be trained to regard themselves as writing on behalf of top management, so that a slovenly letter would be quite inappropriate and a proper degree of care must be shown at all times.

In general we should address our letters so that they are directed at once to the most appropriate person in the organisation to which we are writing. This may be a named individual, or the holder of a particular post. If it is a rule that all correspondence must be addressed to a particular official we can still expedite the letter by putting an *attention line*. Typical attention lines might be as follows:

> Attention of Mr Giles Micawber
> Attention: Brian Senior, Esq., sales director
> CONFIDENTIAL: Attention of the personnel officer
> PERSONAL ATTENTION OF MR T PALMER

The attention line may be underscored for extra emphasis. Although the firm may reserve the right to open all correspondence such letters would usually be put at once into the tray of the person named, and confidential or personal letters would not be opened.

2.3 Styles of address

It is important in business correspondence to use the correct style of address. While some holders of titles and other distinguishing marks of honour or office may be indifferent to their use in the correct style, you cannot possibly know whether this is the case, and it is better to err on the side of formality. Later, a closer acquaintance may enable you to adopt a simpler form.

A useful and economical handbook on such matters is *Titles and Forms of Address – A Guide to Their Correct Use,* published by A & C Black, 35 Bedford Row, London, WC1R 4JH. This book gives both formal and less formal manners of address and is a vital reference book for every office. If your office does not have a copy it is desirable to obtain one.

2.4 The letterhead

Since letters are often elements in the formation of business contracts it is essential to have the addresses of both parties included in every item of business correspondence. Should any contract follow from the correspondence, or any representations made in the letter eventually become important, there is no doubt about the parties concerned. It would be tedious to type the sender's name and address every time a letter was sent, when it is possible to use a printed letterhead bearing this information. By having a printed letterhead a firm ensures that it includes all the necessary details about its own name, address, postcode, telephone number and telex number. In some countries there are regulations about the inclusion of other details. For example the European Community makes each member of the

Community pass a European Communities Act which requires companies to include the following details:

a The place of registration of the company, and its *registered number* as shown on its *certificate of incorporation.*

b The address of the company's registered office, which may not be the same as the address appearing on the letterhead itself.

c The expression 'limited liability' if the company is one that is excused from using the word 'Limited' at the end of its name.

d Any reference to the company's capital must be the paid-up capital and not the 'authorised capital' since sometimes the authorised capital cannot in fact be collected and consequently would give a false impression.

The Companies Acts 1948-81 in the United Kingdom require that the names of the directors of companies shall be given, with their nationality if other than British.

Printed letterheads may include spaces for some details, such as 'Your Reference . . . .' and 'Our Reference . . . .' while a telephone number may finish 'Extension . . . .'.

Several of the letters in this book are reproduced photographically and the details given on the letterhead can be studied. Other letters give the sender's name and address, which the student should type in the top nine lines of space if an A5 portrait paper is being used, or in the top twelve lines of A4 paper.

2.5 Open and full punctuation

The term 'full punctuation' implies that every comma, inverted comma, abbreviation point, etc. will be included as in traditional correspondence. Today the trend is towards reducing all punctuation to a minimum, and thus speeding-up and simplifying the typist's work. Punctuation is only used if it contributes to the reader's understanding of the letter. Thus a celebrated tax in Europe is called Value Added Tax, which when abbreviated and fully punctuated becomes V.A.T. Leaving out these abbreviation points does not reduce our understanding, and the tax is often referred to as VAT. Similarly decorations and honours are understood if the punctuation is omitted; DFC is still understood as Distinguished Flying Cross and GM still stands for George Medal.

Although the majority of business houses favour open punctuation in addresses, references, etc., there is no rule that either method must be used, unless this is laid down as part of the rules for 'house style' by your employer. If a particular executive prefers full punctuation you should use it, but in general open punctuation is acceptable and saves time and paper.

2.6 The use of references

References are essential if we are to be able to trace a particular letter at any time. Disputes about delivery dates, prices, terms and conditions of sale and countless other matters constantly arise, and a sound rebuttal of claims and misrepresentations is only possible if we can quote from earlier correspondence.

The reference usually consists of the initials of the executive who dictated the letter followed by the initials of the secretary who typed it. The executive's initials are usually in upper case (capital) letters; the secretary's initials are sometimes typed in lower case. The two sets of initials may be divided by a solidus (the oblique sign) or a full stop. They may include a file number, or a departmental code of some sort. When giving the reference of a previous letter, to which the present letter is a reply, it is helpful to give the date of the earlier letter. Typical references might therefore be:

Your ref   DHW/AW/22 October 19--
Our ref   PTR/ab

If the letterhead includes a place for references the references will be typed in the space provided, otherwise they are put immediately below the printed letterhead. The reference to earlier correspondence, 'Your ref', etc., should precede 'Our ref', as shown above.

2.7 The date

Every letter should bear a date. Typists and secretaries should always use the actual date of typing unless positively instructed otherwise. If you are dictating letters for someone else to type always give clear instructions about the date if it has any special significance. Where a letter is prepared in advance of a mailing for some reason it may be appropriate to date the letter – Date as postmark.

The recommended order for dates is day, month, year, with open punctuation. Thus 20 November 1982 is perfectly clear, and punctuation would not add anything. In this book the numerous dates given

at the start of the letters are written with the year expressed as 19--.
The reader is asked to type the current year in place of the two dashes.

2.8   The inside name and address

At the top of a letter, below the references and the date, the secretary
types the 'inside name and address'. This is the name and address of
the person to whom the letter is to be sent: the addressee. The name
and address is typed in exactly the same way as on the envelope, in
single spacing, with the town typed in capital letters. Each part of
the address is written on a new line, including the postcode. A
typical address would be:

> Mr T Williamson
> 67 Camside
> Church Street
> Chesterton
> CAMBRIDGE
> CB4 1PQ

Note that this address has been typed with open punctuation.

The inside name and address serves several useful functions. It is of
course the name and address of the other party to the correspondence
and may therefore have to be presented as evidence in the courts at
some future time. It makes the letter complete, so that the envelope
in which the letter was sent ceases to be important and can be dis-
carded by the addressee when it has been opened. The inside address
also enables the secretary to match up the letter after signature with
the envelope typed in readiness for dispatch. It enables any carbon
copies distributed to be understood, and the file copy to be filed
correctly.

2.9   The salutation

A salutation is a greeting. It appears at the start of a letter and will
usually be formal, Dear Sir, Dear Sirs, Dear Madam, Dear Mr Brown,
Dear Mrs Smith, etc. On a less formal note the secretary may be
asked to type in the word Dear . . . leaving the first name of the
addressee to be filled in by the signatory when the letter is signed.
Thus the signatory might write in the word 'John', to read Dear
John. This method also requires a change to the complimentary
closure of the letter (see section 2.14 below). Some types of letter

16

are addressed to the world at large, for example a testimonial given to an employee who is applying for a post elsewhere. In such circumstances we do not know who will be the eventual addressee — the letter may be photocopied and sent to several potential employers. A suitable salutation in such circumstances is 'To Whom it May Concern'.

There is a close link between the salutation, the complimentary close and the signature. This is explained more fully in section 2.14 below.

2.10 The subject heading

The subject heading is inserted after the salutation. In the fully blocked letter (see section 2.17 below) it is usually typed in closed capitals, without underscoring, though if preferred it may be in initial capitals with underscoring. A subject heading should not end with a full stop. Typical subject headings would be:

SALE OF PROPERTY IN THE RIVERSIDE DISTRICT

or:

Catalytic Cracking Tower: Annual Shut-down

2.11 The opening paragraph

The opening paragraph is often only a single sentence. It is introductory in nature and frequently refers to a previous letter, or course of dealings. It should always be courteous, but it should also set the tone of the letter. This may be friendly, or formal, or it may hint at serious matters which the body of the letter will soon make plain.

2.12 The body of the letter

This is the main subject-matter of the letter, and is divided into an appropriate number of paragraphs. Chapter 1 includes some suggestions for writing effective letters. The reader should practise writing many hundreds of letters during a business correspondence course.

2.13 The closing paragraph

The closing paragraph is again usually a single sentence which re-establishes the atmosphere of courtesy whatever has been the nature of the body of the letter. It is frequently used to signal the action which the writer hopes will follow from the letter. The following examples will illustrate the point:

a I am obliged for your help, and look forward to receiving a copy of your speech as soon as the reprints are available from the printer.
b I must repeat that the Board takes a serious view of the situation, and hopes to receive your cheque by return of post.

2.14 The complimentary close

The complimentary close comes at the end of the letter. It usually consists of two words only: Yours faithfully, Yours truly and Yours sincerely being commonly used. Only the first word, Yours, has a capital letter. In cases where the salutation has been written Dear . . . . to allow the signatory to the letter to write a personal salutation, the complimentary close can be left out so that a more personal 'close' can be written in by the signatory before the letter is signed. This personal close would require extra space to be left and should be followed by the remainder of the signature block (see below).

The correct complimentary close to be linked to particular forms of salutation is shown in Table 2.1. Small variations will be found in practice. For the methods of address for royalty, members of the peerage, etc., see the reference book referred to on page 13.

TABLE 2.1

Salutation		Complimentary close
1 Dear Sir, Dear Sirs		Yours faithfully
Dear Madam, Madam, Mesdames	or	Yours truly
2 Sir, Gentlemen,		Your obedient servant
Madam, Mesdames	or	Yours respectfully
3 Dear Mr Jones,		Yours sincerely,
Dear Mrs Jones,	or	Yours truly
Dear Miss Jones,		
4 Dear . . .,		A suitable handwritten
(the first name being handwritten)		close

2.15 The signature block

The signature block consists of the actual signature, the typewritten name of the signatory (since many signatures are almost illegible) and the official position of the signatory — though the latter may be omitted if it is known to the addressee. If you are dictating letters to a central typing pool, where the typist may not know your name, or your official position, it is clearly essential to include this information, including the spelling of your own name if it is at all unusual.

2.16 Enclosures and copies

If a correspondent refers in the body of a letter to the fact that some enclosure is to accompany the letter, such as a brochure, pro-forma invoice, price list, road map for access to premises, etc. it can be very irritating to the addressee if they are omitted. The signature block is followed by a reference to the fact that enclosures are included in the letter. This takes the form of the abbreviation for enclosures, written as ENC, Enc or enc. This may be followed by a reference to the number of enclosures, or better still to their nature. Thus a typical enclosure might read:

Enc
1. Price list
2. Terms and conditions of sale

The number of items listed should be the same as the items enclosed in the letter, so that a double check is made on the enclosures as the letter is put with the enclosures into the envelope.

When carbon copies are taken with a view to sending them to interested parties it is usual to indicate the circulation list at the foot of the letter. There may be occasions when this would not be appropriate, because for some reason (say security) it is undesirable that the addressee should know that a particular party has been notified.

The notification may read copies to: or distribution or more commonly cc: (copies circulated to). The list of those circulated should then follow, with perhaps the department in which they serve. When sent to these individuals the name of the person concerned is either ticked or underlined on the copy, so that it catches the eye of the person attending to incoming mail for that department. It will then be placed in the in-tray of the official concerned.

Registered Address:
39 Parker Street, London WC2B 5PB

Telephone: 01-242 1655
Telex: 261367 Pitman G
Cables: Ipandsons London WC2

Company No: 1268265 England

Pitman Books Limited

BP/jb

27 October 19--

Michael Jefferies Esq BSc(Econ)
15 Camside
Church Street
Chesterton
CAMBRIDGE
CB4 1PQ

Dear Mr Jefferies

PITMAN'S SHORTHAND

Thank you for your letter dated 24 October enquiring about Shorthand publications; I am pleased to enclose the latest Pitman Business Education catalogue.

Pitman 2000 Shorthand - with its lighter learning load and extensive range of ancillary texts, workbooks and cassettes - is recommended as an invaluable skill for tomorrow's secretaries. Indeed the PITMAN 2000 POCKET DICTIONARY, containing approximately 20 000 words and outlines, is to be seen in classrooms and on the desks of top secretaries and personal assistants everywhere.

Our selection of speed development books has recently been extended to include PITMAN'S SHORTHAND SPEED EXAMINATION PRACTICE NO 1 containing a selection of Shorthand examination material at speeds ranging from 50 to 120 wpm, published in New Era or Pitman 2000. The longhand key is counted in tens for dictation.

We strongly recommend TEACHING PITMAN'S SHORTHAND by B W Canning. This valuable text covers the requirements of the Joint Examining Board Teachers Diploma in Shorthand as well as the RSA Shorthand Teachers' Certificate.

I feel sure that you will wish to include on your personal bookshelf the reissued classic by Alfred Baker entitled THE LIFE OF SIR ISAAC PITMAN. Attractively bound in green and gold, this inspiring story is an interesting social document which would also be a most acceptable gift or prize.

Please do not hesitate to write to us again if we can be of further assistance.

Yours sincerely

Betty Perkins

Shorthand Publisher

Encs

cc Service Department Director
   Home Sales Executive

Directors: Nicholas Thompson (Chairman) Navin Sullivan (Vice Chairman) Philip Sturrock (Managing) Donald Davis
J G Johnson Stephen Neal Frank J Roney Neill Ross Alan D Smith

Member of the Pitman Group
London · Toronto · San Francisco · Melbourne · New York · Wellington · Boston
Bath · Avonmouth · Southport.

Fig. 2.1 A letter in fully blocked style

2.17　The fully blocked letter

Fully blocked letters are the easiest to type, because every line begins at the left-hand margin with no indentation. The carriage return ensures that the typescript returns correctly to the same point as each fresh line is typed. Open punctuation is usually used with the fully blocked letter, which again saves time, since punctuation is used only where it makes a positive contribution to the reader's understanding.

The letter reproduced in Fig. 2.1 illustrates the fully blocked style, with open punctuation, and includes many points referred to in sections 2.4-2.16 above. Study this specimen letter carefully, referring back to the sections of this chapter which deal with each part of the letter. Then copy out some of the letters in section 2.18 below, using the fully blocked style.

2.18　Specimen letters in fully blocked style

In this book every chapter includes several specimen letters which cover a very wide range of topics related to the subject-matter of the chapter concerned. For easy reference these letters are designated SL2.1, SL2.2, etc. (SL denotes specimen letter, the first number, 2, indicates Chapter 2, and the final number is the number of the letter in that chapter.) Thus a reference in the text to SL7.5 indicates that the fifth specimen letter in Chapter 7 is being referred to.

The following procedure should be followed with these specimen letters:

a　Read the letter through carefully, particularly with regard to any specialised vocabulary which is used. If you are not sure of the meaning of a particular word use your dictionary.

b　Note the style of the letter, the sender's name and address (which would usually be part of the printed letterhead), the references, the inside address, the salutation, attention line, etc. Note the complimentary close, the signature and any reference to enclosures or the circulation of carbon copies.

c　If you are keen to practise your typing, the letter may be copied on the typewriter.

d　Now turn to the exercises and write one or two similar letters, using the material given in the various exercises.

ESSO PETROLEUM COMPANY LTD

Esso House
Victoria Street
London SW1E 5JW

Telephone: 01-834 6677
Cables: Essopet London SW1
Telex: 24942

Our reference CSG/MH/ap
Extension   2139
Date   21 October 19--

K Hoyle Esq
Thurrock Management Centre
Wood Lane
Aveley
Essex

Dear Mr Hoyle

NORTH SEA LECTURER

I have recently accepted an appointment with Esso Petroleum Company as
a part-time lecturer on North Sea topics. My task is to talk to educational audiences at all levels about developments in the North Sea. I
can discuss the discovery of oil, the development of oil fields, how
the product comes ashore and its significance to the economy of the
United Kingdom. I can adapt my lecture to suit audiences of all ages.

I am prepared to show a film which is a newsreel of the latest activity
in the North Sea and can show vugraphs which will amplify any factual
statements I might wish to make.

This service is fully funded by Esso Petroleum without any financial
commitment by the audience. I am prepared to travel to any location
you wish to give my presentation, subject to accommodating your requirements with those of any other location in your area. If the subject of
my presentation interests you or your colleagues you can contact me via
Esso Petroleum Company (Mr C S Gamage) at the address and telephone
number given.

I look forward to hearing from you.

Yours sincerely

Margaret Hall (Mrs)

CRONER PUBLICATIONS LTD
Croner House, 173 Kingston Road, New Malden, Surrey KT3 3SS
Telephone: 01-9428966

A J Armitage Esq   Your Ref: AJA/PTN
38 Camside   Our Ref: AAS/BEF
Church Street
Chesterton   1 October 19--
CAMBRIDGE
CB4 1PQ

Dear Mr Armitage

CRONER PUBLICATIONS

Thank you for your enquiry about Croner publications, with particular
reference to the export and import trades. We publish a manual in
each of these fields. They are:

Croner's Reference Book for Exporters
Croner's Reference Book for Importers

Manuals of this type take the form of a loose-leaf book with monthly
updates. The information is easy to get at and easy to understand.
The Reference Book for Exporters, for example, is a complete reference
on Export Terms, The British Overseas Trade Board, Export Control,
Export Prohibition, Customs Procedures, Export Finance, Insurance
(ECGD, Marine and War), Postal Information, Documentation, Dangerous
Goods, VAT and Samples. It also includes a survey, an extensive check
list, on every country in the world - Documentation, Import Regulations,
Exchange Control Restrictions, Packing, Banks, etc. etc.

The Reference Book for Importers gives a similar coverage in the field
of imports.

I enclose a brochure giving details of our full range of handbooks,
which incorporates an order/on approval form. I also enclose a current
price list. We shall be pleased to fulfil any order by return of post.

Yours sincerely

A A Symes
Editorial Director

Encl:

CRONER PUBLICATIONS LTD
Croner House, 173 Kingston Road, New Malden, Surrey KT3 3SS
Telephone: 01-9428966

Our Ref: AAS/BEF

24 October 19--

Mr G Robespierre
51 Camside
Chesterton
Cambridge
CB4 1PQ

Dear Geoff

Thank you for agreeing to serve on the Education Committee of The
Society of Shipping Executives. Now that I have been confirmed as
Chairman by the Council, I would like to arrange a meeting as soon as
possible to decide on a programme of action including the present state
of affairs with the Overseas Trade Steering Group (which I am pleased
to say seems to be progressing satisfactorily).

I have listed on the attached sheet a number of dates which are convenient to me. Would you be good enough to tick those dates which are
suitable for you and return the sheet in the enclosed stamped addressed
envelope? The meetings will probably take place in the SITPRO board-
room located near to Piccadilly Circus and therefore should be easily
accessible to everyone. I will confirm the most suitable date when I
have received all the replies.

Thank you for your help and I look forward to seeing you at the first
meeting.

Yours sincerely

Tony Symes

Enc:
1. List of dates
2. SAE

2.19   Exercises on the fully blocked letter

1 The Immaculate Limousine Co Ltd of Royal Way, Acton, London, W10 2DP has received a request from a college for one of its executives to address the engineering students on the subject 'Automation and the Engineering Industry'. You are the public relations officer and write to accept the invitation on behalf of the company. The speaker will be Dr Paul Ericson, PhD, AMIMechE. He is available on two dates, 8 May 19--, and 12 May 19--. His talk will include a slide presentation. He will bring his own equipment, except for a screen which the college is asked to provide. In your concluding sentence remind the lecturer Peter Hayman, BSc(Eng), of Thurrock Technical College, Woodview, Grays, Essex that it is essential for him to confirm which date is convenient for the college.

2 Write to the editor of the magazine *Child Care,* asking for a list of textbooks referred to in an article on 'Residential Care of Children'. The address is 12 024 15th Street, Washington, DC, USA. Explain that you are a lecturer in 'child care' at your college and express your appreciation of their assistance. Refer to three 'international reply coupons' which you enclose to cover the cost of postage by air.

3 Write to the Simplex Advice Bureau, George Vyner Ltd, Mytholm-bridge Mills, Holmfirth, Huddersfield expressing interest in their simple systems of book-keeping for small businesses. Ask them to send you specimen pages of their system and ask for a price list. Mention that you are hoping to set up in business in the near future, and say which trade or profession you propose to follow.

4 You are employed at the Department of the Environment, 2 Marsham Street, London, SW1. A student has written to the Department requesting a supply of brochures, leaflets, etc., about environmental problems. Write a letter regretting that you cannot help her directly, since all such publications are produced by the Stationery Office, and can only be obtained on 'cash with order' terms. Refer in your letter to a 'List of publications' which you are enclosing, and mention that the price is included in the description of each brochure in the list. The student is Miss Mary Lightgood, 217 Flower Court, Grantchester, Cambridgeshire.

5 Using as the basis for your letter any advertisement you like which deals with a nationally known product, write a letter from the sales

manager of the firm concerned to a wholesaler referring to a forth-coming advertising campaign in his area. Ask the wholesaler to order stocks in advance of the campaign, and refer to the special promotion material, display stands, etc., which will be sent with any orders received. Use as the wholesaler's name: Alfred Kemp and Co Ltd, 2138 High Street, in your own home town.

2.20 Appendix on the English language: the paragraph

The paragraph focuses on a particular topic, and amplifies it. The sentences which make up the paragraph may explain and clarify the matter under consideration; they may defend and justify it. In business correspondence paragraphs tend to be short, because flowery speech and literary descriptiveness are rarely appropriate in business letters.

Some rules for writing paragraphs

a Devise a **key sentence** which states the theme of the paragraph clearly. This focuses the attention of the reader on the topic. It will usually be a first sentence in a business letter, but in a report it might be the conclusion, and come at the end of the paragraph.

b The remaining sentences will support the key sentence, and amplify it. *Marshal your ideas coherently,* so that a logical thread runs through the supporting sentences.

c Business correspondence should be *specific and concrete,* rather than vague and abstract. It is better to say 'The consignment will consist of two hundred teak statues' than 'The order will be a con-siderable number of wooden statues'.

d Paragraphs of equal length give a uniform and dull appearance to the finished letter. Vary the lengths of your paragraphs. Occasionally even a single sentence paragraph has its place, which will clearly be a prominent one. In such a case the key sentence *is* the paragraph.

2.21 Exercises on paragraphs

1 Devise a key sentence for each of the situations described below, to be used in a paragraph of advertising material.

a A travel firm has arranged a cheap winter holiday to Majorca. One feature is that the hotel accommodation for four days is free; the charge for the holiday simply covers the air fare. No meal will be served on the aircraft, but refreshments at duty-free prices will be available.

b A breakthrough has been made in solving the tobacco addiction which affects some people. By chewing a nicotine-based chewing gum the smoker reduces his/her craving for a cigarette, and receives the nicotine in a form which does not affect the lungs in any way, and has no adverse environmental effects.

c A new variety of concrete which will harden under water has been developed. Its action depends upon the use of an oil-based preparation to mix the concrete. This preparation does not mix with water and combines chemically with the cement to give high strength and durability.

d The courses at a particular college can be assessed by computer-marked assignments. A student wishing to check on his/her progress can request such an assignment on payment of a fee. This service cannot be requested more frequently than once a month. The results of such tests are not revealed to tutors and consequently do not enter into consideration for course results. Any student who is failed on a course may apply for a review of the final result if he/she can produce computer-marked assignments which seem to indicate that a successful result would be obtained.

2 Rearrange the following groups of sentences to make coherent passages and underline the key sentence:

a I shall lose no time in forwarding to you the net proceeds of the sale. The goods you have sent seem to be of fine quality, and I have no doubt they will command a good price. When clearance is obtained we shall auction them forthwith. Unfortunately they require clearance by the Forest Products Authority. Our commission will be 10 per cent plus 2½ per cent **del credere**.

b He will arrive on the 11.30 am (local time) plane. The purpose of his visit is to familiarise himself with the company's branch in Singapore. He would like to meet local officials and dignitaries. Mr John Smith, who was recently appointed to the post of managing director, will visit you next Friday. Please assist him in every way and give him an opportunity to meet staff at all levels.

c The main feature of the campaign will be a sponsored television entertainment live from the Festival Theatre on April 20th. The next point to consider is the product 'Glamorous'. We propose to mount an extensive advertising campaign in the month of April. Falling sales have led to concern at Head Office recently. We have signed contracts with several celebrities.

3 Voluntary offers and inquiries

3.1 How a business relationship starts

An American proverb tells of the man who invented a better mouse-trap, and the world beat a path to his door. So it may, but only if the news gets around and the world learns the inventor's address. We have to bring our product or our services to the attention of the public in any way we can. We may be able to attract attention by a press release which will lead to the featuring of our product on television, radio or in the press.

If free coverage cannot be obtained because our product is not news we must attract the public's attention by advertisements on the television or radio, or in the popular press, journals and magazines. It may be that the interested 'public' will be a specialised group only, so that we must advertise in the appropriate trade journal.

Never forget that the strength of a business comes from countless contacts, any one of which may lead to an order. Never let a phone ring unanswered; it may be an inquiry that will keep a hundred people busy for two years. Never be indifferent to a phone message, a memo or a letter of inquiry. It may not yield any benefit this time, but a helpful approach may bring another inquiry later. You may be unable to help the potential customer on this occasion, but perhaps you know someone who can, and will be glad of the order. He/she may reciprocate at some time in the future.

3.2 Offer, acceptance and valuable consideration

In English law *a contract is a legally binding agreement between two persons, or more than two persons, which confers rights upon each party in return for the performance of some act by him/her, or some forbearance shown by him/her.*

If a contract is to be legally binding we must be able to prove that one party made an offer, that another party accepted the offer without any reservations, and that some **valuable consideration** will pass between the parties which makes it worth while. A few examples will illustrate this.

A offers his house for sale at £25 000. B accepts the offer and after due legal transfers moves into the house. The purchase price is transferred the same day into A's bank account. There has been a clear offer, a valid acceptance and valuable consideration has passed, so the contract is legally binding.

A says he would like to buy B's car, and inquires what the price might be. B says £1500. A says he is sorry, but that is too dear. In this case A made a simple inquiry, not an offer to buy. B offered the car at a price of £1500 but A rejected the offer. There is no contract.

A says '£800 for your painting by the artist Smith' (an offer). B says '£900 is the least I would take' (a counter-offer). A says 'Done' (an acceptance of the counter-offer). A writes B a cheque for £900, which is cleared into B's bank account (valuable consideration has passed and A is now the owner of the painting). It is a valid contract.

The point about all this is that it is very important in correspondence to make yourself clear to the addressee. Is your letter a simple inquiry? Then make this clear. Is it an offer to buy? If so, use the word 'offer'. If you believe you are accepting an offer, say quite clearly 'I accept your offer to supply a word processor at £1560, free delivered to my premises at . . .'.

3.3 Voluntary offers

A voluntary offer is an invitation to a potential customer to do business with you. There can be no objection to the voluntary offer, which presents the facts about a product or service, especially if the list of addresses used is carefully vetted to include only those likely to be interested. The more careful we are in the mailing, the more attractive the correspondence we send out, and the easier we make it for the addressee to reply, the less likelihood there is that the voluntary offer will finish up in the waste-paper basket. To avoid this we must be positive and businesslike in our offer letter.

Suitable introductory sentences are as follows:

a We have taken the liberty of sending you a copy of our latest catalogue, etc.
b We think you will be interested in the enclosed press release which relates to our new, etc.
c We have pleasure in sending you, etc.

The letter that follows such an introduction should be factual, and give concrete information about the product or service. A press release or other advertising copy should be carefully worded to give the maximum sales promotion value. Several heads are usually better than one, and a specialist advertising agency might need to be called in for advice and help.

3.4 Specimen 'voluntary offer' letters

Study the following letters and use them as typing practice.

SL3.1

Presto Office Equipment Ltd
New Milton, Nr Southampton, Hants. Telephone 04892 82173

```
21 September 19--

The Office Manager
Wright and Co Ltd
2002 Thames House
London EC3 4PW


Dear Sir

We have pleasure in sending you our new catalogue, which includes
particulars of all our products.

May I draw your attention in particular to our Cosmos Vertical Filing
System, which permits quick and easy reference while holding corres-
pondence securely in dustproof, fireproof drawers.  The system has been
subjected to extensive fire experiments with gratifying results.

Should you wish to place an order for any of our products please use
the order form enclosed.  A current price list is also enclosed.
Demonstrations can be arranged by phoning Sue Lawley at our London
showrooms on 01 - 279 3164.

Yours faithfully


T F Draper


Sales Manager


Enc: 1. Order Form
     2. Price List
```

Drapery Sales Ltd

Tower Block House
North Road
Portsmouth
Hants
PO6 4EA

Tel: (0705) 31478

Our Ref RD/JT

29 January 19--

The Chief Buyer
Matteson & Son Ltd
964 South Road
Dorking
Surrey

Dear Sir

We enclose a copy of the new season's catalogue, introducing many
novelties and some variations on the lines which were most popular last
season. Perhaps you would be good enough to study the catalogue now
and outline your requirements for the coming season. This would be of
great assistance to us in adjusting our stocks to the requirements of
our customers, and will ensure early deliveries.

You will see that prices this season are slightly higher, but you will
find that this is offset by marked improvements in almost every line.
We have completely reorganized the supply side of our business and can
confidently claim to have supplies available from the leading manufacturers in the country.

The catalogue incorporates an Order Form (see pages 24-25) and also an
application form for attendance at our open weekend in February (see
page 26). We look forward to meeting many of our customers on that
occasion, and shall be pleased to send tickets by return of post. We
regret that we must limit numbers to three tickets per firm.

Yours faithfully

R Dawson

Sales Manager

ESSO PETROLEUM COMPANY LTD

Esso House
Victoria Street
London SW1E 5JW

Telephone: 01-834 6677
Cables: Essopet London SW1
Telex: 24942

Our reference	CSG/AP
Extension	2139
Date	17 July 19--

PETROLEUM CHEMISTRY, REFINING PROCESSES
AND CHEMICAL MANUFACTURE IN ESSO

Esso Petroleum Company and Esso Chemical have jointly produced this
book to help answer the many enquiries received each day for information on typical refining and chemical manufacturing operations.

The book is based on current practices and has been written by Dr
Barbara Haines of the Schools Information Centre for the Chemical
Industry at the Polytechnic of North London, with the assistance of the
technical staff of both companies. It is designed for sixth form students who have some knowledge of the basic chemistry involved and who
are interested in oil refining and chemical manufacture. It would be
a useful adjunct to any 'A' level topic concerned with refining and
petrochemical operations.

We are pleased to let you have this first copy free of charge, but
subsequent copies will be chargeable at a subsidised price of £1 per
copy. No invoices will be issued and orders will be met on receipt of
a request accompanied by the appropriate cheque or postal order.
Postage and packaging are free and the cost of the publication is
zero-rated for VAT purposes. Cheques or postal orders should be made
out to 'Esso Petroleum Company Limited' and sent to C S Gamage using
the tear-off reply slip below.

Reply slip

PETROLEUM CHEMISTRY, REFINING PROCESSES
AND CHEMICAL MANUFACTURE IN ESSO

Please send me   copies of the book for which I attach £ ....

C S Gamage   Address to which copies are to be sent:
Head of Education Services
Esso Petroleum Co Ltd   ....
Victoria Street
London SW1E 5JW   ....

                              ....

SL3.4

The Office of Fair Trading has asked us to point out that this letter is a circular addressed to a very large mailing list, consisting of all sorts of addressees. The seemingly odd form of address 'IB Misc' refers to the mailing list concerned, and no attempt was made to address the letters to individual addressees.

OFFICE OF FAIR TRADING
Field House Bream's Buildings London EC4A 1PR

Telephone 01-242 2858 ext

IB Misc	**Your reference**
	Our reference
	Date 28 October 19--

OFT PUBLICATION: "THERE'S MORE TO CREDIT THAN JUST HP" (LEAFLET)

I enclose a copy of a new consumer leaflet on credit. Essentially, it advises the reader to 'shop around' for credit, and draws attention to the 'APR' (annual percentage rate of charge for credit) which firms now have to show in quotations and certain advertisements for credit. In addition, the leaflet gives a guide to the main forms of credit available.

The launch of this publication on 30 October 19-- follows the Advertisements and Quotations Regulations under the Consumer Credit Act which came into force on 6 October 19--.

As with many of our publications, we have used a cartoon treatment and a fairly lighthearted style to deal with the main points of a detailed piece of legislation.

Copies of this leaflet and other OFT publications are available from your local Trading Standards, or Consumer Protection, Department, Citizens Advice Bureaux, Consumer Advice Centre and many libraries. Bulk supplies are obtainable from the Central Office of Information, Publications and Design Services Division, LH502, Hercules Road, London SE1 7DU.

In an effort to cut out unnecessary postage costs, we are taking this opportunity to bring our mailing list up to date, and check that our material reaches its destinations. If you wish to continue receiving our publications, please complete and return the slip attached, indicating any out-of-date information or inaccuracies that may be appearing on the address label.

If we do not receive your completed slip by 28 November, we shall assume that you wish your name to be removed from the list.

Yours sincerely

A Harris

A Harris
Information Branch

Fig.3.1 A circular

Registered Address:
39 Parker Street. London WC2B 5PB

Telephone: 01-242 1655
Telex: 261367 Pitman G
Cables: Ipandsons London WC2

Company No: 1268265 England

Pitman Books Limited

Our Ref: BG127 PAW/jhm

Date as postmark

The Lecturer in Charge
Typewriting and Office Practice
All Colleges

Dear Madam/Sir

Pitman Universal Typing - Edith MacKay BA(Hons) FRSA
ISBN 0 273 012436

May I draw your attention to this recently published typewriting manual which
embodies the very latest ideas in keyboard technique, which is beginning to
move out of the traditional secretarial field as new applications and adapta-
tions of the QWERTY keyboard appear in ever-more-sophisticated forms of office
equipment.

The special features include:
1 Systematic layout and the use of a second colour, which add interest, assist
   understanding and make it easy to find one's way about the book.
2 Methodical division into technique sections, units of work and production
   tasks (with target times). It is a learning/teaching whole according to
   the best modern principles.
3 A sound step-by-step treatment of new material by:
   explanation of new work (including model)
   copying the model
   applying the new skill and knowledge.
4 Thorough yet flexible instruction in keyboard/mastery.
5 Comprehensive range of remedial and keyboard/technique drills (one in each
   unit).
6 Complete programme of speed/accuracy development, progressing gradually from
   one-minute to five-minute timings.

Should you wish to see an inspection copy of this important new manual please
complete the attached request slip and a copy will be sent to you by return of
post. (This offer applies to colleges in the United Kingdom only. Other
colleges should apply to their usual supplier for an inspection copy.)

Yours faithfully

P A Wickham (Miss)

Publisher
Secretarial Studies Department

Directors: Nicholas Thompson (Chairman) Navin Sullivan (Vice Chairman) Philip Sturrock (Managing) Donald Davis
J G Johnson Stephen Neal Frank J Roney Neill Ross Alan D Smith

Member of the Pitman Group
London · Toronto · San Francisco · Melbourne · New York · Wellington · Boston
Bath · Avonmouth · Southport.

```
                         Inspection Copy Request Slip

  Please send me by return                                    Please tick

  (a) Pitman Universal Typing - MacKay (ISBN 0 273 012436)    ............

  (b) Catalogue of Secretarial Studies books                 ............

  (c) I am also interested in books on

      English                                                 ............

      Economics                                               ............

      Law                                                     ............

      Mathematics and Business Calculations                  ............

      Other subjects - please state                          ............

                                                              ............

  Name            ........................................

  College Address ........................................

                  ........................................

                  ........................................

  Position held   ........................................

  Note: I agree to return the inspection copy within 30 days if it proves to be
  inappropriate to my courses.  I understand that if an order is placed for 15
  copies or more within 30 days I may retain the inspection copy for college use.

                  Signed ................................
```

Fig. 3.2 A 'voluntary offer' letter with reply slip

3.5   Inquiries

A voluntary offer is made by the seller to a potential buyer. An inquiry is made by the potential customer who is seeking a supply of a particular product, or seeking someone who will perform a service for him/her. The form taken by a letter of inquiry varies with the type of product or service required. It may be sufficient merely to ask for a catalogue and a price list. It may be necessary to specify the range of goods that is of interest. If the buyer has a particular article or product in mind then a specific description of the goods required, the quality, colour and price range will be appropriate. Detailed description reduces the chances of receiving unsuitable goods and avoids further correspondence or telephone calls to clarify the buyer's requirements.

The buyer should beware of turning an inquiry into an order. An offer to buy, which can be accepted at once by the seller to make a firm contract, may prove to be inescapable later. Always make it clear that the letter is an inquiry only, and just a preliminary stage in the negotiations leading up to a contract.

Suitable opening sentences in a letter of inquiry include:

a We shall be glad to receive a catalogue and price list of . . .

b We should be glad to receive details of your terms and conditions of sale for the supply of . . .

c We should appreciate information about . . .

d We are considering the purchase of . . . and are making preliminary inquiries from several suppliers with a view to comparing prices and terms of sale.

e A business friend has given us your name as a reliable firm prepared to supply . . . . We would welcome information about your range of products . . . .

Sometimes the potential customer has no real ideas of the exact article he/she wishes to purchase. It may be of a technical nature, with a variety of products in the market all of which have slightly different features. The customer in these circumstances should make it clear that he/she is relying upon the seller's knowledge and experience to give proper advice and supply goods which are fit for the purpose for which they are intended. In these circumstances it is important to make clear exactly what you wish the product to do. Thus an office copier may be cheap to run but only produce copies at a slow pace. Some are only economical if long production runs are required. To buy the wrong machine for your purpose is a serious handicap to any business. Specify clearly what you require and state quite clearly that you rely upon the supplier's advice and knowledge in making the purchase.

Other matters that may need clarifying are the price, the method of payment, the possibility of discounts and the need for repeat orders in the future. Delivery and packing charges may be involved, and it may be important to decide at the outset who is to bear such charges.

The final sentence of such a letter may be phrased in such a way as to make it clear that no contract can be made at this stage. If the supplier is invited to offer you goods on terms that seem fair to him/her, it will be clear that you are not making an offer to buy at this stage. To be a valid contract we have to have an offer which has been clearly accepted. If you ask the supplier to make an offer you make it clear that you reserve the right to accept it, or reject it at a later date.

3.6 Specimen letters of inquiry

Study the following letters of inquiry and use them as typing practice.

SL3.6

Robespierre Haulage Co Ltd
51 Camside, Cambridge, CB4 1PQ. Tel: 23543

Our Ref: GVR/ab

30 November 19--

Pye Telecommunications Ltd
St Andrews Road
Cambridge CB4 1BR

Dear Sirs

I should like to receive a copy of your brochure 'A Look at Business
Communications Costs' referred to in Business Systems and Equipment this
week. We are long distance hauliers operating a fleet of 12 40 foot
trailers, and it appears your system might have distinct advantages.

Yours faithfully

G V Robespierre
Fleet Manager

SL3.7

LEE AND CO   14856 Harbour Drive, Singapore

Our Ref. ML/AB   1 August 19--

Dear Sirs

We should be grateful for a copy of your latest catalogue and a price
list. We are about to open a branch office and may need to order a
range of goods very soon. Please ensure that the catalogue is sent
air mail not surface mail.

Yours faithfully

Man Lee
Purchasing Officer

SL3.8

Charlesworth Engineering (Southampton) Ltd

1745 Dock Road, Southampton. Tel: 37800

```
Our Ref: RJDC/TS
17 April 19--

G K N Sankey Ltd
Marketing Department
St John's House
St John's Square
Wolverhampton  WV2 4BH

Dear Sirs

Supernova Vending Machine

I saw this new machine in the Management Training Centre and would like
to have information about it, with a view to adopting it in our premises
where we employ some 300 staff.  Please send us full details.

Yours faithfully


R J D Charlesworth
Personnel Director
```

SL3.9

Educational Mailings (Southampton) Ltd

1784 Richville Road, Southampton, Tel. 90784

```
Our Ref: DG/JH/2                                    31 October 19--

Polythene Envelopes Ltd
2494 Market Hall
Cambridge  CB2 1PV

Dear Sirs

Please send samples of your A4 and A5 polythene envelopes as recently
advertised in Business Systems and Equipment.  At present we use opaque
envelopes for our mailings, and feel that many of our brightly coloured
brochures would have greater impact in a polythene cover.

A catalogue and price list would greatly assist us.


Yours faithfully


D Grantley
Mailings Supervisor
```

Gooch Cutlery Ltd

93 Hallam Grange Rise, Upper Fulwood, Sheffield 10. Tel: (0742) 39051

```
Press and Information Office                    Our Ref: DB/cd
City of Solingen
POB 100165                                      31 October 19--
D5650 Solingen
West Germany

Dear Sir

Your advertisement in the 'Economist' interests us greatly.  We are
manufacturers of fine cutlery in Sheffield, and should very much like
to bring a party of about 24 people over to spend a weekend in Solingen
and visit your Museum of Blades.

Could you please send me a brochure about Solingen and a few details
about accommodation etc.

Yours faithfully



Daniel Gooch
Director
```

3.7 Exercises on voluntary offers and inquiries

1 Write to Bettamarket Ltd, who are opening a supermarket at 224 High Road in your own home town. Offer your services as a contract window cleaner. Point out that your charges are based on shop window cleaning only, other windows in offices and storerooms being cleaned free of charge. Ask if you may visit the premises to measure the windows, submit an estimate and discuss the frequency of cleaning required. If the estimate proved to be acceptable accounts would be rendered monthly, payable within 7 days.

2 Write to Brassware (Chittagong) Ltd offering supplies of sheet brass on favourable terms due to cancellation of a major order from a

defence establishment. The prices and other details are as follows:

Sheets (2 m × 1 m × 0.005 m) 160 Rupees per sheet
Sheets (2 m × 1 m × 0.003 m) 140 Rupees per sheet

Freight and insurance would be for the customer's account.

3 Watson & Co Ltd, 797 High Street, Bristol, who have for many years placed orders for bond and bank paper and carbon paper with Stationery Supplies Ltd, 1331 Kingsway, London, WC2, have suddenly ceased to do business with them. Stationery Supplies Ltd ask why their customers have taken this course and they make them a special offer, calculated to regain their custom.

4 Labour-Savers Ltd, 23 High Street, Comfrey, who have introduced a new cleaning powder, wish to circularise retail hardware dealers with a view to inducing them to handle the new product. Draft the letter for them. Invent a suitable name for the powder, mention its special merits, its price, the trade discount available (45 per cent) and the heavy campaign of television advertising to be commenced shortly.

5 Imagine you are working for the publisher of your favourite magazine. Write a circular to firms in the fashion trades drawing their attention to the specimen copy enclosed and suggesting that they consider advertising in the magazine. Refer to the rate card also enclosed and offer them a 25 per cent discount for advertisements placed within one month of the date on your letter.

6 Cassettes and Tapes Ltd, of 759 Overcliff Road, Frinton on Sea, circularise college student unions with a special offer of blank cassettes. Students can buy cassettes at the following prices:

Playing time	Price (inc. VAT)
T60 (30 minutes each side)	59p
T90 (45 minutes each side)	79p
T120 (60 minutes each side)	£1.09

Student Union officials who submit bulk orders on behalf of members may deduct 20 per cent of the total order value for Student Union funds. All orders must be accompanied by a statement from the college principal that the correspondent is indeed a member of the Student Union Committee. Write a suitable circular letter.

7 Write a letter of inquiry to your local garage asking whether they would be prepared to display your motor vehicle on their forecourt for sale, and the terms and conditions for acting on your behalf. Give full details of the vehicle.

8 Your firm is interested in purchasing or renting a photocopying machine which will print and collate house journals, reports and training materials. It must also be available for one-off copies at all times of the day. Write to a local firm of office suppliers asking them for suggestions, prices and demonstrations of suitable machines. Emphasise that the need is urgent, but this is only a preliminary inquiry.

9 Write as the personnel officer of a major firm in the locality to the secretary of a local tennis club for details of personal membership and company memberships. Mention the possibility of sponsoring local tournaments.

10 Write to a local travel agent asking for particulars of trips to Holland and Germany for parties of 30 or more. You envisage training visits by parties of employees in connection with a training programme entitled 'Meeting the Challenge from the Continent'.

3.8 Appendix on the English language: the tense of verbs

The tense of a verb shows the time of the action — present, past or future. In order to describe all events adequately as to time we need to have six tenses — three **simple** tenses and three **perfect** tenses. To illustrate these tenses we will use two verbs, the verb 'to carry' and the verb 'to visit':

Simple tenses	To carry	To visit
Present tense	I carry	I visit
Past tense	I carried	I visited
Future tense	I shall carry	I shall visit

Note: The simple present tense shows that an action takes place now:

I carry the water into the barn for the cattle.
I visit my daughter every day.

The simple past tense shows that an action took place at some time in the past:

> I carried the unconscious child into the surgery.
> I visited the deceased man's wife and conveyed the condolences of the committee.

The simple future tense shows that an action will take place in the future (first person takes 'shall', second and third persons take 'will'):

> I shall carry the banner in the parade.
> I shall visit my mother next weekend.

Perfect tenses show that an action is complete (perfect) at the time in question. They are formed by prefixing have or has (present perfect), had (past perfect), and shall have or will have (future perfect) to the past participle of the verb. To illustrate these tenses using the same verbs we have:

Perfect tenses	To carry	To visit
Present perfect	I have carried	I have visited
Past perfect	I had carried	I had visited
Future perfect	I shall have carried	I shall have visited

Note: The present perfect tense shows that the action was perfectly complete at the present time:

> I have carried in all the harvest for this year.
> I have visited my sick child every day for the last week.

The past perfect tense shows that an action was perfectly complete at the same time in the past:

> I had carried the wounded men into the shelter when a further bombardment started.
> I had visited the nuclear reactor some years earlier.

The future perfect tense shows that an action will be completed before some future time:

> I shall have carried the equipment in by the time the test is due to be carried out.
> I shall have visited the few remaining sentry posts before the brigadier arrives.

3.9 Exercises about the tense of verbs

1 Give the tense of each verb in *italics* in the ten sentences below. You need not copy out the sentences.
   a 'I *drink* to your very good health.'
   b The intoxicated rider *had collided* with the stationary vehicle.
   c The engineer *will assess* the problem as soon as he arrives and report to you.
   d The government *had achieved* its economic targets.
   e I *shall have concluded* my lecture by 7.30 pm.
   f In response to the choirmaster we all *sing* cheerfully.
   g They went and told the sexton and the sexton *tolled* the bell.
   h By good fortune she *has survived* unharmed.
   i We *will arrive* at 3.30 pm.
   j I *have loaded* the vehicle and we can depart.

2 Change this passage into the past tense:
   The typewriters rattle away in the typing pool as the audiotypists finish the day's correspondence. On the supervisor's desk the telephone rings. The editor wants her letters before 3 pm every day but they have not arrived and she has an important conference in half an hour. Mrs Clarke sends the messenger up with them and tells him to hurry. The other trays of completed correspondence are taken up to their respective destinations. It is time to go home.

3 Complete the past perfect tense of the verbs 'to type', 'to export' and 'to organise', using the following list of persons. The first line has been done for you.

1st	person singular	I had typed
2nd	person singular	You . . . .
3rd	person singular	He . . . .
		She . . . .
1st	person plural	We . . . .
2nd	person plural	You . . . .
3rd	person plural	They . . . .

4 Responding to inquiries: estimates and quotations

4.1 The general nature of responses

There are an infinite variety of inquiries each of which must be responded to in an appropriate manner. In the present age of instantaneous communication the most effective response to an inquiry is a telephone call. For example the letter of inquiry sent to G K N Sankey (see SL3.8) would not in the normal way be responded to in letter form. The standard response by this firm to all such inquiries is a telephone call in which the telephonist asks the inquirer to answer one or two standard questions which give the firm some ideas of the type of installation that might be needed. The inquiry is then passed to the company's marketing staff in the particular area, who are asked to arrange an appointment to inspect the premises concerned, with a view to making a firm proposal for siting and installing the machines required. This proposal would be the written response to the original inquiry but several weeks might have elapsed before this firm proposal, or quotation, could be made.

The need to answer each inquiry entirely on its merits is the chief reason for developing a good style in business correspondence, and the reader is urged to write as many original letters as possible. To assist with this aim the letters in this chapter include suggested replies to certain common types of inquiry. They are as follows:

a The dispatch of brochures, price lists, etc., with a compliments slip only.
b The dispatch of brochures, price lists, etc., with a covering letter of a routine nature, in 'standard reply' form.
c Detailed replies to a specific inquiry.
d A reply which constitutes an offer to sell or supply a service.
e An estimate or quotation.

4.2 Replies using compliments slips

A compliments slip is a small sheet of paper with the full details of a firm's name, address, telephone number, etc., in a form very similar to the firm's letterheading. It then has the words 'WITH COMPLIMENTS' or perhaps 'WITH THE COMPLIMENTS OF'. The latter wording gives the official of the company concerned the opportunity to introduce a personal note by giving his/her name. The rest of the slip is blank, leaving enough space to type a simple message, should one be necessary. An example is reproduced in Fig.4.1.

Pitman Books Limited

128 Long Acre, London WC2E 9AN

Telephone: 01-379 7383

With Compliments

Fig. 4.1 A compliments slip

The type of routine inquiry which requests catalogues, brochures or price lists would be answered by sending the items required with a compliments slip. If there is any defect in the response, for example if a particular brochure is not enclosed because it is out of print, a short note could be written or typed on the compliments slip to explain the matter. Typical responses are as follows:

SL4.1

WITH COMPLIMENTS

21 October 19--

We regret that the brochure on Copyfast photocopiers is reprinting.
We hope to send this to you within two weeks.

G M Walker
Publicity Department

SL4.2

With the compliments of

G M Walker   21 October 19--

Would you please note that the price of the De Luxe model has been
reduced by 5 per cent, to £30.40, free delivered. Otherwise the price
list is correct.

SL4.3

WITH COMPLIMENTS

21 October 19--

If you wish to see a demonstration of this equipment please telephone
our local sales representative, Sally Oppenheimer on 01021-25168.

G M Walker
Publicity Department

4.3   'Standard-form' responses

Frequently a standard-form letter provides the most adequate response
to a wide variety of requests, because all that is necessary is to mark
in the appropriate box the reply which you wish to send. Such a
standard letter to deal with requests for brochures, etc. is frequently
used, as in SL4.4.

Linden Lea Naturalist Society

The Meadow House
Linden Lea
Suffolk
England
Telephone: 46145

Date as postmark

Brochures on Linden Lea

Thank you for your letter requesting brochures. Please refer to the
heading marked with a cross on the right hand side of the page.

	Attention
1. The free brochures you requested are enclosed with our compliments and best wishes	....
2. We regret that the brochures you have requested can only be sent if we receive cash with order. Would you please send a cheque or postal orders to the amount of £........ when we shall be happy to fulfil your order by return of post.	....
3. Your order is only part complete. The balance will be sent as soon as supplies are available.	....
4. We regret that the supplies you requested are out of print. Please find enclosed a cheque for £........ to return your remittance.	....

Yours faithfully

T Shoreham

Curator

This type of response is applicable to many situations. SL4.5 shows a
typical letter answering inquiries about an order sent in earlier.

MEGAPOLIS MAIL ORDER CO LTD

27 The Quay, Megapolis, Hampshire, England.   Tel: 75402

```
Your Reference: Letter dated 17 October 19--
Our Reference:  MOB/ab

21 October 19--

Dear Sir/Madam

The answer to your letter is given on the line marked X below.
```

Please note
the line marked
X below

1. Your order has already been sent. It left
   our Cayton Street depot on ....

2. Your order was sent today. We regret the
   delay which was caused by ....

3. Your order has been delayed due to difficulties of supply overseas. We hope to be
   able to fulfil it by ....

4. Your order has been held up on the instructions of our credit controller. She tells
   me that you were written to about this
   matter on .... Would you please
   check your files on this matter. In case
   of difficulty please phone Mrs Taylor on
   Extension 291. ....

5. We can find no trace at all of your order.
   Please send us further details and if
   necessary consult your local post office
   if a loss of money in the post may have
   occurred. ....

```
Yours faithfully




M O'Brien
Sales Department
```

4.4 Letters in answer to a specific request

When answering a specific request one can only deal with the facts of that particular case. In real life there is usually no difficulty; in textbooks it is sometimes more difficult to provide all the facts for students so that they can write a satisfactory letter. To some extent the student must use his/her imagination to clothe the skeleton of facts provided. Some typical answers from businesses are given in the letters below. In some cases the request letter precedes the answer so that the correspondence can be followed.

SL4.6

ESSO PETROLEUM COMPANY LTD

Esso House
Victoria Street
London SW1E 5JW

Telephone: 01-834 6677
Cables: Essopet London SW1
Telex: 24942

Our reference CSG/DA
Extension 2139
Date 21 October 19--

Dear Sir/Madam

CHRONICLE OF EARTH HISTORY

Thank you for your request for this wallchart. Demand has been so great that we have exhausted our stock earlier than expected. We will be reprinting this wallchart early next year and shall answer outstanding requests as soon as new supplies become available.

We very much appreciate the interest you have shown in this particular educational item and regret that we cannot help you at present.

Yours faithfully

C S Gamage

Head of Educational Services

South of England Technical College

Newstead Road
Abbotsbury
Dorset
DT4 0DG

Telephone: Abbotsbury 3424

22 October 19--

George Vyner Ltd
Simplex House
Mytholmbridge Mills
Mytholmbridge
Holmfirth
Huddersfield
HD7 2AT

Dear Sirs

Free sets loose pages - Simplex Accounts Books

I understand from a colleague that you supply free sets of loose pages
of your Simplex Accounts Books for use on courses for businessmen.
Our course 'How to run a small business' starts on 8 December.

I should very much appreciate a supply sufficient for 40 students, and
if you have any literature explaining your simplex systems I should
appreciate any advice or guidance you can give.

Yours faithfully

A R Morse
Head of Courses for the Community
Business Studies Department

THE VYNER GROUP

INTERNATIONAL DISTRIBUTORS	SIMPLEX	SPECIALISED ACCOUNT BOOKS

GEORGE VYNER LTD   **GEORGE VYNER** (EXPORTS) **LTD**   **GEORGE VYNER** (DISTRIBUTORS) **LTD**

P.O. BOX No. 1
HOLMFIRTH
HUDDERSFIELD HD7 2RP

TEL. No. HOLMFIRTH
(STD 048489) 5221
CABLES VYNER HUDDERSFIELD

Our ref: BS/AB

Your ref: –

30th October 19--

Mr. A. R. Morse,
Head of Courses for the Community,
South of England Technical College,
Newstead Road,
Abbotsbury,
Dorset, DT4 0DG.

Dear Mr. Morse,

I thank you for your letter of 22nd October and have pleasure in confirming that a parcel containing 40 sets of loose pages of Simplex Books has been sent to you under separate cover. I trust they prove useful and if at any time you would like a further supply, please do not hesitate to contact me.

Enclosed with this letter is a sample copy of <u>Simplified Book-keeping for Small Businesses</u>. This book explains simply, yet comprehensively, how Simplex Books should be kept. It is essential to new small-business owners and at £3.20 per copy including postage, is good value for money. Copies are available from us should any student be interested.

Yours sincerely,

B. Senior
General Manager

SIMPLEX BRAND PRODUCTS ARE DISTRIBUTED AND COPYRIGHT THROUGHOUT THE WORLD

Fig. 4.2 A letter in response to a request

SL4.9 (Response to SL3.10)

Stadt

Solingen

Der Oberstadtdirektor

Stadtverwaltung Amt: 13 Postfach 1001 65 · 5650 Solingen 1

Mr.
Daniel Gooch
93 Hallam Grange Rise
Upper Fulwood
Sheffield 10

Amt	Presse- u. Informations-amt
Gebäude	Rathaus Potsdamer Str.
Zimmer	38 a
Ruf (02122) 191	
bei Durchwahl	19 2207
Sprechzeiten	
Auskunft erteilt	Herr Laute

Ihr Schreiben
DG: cd
of 31st October 19--

Mein Zeichen
13-2 k-1a

Tag
7th November 19--

Dear Mr. Gooch,

we acknowledge receipt of your kind inquiry of 31st October. It
is, of course, a particular pleasure for us to hear that visitors
from Sheffield, Great Britain's hardware town, wish to come over
to Solingen which is called the town of blades. Given this
relationship we are anxious to support your interest in visiting
Germany's unique Museum of Blades. For your information we enclose
folders about the Museum of Blades with a detailed description
of the collections ranging from edged weapons and sets of table-
ware to cutting instruments from all epochs and cultures. You are
sure to discover soon that a visit to this Museum alone will make
your trip to Solingen worthwhile.

Furthermore your will find enclosed some general information about
Solingen as well as a list of hotels providing you with addresses,
standards and prices and even special weekend offers.

We hope that you will find these data useful and wish you a very
enjoyable stay in Solingen.

Yours faithfully
By order of

Hansjörg Laute

Altpapier sammeln - Umweltschutzpapier benutzen.

Zahlungen arbeten auf die Konten Stadt-Sparkasse Landeszentralbank Postscheckamt Köln Fernschreiber
der Stadtkasse Solingen Solingen Nr. 2766 Solingen 342 01700 Nr. 185 99-503 8 514 777

Fig. 4.3 A letter from a municipal authority

College of Sea Studies

Woodview, Grays, Essex, England.
Telephone number: 93767

Our Ref TD/LR

4 November 19--

G Kydonakis Esq
1075 Ag Sofias St
Corfu
Greece

Dear Mr Kydonakis

Thank you for your letter requesting admission details of this college.
I enclose brochures giving details of our courses, but must advise you
that these are high level courses leading to full professional qualifications in professional institutes in the shipping and freight forwarding fields. We have to exercise rigorous controls over entry qualifications to ensure that overseas students are of the right level of
ability and that the qualifications you have at present are officially
comparable with United Kingdom qualifications.

In order to ensure that this is so it is necessary for you to be inter-
viewed by an Education Officer in Greece. I am not sure whether this
is possible in Corfu itself but almost certainly it is. Will you
please approach the British Consul in Corfu and discuss your proposal
to come to Grays with him. If he is prepared to confirm that your
qualifications are appropriate you may complete the form at the back
of the brochure and present it to him. He will then forward it
officially to us.

I hope we may welcome you to Grays in due course.

Yours sincerely

T Donaldson
Course Lecturer: Shipping

Enc: 2 brochures

4.5 Estimates and quotations

Frequently when a firm is asked to supply goods or services it is asked for an estimate, though some customers might ask for a quotation. There is not much difference between the two but a quotation is more formal than an estimate and is susceptible to immediate acceptance. We have already learned that in a contract there must be an offer, followed by unconditional acceptance of the offer, and somewhere in the arrangements there will also be valuable consideration (which usually means a payment of money).

An estimate is prepared at a given moment in time for the information of the inquirer, and it is certainly possible to use it as a basis for a contract. The inquirer says 'Thank you for your estimate. I should like to buy the goods listed in your estimate and agree to pay for the installation work, etc.' Some wording of this sort is clearly based upon the estimate, but it is the customer who is offering to buy. The supplier may then accept this offer and the contract is made. Suppose that an estimate submitted in July is not responded to until December. Much may have happened in the meantime; prices may have risen and the estimate may be quite unrealistic now. The supplier will therefore refuse the offer to buy. He or she will respond 'I regret that I cannot accept your offer to buy on the basis of the estimate made last July. I am sure you will realise that prices have changed, etc.' An estimate is not an offer, which is capable of being accepted. It is an 'invitation to treat', which means that it is an invitation to do business. If the customer is interested he/she can make an offer, and the trader will then accept or refuse the offer as he/she is so inclined.

A quotation, by contrast, is an offer to sell or supply and is capable of being accepted immediately. As an 'offer' it is very important that it is correctly expressed, in all its details. One exporter sent a quotation to a foreign customer living in the United Kingdom offering to sell goods at a certain price, free delivery to any named address. The customer accepted promptly, and named an address in Singapore, involving several hundred pounds delivery charges. This is the sort of thing that happens if great care is not taken to think the whole quotation through to its logical conclusion. The only safe way is to insert standard terms and conditions in a quotation which cover all the likely events.

4.6 Standard terms and conditions

Standard terms and conditions for any sort of contract are drawn up by the party interested, usually on legal advice. They attempt to cover all the eventualities that may arise, and in the past have given rise to a good deal of conflict because they could be used to exclude liability of every sort. In the United Kingdom this has led to the enactment by Parliament of the *Unfair Contract Terms Act 1977* which attempts to reduce the unfairness of these kinds of terms and conditions.

Frequently the terms are referred to on the front of the quotation, but are printed in fine print on the back – often in pale ink which is difficult to read. Hence the warning, often given, to 'read the fine print' in any contract. Sometimes sets of 'Standard conditions' are drawn up by the trade association for a particular industry, and all members use the same set of foolproof standard conditions. A well-known example is the Road Haulage Association's **Conditions of Carriage**, which covers every eventuality in the carriage of goods by road.

4.7 Typical standard paragraphs

Typical standard clauses might read:

Price variation Quotations are based on the trader's current costs of production and, unless otherwise agreed, are subject to amendment on, or at any time after, acceptance to meet any rise (or fall) in such costs.

Liability The trader shall not be liable for any loss to the customer arising from delay in arrival, unless it can be clearly established that the delay was the fault of the trader.

Illegal matter The printer shall not be asked or obliged to print any illegal matter, or matter which in his/her opinion is of a libellous nature or likely to infringe the rights of any third party whatsoever.

Third party or other claims We will accept no liability for any indirect loss or third party claim howsoever caused which arises from any delay in completing the work or from any delay in transit. In the event of any defect in the work, including negligence, our liability (if any) will be limited to rectifying the defect.

(*Note:* Under the Unfair Contract Terms Act 1977 the limitation of liability for negligence only extends to cases where the test of reasonableness applies. Thus where a tailor fails to put a ticket pocket in a jacket it might be reasonable to accept that this negligence only needs to be corrected, and does not call for compensation. If the tailor leaves a sleeve out of the jacket this would hardly be 'reasonable' and the exclusionary clause would be invalid, and the tailor liable.)

4.8 Specimen quotations

SL4.11

Specialist Printers (Cottenham) Ltd

Castle Hill, Cottenham, Cambridgeshire.   Tel. 55255

```
Your Ref   TD/AB
Our Ref    GRP/NC/RH

10 October 19--

Shiny Surfaces Ltd
King Street
Cambridge
CB2 1QR

Dear Sirs

QUOTATION 1854

Thank you for your enquiry.  We have pleasure in submitting our
quotation subject to the standard conditions shown below and overleaf.

Revision of estimate number 1854
CIRCULAR
Size 297 x 210 mm (A4).
Printed black ink one side only on 100 gsm white bond paper.
3000 copies £40.00

Yours faithfully


G K Parker - Estimator

Terms (also see Standard Conditions overleaf)

The above estimate is based on the present day cost of materials and
labour and is subject to amendment in the event of any increases
between now and the completion of the work.

Payment Terms: Net 30 days

When accepting please state Quotation No 1854
```

CLEARFLASH LTD

27 Morden Road
Mitcham
Surrey
CR4 4XB

Telephone: 43434

Wenngens A B
1077 Nybroksajen
Stockholm
Sweden

Your Ref AJP/QR
Our Ref HTV/SA

17 June 19--

Dear Sirs

Quotation 12357 Electronic Camera

Thank you for your enquiry of 4 June 19--. We are pleased to quote as
follows for the supply of:

	£
1 Electronicamera 227	854.00
20 (26) films to fit	60.00
20 (12) films to fit	28.00
	942.00
Less trade discount 45%	423.90
	518.10
Air freight	20.00
	£538.10

Please note that all our quotations are subject to our standard terms
and conditions which are stated overleaf. In addition this quotation
is subject to the special terms and conditions stated below. Acceptance of this offer to supply implies acceptance of our conditions.
When accepting this quotation please refer to Quotation 12357.

Yours faithfully

A J Perkins
Sales Manager

Terms
Payment: Net cash 7 days of receipt of air freight package.

Acceptance: If this quotation is not accepted within 30 days of the
date shown above we reserve the right to raise the price according to
the official inflation index.

Film Dispensers (Newcastle) Ltd

1024 Grey Street, Newcastle 1.
Telephone: 233797

Your Ref MK/AB 27 April 19--
Our Ref JJT/AH

11 May 19--

Mustafa Mitsul and Co Ltd
725-37 Einek H
Istanbul
Turkey

Dear Sirs

Quotation 2541

We are pleased to respond to your letter with the following
quotation:

		£
100 Film Dispensers (Stopwaste Model) at £16	=	1600
5 Exposure Control Units at £85	=	425
		2025
Less Trade Discount 35%	=	708.75
		£1316.25

We agree to present the goods for inspection to the independent
evaluators Filmstudy Ltd and to pay their inspection charges. Their
packing, freight and insurance charges to be for your account alone,
and no part of our quotation.

Please note our standard terms and conditions on the reverse side of
this quotation. If you decide to accept this quotation please do so
by telex, and confirm by air mail, within 30 days of the date shown.

Yours faithfully

J J Treherne
Marketing Assistant

Office Equipment Hire (Whitley) Ltd

84 Stile Road, Whitley, Tyne and Wear.   Telephone: 937888

Your Ref: AJM/DG
Our Ref: Lsg 1294/TSH/AB

27 August 19--

JAJ Fuel Supplies (Hexham) Ltd
Haining Alley
Hexham
Tyne and Wear

Dear Sir

Furniture Leasing: Quotation 1294/1

After our visit to your premises last week we are pleased to quote you
as follows:

	£
Purchase price of your existing office equipment	6500
Purchase price of new machines etc. to be supplied by Neatoffice (Newcastle) Ltd	6500
	£13000
The above equipment to be leased back to you for a monthly payment of	£156.25

We have already drawn your attention to our standard terms and conditions, a further copy of which is enclosed. Acceptance of this quotation implies acceptance of our conditions.

In accordance with our discussions last week your acceptance of this
quotation must be made by 5 September 19--, so that we can place an
order for your new machines with Neatoffice (Newcastle) Ltd before the
deadline of 15 September. Our cheque in full settlement of the
purchase price of your existing furniture will reach you on 15
September provided we have received our 'direct debit' mandate permitting us to claim the monthly payment on the 27th day of each month.
This mandate must be signed by both directors.

Yours faithfully

T S Hargreaves
Financial Director

Enc: Standard Leasing Terms and Conditions

GKN Sankey Limited

AUTOMATIC VENDING DIVISION,
Roebuck Road, Chessington, Surrey, KT9 1LF
Tel: Sales - 01-391-1551
Tel: Service - 01-397-8184 (24 hour)   Telex: 929716

Your Ref: RJDC/TS
Our Ref: WM/LMW

30 April 19--

R J D Charlesworth Esq
Charlesworth Engineering (Southampton) Ltd
1745 Dock Road
Southampton

Dear Mr Charlesworth

Proposal for Installation of Vending Equipment

I refer to our recent meeting and discussion at your premises in Dock Road.
Based on the information you supplied I enclose for your consideration and
action a proposal for the installation of vending equipment which will
enable you to achieve your objectives in an efficient and economical way.

You will see that the proposal contains an evaluation of your objectives;
our recommendations and a full description of our service, maintenance and
costings. I hope this information will be sufficient to enable your Board
to approve the proposal. We would then proceed to the installation stage
at a convenient date.

Thank you for your hospitality on 25th; it was much appreciated.

Yours sincerely

W Morrison
Sales Consultant
Vending Operations

Enclosure: Proposal for 1745 Dock Road

AREA OFFICES THROUGHOUT THE COUNTRY
A Member of the GKN Group of Companies
Registered in London under No. 74901. Registered Office: Hadley Castle Works, Telford, Salop, TF1 4RE

Fig. 4.4 A proposal resulting from an enquiry

4.9   Exercises on responses to inquiries

1 You are responsible for the dispatch of brochures, small booklets, etc. Write a compliments slip to deal with each of the following. Each slip is to bear your own name, and the phrase i/c Brochures and Small Sales Department. I/c is short for 'in charge of':

  a A request for brochures, all of which are available.

  b A request for brochures and a price list. The price list is reprinting and will have to be sent separately later.

  c A request for three wall maps. You are sending two of them; the third will be sent direct from the printers within a few days. The printers are Smartmaps Ltd, Ancient Ley Works, Aveley, Essex.

  d A request for free booklets. Only one of them is free, which you enclose. The other three are priced at £1 each, and you offer to send them on receipt of a cheque for £3.

2 Draw up a short 'standard-form' response from your firm, Clerical Aids (Ipswich) Ltd, 7 Lady Lane, Ipswich, Suffolk to deal with the following problems which prevent the fulfilment of many small orders:

  a People write to ask for goods and enclose the money but forget to say what the goods are that they wish to receive.

  b People say what the goods are but fail to enclose the money they promised.

  c People send cheques that are not signed.

  d People send cheques that are not dated.

3 Draw up a short 'standard reply' which deals with the following problems. You supply wall maps for educational purposes; some are free and some are charged at a nominal price.

  a School or college staff fail to say which map they require.

  b They specify the free map they require but do not say whether they need the small chart or the large one.

  c They request a map which is out of print and you want to let them know that it will be sent on in due course.

  d They request a map which has been discontinued and you want to return their money to them.

4 Metal Tops (Nottingham) Ltd have asked Aurora Lighting Ltd to visit their premises and advise on the installation of glare-proof

overhead lighting, bench and workshop lighting and office desk lighting. You are the estimator for Aurora Lighting and submit a quotation for fittings costing in all £3500 and installation work costing £1650. Refer to a proposed starting date, your standard terms and conditions and the need to get the sanction of the factory inspectorate. This will only be a formality but makes it essential to apply as quickly as possible if delay is to be avoided.

5 The editor of *Business Equipment Times* quotes charges for two full-page advertisements and one half-page advertisement (£250 full-page, £150 half-page) to Better Office Drinks Ltd, and mentions a discount of 50 per cent for those advertisers who take a regular run of the same advertisement for six consecutive months. Invent suitable addresses. Refer to your standard terms and conditions, a copy of which is enclosed.

6 In reply to the inquiry of the Metropolitan Stores Ltd, the Wykeham Press quotes the price at which it is prepared to supply 20 000 catalogues of their design submitted. They suggest other designs also, and emphasise their merits.

7 You work for Camside Demolitions (Loamshire) Ltd, who submit an estimate to Loamshire City Council for the demolition of slum properties and site clearing in the city centre. The work is to include the salvaging of bricks, lead piping, ironware and other resources, all of which will become the property of Camside Demolitions. The total cost is £250 000, less £50 000 for the salvaged material. Refer to your standard terms and conditions and your agreement to comply with local government bye-laws in the employment of safety personnel (one fireman, one gas fitter and one member of the staff qualified in first aid) for the period of the contract. Such staff to be provided by the Council, on secondment to Camside Demolitions Ltd.

8 You are employed as an estimator by Motor Repairs (Granby) Ltd. You send an estimate to a motor cyclist, Tom Williams, who is at present in the orthopaedic ward of St Luke's Hospital. Your estimate for repairs totals £450.50, but you are able to tell him that the insurance company of the motorist who was to blame has inspected the vehicle and unofficially offered £350 in full compensation to avoid legal action. Impress on Mr Williams that the work

you propose involves the use of new parts only (as supplied by the manufacturer) and your mechanics are all fully qualified and manufacturer-trained.

9 Sewsharp Discount Warehouse Ltd quote Personal Appearance Ltd for the supply of five of their latest 'Hi-power' Sewing Machines at £850 each. A deposit of one-fifth of the purchase price is required by law on acceptance of the quotation. Interest will be added to the outstanding balance at a flat rate of 12 per cent for three years, and then payable by monthly instalments. It will be necessary to sign a hire purchase agreement, and it is preferred that payment is made by standing order.

10 Electro-type (Hong Kong) Ltd quote for the supply of 120 Orient-Europa electronic typewriters at £105 each to Hucknall Business Machines Ltd, Hucknall, Nottinghamshire. The terms quoted are **FOB** Hong Kong, all freight and insurance charges to be for the account of Hucknall Business Machines Ltd. You work for Electro-type Ltd, and are to write a letter giving the quotation, referring to your standard terms and conditions, which are printed on the reverse side of the letter.

4.10 Appendix on the English language: confusion of tenses

It is important that there should be no mistaken mixing of tenses in any form of business communication, as an illogical use of tenses within a sentence or from one sentence to another is an elementary error of style. Students sometimes fail to maintain a logical sequence of tenses between a main clause in a sentence and the subordinate clause(s). A clause is a group of words which has a subject and a verb. If the group of words can stand on its own it is a *main clause,* but if it is dependent on another group of words for its meaning then it is called a *subordinate clause.* For example, in the sentence '*The manager will be visiting the department* which is about to be re-organised' the words in italic form the main clause while the rest of the sentence is a subordinate clause describing 'the department'. *As far as the confusion of tenses within a sentence is concerned, the general rule is that a present or future tense in the main clause can be followed by any tense in the subordinate clause(s).* For example:

The customer says (present tense) that the goods are satisfactory (present tense).

The customer says (present tense) that the goods were satisfactory (past tense).

The customer says (present tense) that the goods will be satisfactory (future tense).

However, if the *past tense is used in the main clause the same tense must be used in any following subordinate clause.* For example, the sentence 'The consignment was damaged during unloading which takes place at the store's yard' is clearly illogical, as the tenses of the main clause and the subordinate clause are different. The sentence should read 'The consignment was damaged during unloading, which took place in the store's yard'. The main exception to this rule regarding the confusion of tenses when the main clause uses a past tense is in the reporting of speech. For example, it is quite usual to say 'The purchaser informed us that the goods will be appropriate for their needs.'

Just as it is important to maintain a logical development of tenses within a sentence, so it is necessary to avoid confusion of tenses within a longer piece of writing. For example, when compiling a report, it is a mistake to switch tenses mid-way through your writing, perhaps from the past tense to the present tense and back again. Look at this example:

The machinery was in a poor mechanical condition. The fly wheel was loose and the instrument panels obscured by dirt. *No safety guard is fitted.* The rubber mountings were badly worn.

The error in this report is to be found in the sentence in italics, for although most of the report is written in the past tense, this sentence uses the present tense, and is therefore out of step with the rest of the report.

It is important to remember to re-read all written communications before they are sent, and to check for errors, such as a confusion of tenses, both within individual sentences and in longer pieces of writing as a whole. A logical use of tenses is important if a letter or other communication is not to be confusing or vague.

4.11 Exercises on tenses

1 In each of the following sentences choose the correct form of tense for the clause in italics. If either form is correct write 'Either (or any) form will be satisfactory', and why:

a The director believed *that he* (*is capable, was capable*) *of making the decision.*

b The marketing director laid down the regulation *which* (*was ignored, is ignored, will be ignored*).

c The judge understood *that the cargo* (*is stored, had been stored*) *on the open deck.*

d He was trusted *although his record* (*is poor, was poor*).

e The transport manager believed *that the lorries* (*are parked, were parked*) *before midnight.*

f He is reliable on financial matters *although he* (*is poor, was poor, has been poor*).

g He had argued *that the postal service* (*is unreliable, was unreliable*) *in developing countries.*

h He pretended *that he* (*is, was*) *the general manager.*

i He believes *that he* (*will float, has floated*) *the cargo safely through the rapids.*

j I had achieved the result *for which everyone* (*hoped, will hope*).

2 a Read the following report and state which verbs have been written in the wrong tense:

> The ocean liner was bound for the West Indies. It had on board eight hundred passengers, many of whom were planning to return to England on the vessel. The facilities for entertainment and recreation are excellent, although some criticisms were made about the absence of a singer who had had to withdraw due to ill-health. The passengers can use any of the ship's bars and ball rooms, but they were restricted in their choice of dining area.

b Now rewrite the report:
   i in the present tense, and then
   ii in the past tense.

5 Orders

5.1 The nature of orders

Orders may be offers to buy goods, or acceptances of offers to sell goods. Frequently this involves the acceptance of a quotation, as described in Chapter 4. The initial difficulties of selling have been overcome and the customer has been persuaded to purchase the product. A valid contract is about to be made. If the order is an offer to buy, the seller will be able to accept the offer and supply the goods. If the order is an acceptance of a previous offer to sell, or of a formal quotation, then the contract is made under English law when the order is put into the post. The seller will proceed to supply the goods as soon as the order arrives.

Since the placing of an order is such an important part of a contract for the sale of goods, it is necessary to be cautious, particularly if the order is the first one to be placed by the buyer, and has been preceded by lengthy pre-contract negotiations. It is advisable to be absolutely precise about the important elements in the pre-contract negotiations so that no difficulty can arise. A salesman might, for example, tell the buyer one thing and his employer another. A buyer who has been led to believe that goods will be delivered **carriage paid** is going to be very annoyed if they arrive **carriage forward**, so that the carrier will not deliver them until the carriage charges have been paid. Therefore always begin your correspondence with firm statements about the terms on which you are placing the order. Typical opening sentences might be:

1 I wish to place an order for . . . as a result of my discussions with your representative Mr . . .
2 After representations made by your employee Mr . . . I am prepared to order . . . provided . . .

The businesslike nature of these opening sentences conveys the impression that the buyer is an experienced and competent business-man/woman.

The letter should then proceed to recapitulate the discussions held with the representative and most of the following points should be made:

a The exact description of the goods required, with any codes or part numbers or other technical details clearly stated. The description may refer to quality, materials, colour, weight, size, etc.

b The price agreed, or the way in which the price is to be calculated. Sometimes it may require that an independent valuer will value the object concerned, to ensure a fair price. The time and method of payment should also be made clear.

c Any conditions of delivery should be stated, and especially if time is of the essence of the contract. Thus if late delivery is as bad as non-delivery and amounts to breach of contract you must make this absolutely clear — otherwise a reasonable time is allowed and this will be governed by the usual dealings in this particular trade or industry. What is considered to be a reasonable delivery sche-dule for a consignment of hen's eggs would not usually be thought reasonable in the case of an order for the construction of a passen-ger ship.

d The question of carriage of the goods is important, and who is to pay the carriage on them.

e Every eventuality which could affect the order should be consid-ered. For example, it may be helpful to give an order number (to assist in tracing the order if necessary). A named individual, perhaps the purchasing officer, should be designated as a liaison for any problems that arise. In technical matters it may be pre-ferable to name a suitably qualified technician, and give his/her telephone number and extension. Several of the specimen letters below contain such details. These letters should now be studied carefully.

SL5.1

Rosythe Commercial Vehicles Ltd
Syston Road, Ilkeston, Derbyshire. Telephone: Ilkeston 25749

Our Ref GHJ/HT

3 December 19--

Rapidity Business Machines (UK) Ltd
Freepost
Waddell House
Waddell Gardens
Croydon
CR9 9ES

Dear Sirs

Order
T201 Copying Machine; Lime Green

Thank you for arranging for us to visit your showrooms in London to see
a demonstration of your range of copying machines. After discussions
with your representative Mr Palmer we have decided on the latest T201
fibre optics machine, with micro-computer technology; colour lime green.

The price quoted to us by Mr Palmer was £560, with a trade in allowance of £60 on our obsolete machine. Your representative is to deliver
and install the machine, and take away the machine to be traded in, at
your expense. We would give him a cheque for the full balance (£500)
payable to Rapidity Business Machines (UK) Ltd.

We also understand that your annual service agreement will reach us
within 30 days, together with an invoice which we shall pay by return.
This entitles us to call for immediate service from the date of
delivery of the machine for one year.

Would you please put this order in hand at once, as we require delivery
before 15 December, when we start a major mailing to vehicle users.

Yours faithfully

G H Johnson
Administrative Officer

Robert Armstrong (Sunderland) Ltd

24 Cheyney Rise, Sunderland, Tyne and Wear, England

Investment Jewellers to the North of England

Phone: Little Sunder 789756

Our Ref: RTA/CB

4 December 19--

Boucher et Boucher
178 Place Vendome
Paris 75
France

Cher M. Boucher

Order: Pear-shaped Diamonds

Thank you for your hospitality on my recent visit to Paris. It was
delightful to renew our acquaintance after so many years and I look
forward to returning your hospitality when you next visit the United
Kingdom.

We have a client who is interested in purchasing 20 pear-shaped
diamonds of 1.3 - 1.5 carats. The order is quite firm, but we must
impress on you that we rely on your skill and judgment in the selection of suitable stones, particularly with regard to colour and cut,
since the purpose of the purchase is investment.

We shall arrange a letter of credit covering the cost of the diamonds
and the insurance and other costs, as soon as you give us your estimate
of the amount required. We will then arrange the credit for 20% more
than the estimate, so that if you subsequently obtain better stones
you will not be prejudiced by selecting them. We rely on you to draw
from the credit a fair price only.

Your early attention to this order would be greatly appreciated.

Yours sincerely

Robert T Armstrong
Investment Manager

Acme Plumbing and Heating (Hornsey) Ltd

1224 Coppetts Road, Muswell Hill, London N 10
Telephone: 01 - 546 79345

Your Ref -
Our Ref TSD/AB/1089

29 July 19--

Roofing Insulation (Billingham) Ltd
1074 Harbour View
Billingham on Tees

Dear Sirs

Order No 1089

Your representative Peter Carter who called on us recently quoted us a
price of £450 free delivery for one container load (256 rolls) of
Super-insulate roof insulation. We understand this insulation is
packed in polythene sacks of sound quality and may be stored in the
open. This is of great importance to us as we have limited warehouse
space at present.

We enclose as requested by Peter Carter a letter from our bankers
Midland Bank Ltd confirming that we are financially sound and suitable
customers for your ordinary terms of trading. We have been told that
these are cash 30 days after rendering of the monthly statement, which
we understand is sent out under your cyclical billing system on the
4th of each month for customers with the initial A.

We therefore place a formal order for:

   256 rolls Super-insulate Roof Insulation @ £450

We hope to become regular customers, and to repeat this order many
times in the years ahead.

Yours faithfully

Thomas S Doddinghurst
Managing Director

BABCOCK SUN TOPS LTD
Purley Way
Aveley
Essex

Your Ref –
Our Ref TC/ML

Date 24 August 19--

Confection Moderne
1722 Rue de la Maison Blanche
Alger
Algerie

Dear Sirs

Attention of Abdul Ajakaiye: Order

With reference to your recent visit to the United Kingdom and the
sample garments you submitted at that time, we wish to place an
order for the following:

5000 Mademoiselle Jolie blouses
     (five colours and five sizes as discussed on your visit)
5000 Carnac-Plage suntops
     (also in five colours and five sizes)

The terms are agreed to be as follows:

(a) DDP our premises at Aveley.
(b) Insurance to be arranged by you with a Lloyd's broker only
    through your London agents, for £16 500.
(c) Payment to be made in Sterling (£15 000) to your London agents
    within one month of the arrival of the goods at Aveley.

We should appreciate prompt attention to this order which is urgently
required. We hope to establish a regular connection for the future
if this first consignment proves to conform to the samples supplied.

Yours faithfully

Thomas Cookson
Purchasing Officer

Arthur Telford (Birmingham) Ltd

2022 Aston Road, Wednesbury, Staffs

Home and Office Designs for the Midlands Area

Agavox Answering
4 Sydenham Road
London SE26 5QY

Your ref: AT/JM
Our ref: Visit by Alan Rudman

Date: 17 October 19--

Dear Sirs

Order: C385 Answering Machine

Thank you for arranging that your representative Alan Rudman should
demonstrate your answering machines to us. We were very impressed
with their performance and wish to place an order for one C385 machine
as demonstrated.

We prefer to lease rather than buy, and are prepared to sign your
standard 3 year agreement as explained by Mr Rudman. We understand
that this takes some weeks to prepare but that you are prepared to
install the machine at once. This would help us, as we start a major
design project on 28 October which will mean that our offices are
likely to be unattended for some parts of the day.

Thank you for your courtesy and cooperation.

Yours sincerely

A Telford
Managing Director

5.3   The advantages of order forms

Of course, the real aim of all salesmen is to establish an enduring business relationship with every customer. In many trades the wholesaler-
retailer relationship is one which, after being initially established by
an enthusiastic and perceptive salesman, develops into a regular trading relationship with goodwill on both sides. With such an established
connection it will not be necessary to remind the seller of the terms
of the original negotiations, and reliance can be placed on evidence
of an established course of dealings should any dispute arise. In these

DELIVERY NOTE NO. 13301

BAILEY MILK PRODUCTS LTD

29 BRIGHTON ROAD · CRAWLEY · WEST SUSSEX · RH10 6AE
Tel: CRAWLEY(0293) 511311 · Telex: 87464 · Regd. No. 1524937 England

INVOICE TO:	DELIVER TO:
Speedy Dairies Ltd	The Wellcome Dairy
Old Mill Road	2174 Camside
Cambridge	Chesterton
CB2 1SQ	Cambridge
	CB4 1PQ

ACCOUNT NUMBER	BRANCH NUMBER	CUSTOMER ORDER No.	ORDER DATE	CUSTOMER CATEGORY
01 4892_ _ _	4	D 1037	11.12.--	C

CODE	PRODUCT DESCRIPTION	QUANTITY PER TRAY	NO. OF TRAYS ORDERED	NO. OF TRAYS RECEIVED	REMARKS
Y01-	'Frutti' Yogurt Multi-pack Cherry/Strawberry	6 x 4 x 125g	180		
Y02-	'Frutti' Yogurt Multi-pack Apple/Orange Cherry/Orange	6 x 4 x 125g	180		
Y03-	'Frutti' Yogurt Multi-pack Cherry/Strawberry/Apricot	8 x 3 x 125g			
Y04-					
Y05-	'Fruit Basket' Yogurt Kiwi/Gooseberry Apricot/Mango	20 x 150g			
Y06-	'Fruit Basket' Yogurt Morello Cherry/Elderberry Plum/Walnut	20 x 150g			
Y07-	Fruit Yogurt Cherry 500g	12 x 500g			
Y08-	Fruit Yogurt Strawberry 500g	12 x 500g			
Y09-	Fruit Yogurt Apricot 500g	12 x 500g			
Y10-	Fruit Yogurt Mixed Fruit 500g	12 x 500g			
Y11-	'Frutti' Yogurt 150g pots Cherry/Strawberry	20 x 150g			
Y12-					
Y13-					
Y14-					
D01-	'Puddi' Chocolate Dessert	12 x 2 x 125g	90		
D02-					
D03-	Chocolate Dessert with Cream	20 x 125g			
M01-	'Drink Me' Banana Milk Drink	24 x 200ml			
M02-	'Drink Me' Strawberry Milk Drink	24 x 200ml			
M03-	'Drink Me' Chocolate Milk Drink	24 x 200ml			
M04-					
C01-	U.H.T. Whipping Cream 35% Fat	24 x 200ml			
C02-					
C03-					
		TOTAL TRAYS	450		

SPECIAL DELIVERY INSTRUCTIONS	RECEIVED VIA:	CUSTOMER SIGNATURE OR P.O.D. STAMP
ASAP and no later than 17.12.--	LOWFIELD DISTRIBUTION LTD.	
	TERMS: NETT PAYABLE 30 DAYS FROM ACTUAL DELIVERY DATE	DATE DELIVERED:.................................

Fig. 5.1 An order form

circumstances the use of *order forms* to speed up the processes of ordering and the dispatch of orders becomes a possibility.

Orders are frequently placed by using special order forms provided by the seller. The advantage is that the seller can list the items on the order form in such a way as to fit his/her distribution system.

Sometimes in these days of high-speed communication, orders are taken by telephone. The seller's order clerk completes the order form as the order is phoned in, and the order form becomes a *proof of delivery note* which accompanies the goods in transit. In this way an order for fresh foods, for example, can be phoned through to the order clerks in the dispatch depot of the supplier. The goods can be placed at once in the delivery vans (often refrigerated vehicles) for dispatch the same day. Such a form is reproduced in Fig.5.1.

In other cases the order form is supplied to the potential customer, who fills in the quantities required in the spaces provided. This order can then be easily processed by the supplier's dispatch department.

When sending an order on a prepared order form it will often be sufficient merely to attach a compliments slip, with a few typed words of instruction. In other cases a relatively short covering letter will be sufficient.

5.4   Covering letters for orders on official order forms

SL5.6

Pitman Books Limited   128 Long Acre, London WC2E 9AN

Telephone: 01-379 7383

```
Fisher Reprographics (Kilburn) Ltd
1024 Newstal Road
Kilburn, London NW6                       27 May 19--

The goods listed on the attached official order form are
required urgently.  Would you please fulfil this order as
soon as possible.
```

With Compliments

Fig. 5.2 A compliments slip to accompany an order

With compliments

Teatime Restaurants (Whickham) Ltd

27 Fellside Road, Whickham, Tyne and Wear

Scottish Meats and Pies Ltd
Coldstream, Scotland   19 October 19--

Your official order attached: would you please note that a shortage of
2 cases of corned beef from our September order is to be included in
the present consignment and not charged (paid, our cheque 5 October).

SL5.8 (Response to SL3.1)

Wright and Co Ltd

**2002 Thames House
London EC3 4PW
Tel: 01 - 342 2656**

1 October 19--

Presto Office Equipment   Your Ref: -
New Milton   Our Ref: TBC/DW
Hants

Dear Sir

<u>Order</u>

Thank you for the catalogue and price list you sent us recently, and
the demonstration arranged for us by Sue Lawley at your London
showrooms.

We have decided to equip one of our offices with your equipment and
accordingly enclose an order on your official Order Form. Would you
please arrange early delivery as the office concerned is being re-
decorated and should be ready for occupation on 12 October. If
delivery could be arranged for 8 October it would be most helpful.

As this is our first order, and we would like to pay on the usual trade
terms, i.e. cash 30 days after monthly statement received, I am sending
you a banker's reference as evidence of our reliable financial position.

Yours faithfully

T B Cornwallis
Purchasing Officer

Enc: 1. Order Form
      2. Banker's reference

MATTESON AND SON LTD

964 SOUTH ROAD
DORKING
SURREY

Tel: Dorking 35214

Your ref: RD/JT 29 January 19--
Our ref: MAP/JTC

Date: 18 February 19--

R Dawson Esq
Sales Manager
Drapery Sales Ltd
Tower Block House
North Road
Portsmouth
Hants

Dear Sir

Order

Thank you for the catalogue you recently sent to us, and for the
invitation to your 'Open Day' in Portsmouth. Unfortunately, due to
staff sickness, we shall not be able to attend this year, but we hope
you will have a successful day.

An order for the forthcoming season is enclosed. We should appreciate
reasonably prompt attention to this order since our stocks are low,
but we understand that some of the new lines may not yet have reached
you from your suppliers. If you have a part load coming this way for
another customer and could usefully send us such goods as are readily
available we should appreciate it.

Yours faithfully

Michael A Partington
Supplies Officer

Educational Mailings (Southampton) Ltd

1784 Richville Road, Southampton, Tel. 90784

Our Ref   DG/JH/2   14 November 19--

Polythene Envelopes Ltd
2494 Market Hall
Cambridge
CB2 1PV

Dear Sirs

<u>Order</u>

Thank you for the sample envelopes you sent in response to our enquiry
of 31 October. We feel that these are certainly a useful alternative
to our present mailing envelopes and accordingly we have completed your
order form which we return herewith.

We start a major mailing on 29 November, so it would be most helpful if
these envelopes could reach us by 28 November at the latest. If this
presents any difficulty please phone Mr Goddard on (0703) 0129.

Yours faithfully

D Grantley
Mailings Supervisor

Enc: Order Form

5.5   Exercises on orders

1 You send an order to J T C Westcott (Liverpool) Ltd on their
official order form, with a compliments slip. This draws their
attention to the promise they made over the telephone to send the
order within seven days of receipt. Type, or write this compliments
slip, using your own name and address as customer.

2 Messrs Hartley Bros recognise that the National Paint Co Ltd cannot send goods carriage paid. As they are interested in the paint, however, they are prepared to take a trial lot of Colourine No. 37, carriage forward, which must be delivered at their Slough factory within seven days.

3 Write a letter, pointing out and apologising for certain errors in an order dispatched the previous day to Golden Glow Cosmetics Ltd. The orders are to be amended to 100 of each item ordered, instead of 10. This will entitle you to a special trade discount of 60 per cent on the retail price. Express the hope that the supplier will be able to trace the order and amend it in time.

4 Place an order for goods that you need urgently. Emphasise this fact and give instructions for their forwarding.

5 Assume that you are a representative who has been able to obtain a large contract for the supply of ink and stationery. Send the first order form with a covering letter to your head office.

6 Messrs Henry Baxter & Son, Bedford, wish to cancel an order they have placed with the Excelsior Trading Co Ltd, Nottingham, unless the company is willing to hold the goods at their disposal until they have sufficient storage space available.

7 Windermere Bros Ltd thank Messrs Astley & Sons for their quotation, and enclose an order for 500 tonnes of Red Diamond Cement (Hydrofast Type) at £20 per tonne, to be delivered in 50-tonne lots at intervals of 10 days dating from 1 August. All accounts will be settled monthly.

8 Watson & Co Ltd write a friendly letter to Stationery Supplies Ltd, stating that they are pleased to place an order (order form enclosed) and explaining why they have not placed orders for some time.

5.6 Appendix on the English language: 'shall' and 'will'

Many students find 'shall' and 'will' difficult words to use correctly, and no-one can deny that the rules behind their use are a little involved, but as the correct use of these words enables us to convey many delicate shades of meaning it is well worth the trouble of mastering them. There are two uses for these words. They are:

a As auxiliary verbs to form the future tense. (An auxiliary verb is one that is used to help form the tenses of other verbs, e.g. am, was, been, have, shall and will.)

b When not used to form the future tense they show personal determination in the first person and commands or promises in the second and third person.

For future tense 'shall' is used for the first person, and 'will' for the second and third person.

Future tense

Singular

a I shall go to the bank for some money.

b You will go to the bank for some money.

c He, she will go to the bank for some money.

Plural

a We shall go to the bank for some money.

b You will go to the bank for some money.

c They will go to the bank for some money.

Personal determination

When 'shall' and 'will' are not used as auxiliary verbs to form the future tense, but are used to show determination on someone's part, their roles are reversed from the above. 'Will' shows personal determination in the first person singular and plural.

Singular and plural

a I will go to the police and report the matter.

b We will consult a solicitor, even if you think it unnecessary.

Commands and promises

'Shall' denotes a command to, or a promise to, the second or third persons.

Singular and plural

a You shall go to the dentist, however much you dislike it.

b He (she) shall be rewarded for his (her) generosity.

c You shall seek legal advice; you are both in danger of prosecution.

d They shall be promoted as a reward for their gallantry.

'Shall' is also used interrogatively (i.e. to ask a question) in the second person; for example:

Question: Shall you go out tonight?
Answer: Yes, I think I shall.

Abbreviations of 'will' and 'shall'

In informal circumstances such as everyday speech 'I will' and 'I shall' become 'I'll'. Similarly we can have 'you'll', 'he'll', 'she'll', 'it'll', 'we'll' and 'they'll'. The negative 'will not' becomes 'won't' and the negative 'shall not' becomes 'shan't'.

In business correspondence we keep to formal English and it would therefore not be appropriate to write these abbreviations. The words should be written out in full: 'I regret that I shall not be able to attend', etc.

5.7   Exercises on 'shall' and 'will'

1 What is an auxiliary verb? Use the verbs 'shall' and 'will' to form the future tense of the following verbs (all six persons).
   a To correspond.
   b To deliver.

2 Make up a sentence about some aspect of overseas trade for each of the verbs listed below. Use any person, in the future tense.
   a To telex.
   b To insure.
   c To dispatch.
   d To consign.

3 Choose the correct form of the verb in each of the following sentences.
   a I (shall, will) send the goods to the freight forwarder tomorrow.
   b You (shall, will) be able to alter the letter of credit if you consult your banker.
   c If the goods are lost, no-one (shall, will) recompense me.
   d The hazardous goods (shall, will) be stored on deck.
   e I (shall, will) go, whatever you say.
   f They (shall, will) be rewarded for their honesty.
   g (Shall, Will) you travel to the conference tomorrow?
   h We (shall, will) commence exporting to Europe next month.

6 The acknowledgment and acceptance of orders

6.1 The legal implications of accepting an order

We have already seen that a contract is made when a valid offer is accepted unconditionally and valuable consideration is an element in the agreement. An 'order' is an offer to buy, so that if this is accepted a binding contract will immediately be made, so long as valuable consideration (the price) is an element in the agreement between the parties. We must always be cautious therefore in 'accepting' an order, since acceptance has legal consequences. Never 'accept' an order until you have checked it with the pre-contract negotiations, for the customer may have deliberately mis-stated the price quoted, or altered the terms of delivery or of payment in some subtle way, and to 'accept' the order would be to accept these changed conditions. In strict law it might be possible to argue one's way out of a contract made in error, but it is much safer to avoid the trouble by careful correspondence in the first place.

It follows that we do not 'accept' orders straight away, we only *acknowledge* their receipt and promise a letter of acceptance in a few days' time. Of course there will be many occasions when an order can be accepted at once and dispatched the same day. For example, when we are dealing with a trusted and respected customer, known to be absolutely reliable, within a framework of established trading practices, there is no problem at all. Our customer would not wish us to suffer loss on his/her account, any more than we would wish to damage our goodwill as far as he/she is concerned. Good business associates never go to law if they can avoid it, but settle disputes in an agreeable way. No difficulty arises where an order is being made on a standard order form, for the framework of business relations has been clearly understood before the order form is completed. Problems do arise where an order is for a non-routine transaction, for example a specialised production job, or an export order involving documentation, etc., or a service arrangement where the actual work to be done cannot be accurately forecast. In all these cases a check on the order is essential and 'acceptance' becomes a more formal matter where we clearly undertake the legal consequences which follow from the words 'We accept your order.' Until the check has been made we only send a letter of acknowledgment.

6.2 The acknowledgment of an order

In the letters that follow an order has been acknowledged, but not accepted. The acknowledgment letter lets the customer know the order has arrived safely, but does not constitute an acceptance, and the legal consequences of an acceptance do not therefore follow. Such letters are usually fairly brief, and in some cases a **preprinted postcard** with spaces left for typing in a few relevant details may be adequate for the purpose. In others a **standard letter** may be used, with a few details typed or written in. The advantage of such pre-printed standard formats is that they can include phrases which clarify the legal position – such as 'Our formal acceptance will follow in a few days.'

The first two pieces of correspondence shown, SL6.1 and SL6.2, are blank. They are a preprinted postcard and a standard-form letter which could be used as routine acknowledgments for many types of orders.

6.3 Specimen letters of acknowledgment

SL6.1 (A pre-printed postcard)

Aluminium Manufacturers Ltd

Victory Road, Southwell, Notts
Telephone (0635) 01496

.... 19--

We acknowledge the receipt of your order no .... which is
receiving attention. Our letter of acceptance will reach you in a
few days.

                                    Signed ....

SL6.2 (A standard-form letter)

Machinery Reconditioners Ltd

Greasely Street, Bulwell, Nottingham.
Telephone 0602 0123

.... 19--

To

Dear Sirs

Acknowledgment of Order No

We acknowledge the receipt of your order as shown above which reached
us on .... Please note the information marked with a
X on the right hand side.

<u>Note X below</u>

a Our acceptance of this order will follow in
   a few days.   ....
b This order does not conform to the pre-contract
   negotiations and a letter of clarification will
   reach you within a few days.   ....
c The order is defective for the following reason/s
   and is returned herewith for your attention.
   i Not dated   ....

  ii Not signed   ....

 iii Technical details unclear. Please note:

      ....
      ....

  iv Prices incorrect. The correct prices are:

      ....
      ....

   v Other reasons: ....

      ....

If you resubmit the order we shall be happy to supply you.

Yours faithfully

Sales Manager

Aluminium Components (Kings Lynn) Ltd

Hythe Road, Wormgay, Norfolk. Tel: 47799

Your Ref: Order No 1204 24 April 19--
Our Ref: TP/dg

27 April 19--

Sports Stadium Construction Ltd
594 Kings Road
Cambridge
CB2 2HJ

Dear Sirs

Acknowledgment of Order No 1024

Thank you for your order received today, for aluminium units for the
college sports stadium. The order has been passed to our designer
Peter Phillips who co-operated with Mrs Shiner on the proposed
building. He will send you our formal acceptance within a few days,
and we have no doubt that the work can be put in hand in good time
for the vacation dates you mentioned.

Yours faithfully

T Poynter
Order Progress Clerk

6.4   Letters of regret

It occasionally happens that an order cannot be accepted for some
reason. The established arrangements of firms may be affected by
international problems, wars, natural disasters, changes in the ownership of companies, etc. In these circumstances letters of regret must
be sent to let the customer know of the changed circumstances. Such
an interruption in established relationships can be very serious for
the firms concerned and it would be helpful to suggest alternative
suppliers or even alternative materials that might be used as a sub-
stitute. Some attempts to preserve the goodwill of the customer
should be made.

Middle East Fruit Corporation Ltd

Lower Wharf, Greenwich, London SE10 7SU
Telephone: 01 - 760 4377

Your Ref: AST/DB 21 November 19--
Our Ref: JQ/RF

Date: 23 November 19--

Metrofruit (Croydon) Ltd
2274 High Street
Croydon
CR9 1JA

Dear Sirs

We very much regret that it is impossible for us to accept your order
for Christmas packs of 'Old Sinbad' dates as supplied in previous
years.

We are sure you will appreciate that the troubled situation in the
Near-East has made it impossible to purchase supplies at economic
prices. Such purchases as we have made were at prices well above last
year's prices, and these supplies were taken at once by one fashion-
able West End store.

We do have negotiations in hand with a Californian supplier to provide
American dates. These are not packaged in the traditional way - the
dates are individual, separated from the stem, and packed in cartons
with polythene tops. The price of these is likely to be 20% higher
than last year's Middle East prices. Would you please reply at once
if these interest you. In view of our long business connection I will
definitely keep supplies available for you if you place an order
within seven days.

Yours faithfully

J Quintall
Import Manager

MOTOR SPARES (Norwich) Ltd

1751 Earlham Way, Norwich, Norfolk, United Kingdom

Telephone: Norwich 73569

```
Your Ref   MM/TJ   7 April 19--
Our Ref    SAB/TT

25 April 19--


Mustafa Mutnil and Co Ltd
725-37 Emek H
Istanbul
Turkey
```

Dear Sirs

Spare Parts: Invalid Vehicles

We very much regret that we are unable to supply you with the spare
parts for the invalid vehicles referred to in your Order No 1275.
These machines ceased to be manufactured some fifteen years ago and
our undertaking to provide spare parts for ten years after the date of
manufacture therefore expired some time ago.

The decision to cease production of these spare parts was reinforced
by new safety regulations introduced in the United Kingdom about the
same time which made the machines unsuitable for use any further in
the United Kingdom.

Improved machines are now available from another company, Invachair
(Wymondham) Ltd, who will be happy to send you brochures. Their
address is College Lane, Morley, Near Wymondham, Norfolk.

With sincere apologies for our inability to assist you.

Yours faithfully

S A Bartram
Chief Engineer and Sales Manager

6.5 Checking an order

An order must be checked from the following points of view:

a Is it in accordance with the pre-contract negotiations with regard to:

   i technical specifications
   ii price
   iii payment terms
   iv time for delivery
   v delivery terms
   vi post-completion problems, such as maintenance or service clauses, etc?

If not, what is the nature of the discrepancy? Action must be taken to point out discrepancies, raise any queries and secure amendment to the order before it is accepted.

b Is it possible to fulfil the order either from goods in stock, or from goods to be manufactured before the designated completion date? You must check the supply position.

c Is the customer creditworthy? Even an established customer can become a credit risk and a pattern of behaviour may be revealed by his/her orders. Frequently a trader will increase orders for saleable goods and use the proceeds to pay other suppliers whose goods have not sold well. New customers should always be investigated, and references taken up from bankers, other major trade suppliers, etc. You should consult your own **trade association** for any record of a prospective new customer's dealings with other members. It is not unknown for an established trader who has become unreliable and failed to pay his/her present suppliers to seek supplies from other sources. If the customer is an established trader why have the established suppliers ceased to supply? Your trade association will usually know.

Any of these matters may call for letters of clarification.

6.6 Letters of clarification

SL6.6

ESSO PETROLEUM COMPANY LTD

Esso House
Victoria Street
London SW1E 5JW

Telephone: 01-834 6677
Cables: Essopet London SW1
Telex: 24942

Your reference	TD/SA/16 June
Our reference	CSG/LB
Extension	2139
Date	21 June 19--

Dear Miss Donaldson

CHART OF THE NUCLIDES

Thank you for your recent order for the Chart of the Nuclides.

We hold stocks of the most recent version of this chart, which is
printed in Germany. As we have been put to considerable expense to
purchase and import these charts, which are not directly concerned
with our business but which are of use to a great many people in the
United Kingdom, I am asking everyone who is interested in obtaining
them to pay a small charge which will go towards these costs. We
imported further supplies of these charts in August 19-- and the
prices have had to be increased to reflect the increase in costs
since the original purchase in 19--.

The material is available in the form of explanatory books (A4 size)
with a folded chart inside the back cover, and a separate wall display
chart. The charge for each book containing a folded chart is £1.50
and for each wall chart £1.00.

Would you please let me have your cheque or postal order to cover the
order. I wish to make the transaction as simple as possible and will
not issue invoices or receipts. I will respond to your request
within seven days and enclose a suitable reply slip for your use.
Each item is zero rated for VAT purposes.

Yours sincerely

C S Gamage
Head of Education Services
Public Affairs Department

Enc. Reply slip

CONFECTION MODERNE

1722 Rue de la Maison Blanche, Alger, Algérie

Your Ref TC/ML 24 August 19--
Our Ref Order No U.K.177 AA/td

31 August 19--

Babcock Sun Tops Ltd
Purley Way
Aveley
Essex
England

Attention of Thomas Cookson, Purchasing Officer

Dear Mr Cookson

Thank you for your recent order which we shall be happy to fulfil as
soon as a major error in your pricing is corrected. I am sure it is
just an oversight on your part, but the price you quote is the price
of the blouses only - you will recall that at our meeting in England
we quoted £3 per blouse.

The suntops were priced at £1.50 each - an additional £7500 in all.

To be correct the total cost to you is therefore £22 500 and we
should insure the consignment for cost plus 10% i.e. £24 750. Would
you please telex your agreement to these figures and we will telex
our acceptance of the order within 24 hours.

We are very glad that our visit to you has produced this order, and
you will have no reason to feel that the final product falls short of
the samples supplied.

Yours very sincerely

Abdul Ajakaiye
Export Manager

Nippon Electronics (Kyoto) Ltd

2-13 Shinsuna 1, Kyoto, Japan

```
Your Ref   Order No 1275
Our Ref    TY/db
31 October 19--
```

```
Electrotones (Waterbeach) Ltd
Cambridge Road
Waterbeach
Cambs
United Kingdom
```

Dear Sirs

1 <u>Disparity in Price</u>
2 <u>Delivery Difficulty</u>

Thank you for your order for 40 electronic organs, dated 27 October 19--. Two difficulties arise over this order.

1 The price quoted is £46.50 per instrument, whereas our salesman Mr Yoshida quoted you £56.50 in his telex of 15 October. It is possible that this is simply a typing slip, but it makes a very considerable difference to the total cost of the order. Will you please telex us confirming that you are prepared to honour the full price of £56.50.

2 You ask us to arrange for the goods to be sent in a single container by the Trans-Siberian Railway route. These organs are packed in crates measuring 4 feet x 4 feet x 5 feet (1.219 m x 1.219 m x 1.524 m). Thirty-two of these crates fit exactly into one 40 foot container. To complete an order for 36 instruments we must use more than one container. You could therefore
  i Reduce your order to 32 organs
 ii Increase your order to 48 organs - which would occupy 1 x 40 foot container and 1 x 20 foot container
iii Leave the order at its present size and allow us to send 8 crates as general cargo, non-containerised, (although in fact the freight forwarder would probably containerise them with other general cargo).

Would you please telex us a decision on these points too.

Yours faithfully

```
T Yamamoto
Sales Manager
```

Agricessories (Long Eaton) Ltd

Long Road Foundries, Long Eaton, Notts.   **Tel: 060 76 80434**

The Manager
Big Four Bankers Ltd
Riverside
Matlock
Derbyshire

Your Ref:
Our Ref: JTD/BA

Date   30 November 19--

Dear Sirs

Re P W Norfolk (Matlock) Ltd, Agricultural Suppliers

We have been given your bank as a referee to whom we might apply for a
credit-worthiness reference. Mr P W Norfolk, managing director of the
above company states that the company has dealt with you over many
years and is in a thoroughly reliable financial position.

The order placed with us is for a considerable quantity of agricultural
spare parts - the total value is £13 500, payable within 30 days of
delivery. Delivery is to be in three parts, £5000 on 1 January, £5000
on 1 March and £3500 on 1 April next. Would you be able to confirm
that P W Norfolk (Matlock) Ltd are likely to be in a position to meet
such bills. As Mr Norfolk has been in business for many years and must
have had other suppliers we wonder why he has changed to us, rather
than his usual suppliers. We are only too ready to supply him, but
since he offered your name as a referee we feel it is prudent to seek
your confirmation of the firm's reliability.

Yours faithfully

J T Doncaster
Financial Director

6.7   Letters accepting an order

The letter of acceptance constitutes the formal recognition that a
binding contract now exists between the two parties. The supplier
agrees to supply on the terms and conditions specified in the order,
or arranged during the pre-contract negotiations. The buyer agrees
to pay the price, and abide by the conditions of payment. Until the
letter of acceptance is put into the post there is no binding contract
– silence cannot be taken as consent. The offeror (the customer) is
free to withdraw the order at any time up to acceptance by the

offeree (the supplier). In that case there will of course be no order to accept. Once the order has been accepted there is a binding contract and if either party tries to withdraw from the contract the other party may bring an action for breach of contract. It does not follow that such an action will be brought — sometimes a cancelled order will be accepted, but more frequently a failure to carry out a bargain is followed by an action for damages for breach of contract.

Frequently a letter of acceptance can be quite short; just stating that steps will be taken immediately to fulfil the order.

6.8 Specimen letters of acceptance

SL6.10

J Smithson & Co (Castle Donnington) Ltd
Derby Road, Castle Donnington, Nr Derby
Telephone: Derby 65724

```
Your Ref   AJ/PT/21 May 19--
Our Ref    RB/BA

24 May 19--


Malcolm Carter Esq
200 High Street
Manchester 14

Dear Sir

Thank you for your order for a Sunway motor caravan.  We refer to our
telephone conversation of 23 May in which you agreed to accept delivery
of a primrose yellow caravan, instead of the daffodil colour requested
in your order.  This being agreed, at no change in price, we accord-
ingly accept your order and will arrange delivery for Friday next, 29
May 19--.

Our driver should reach you about 2.00 pm and will give you a full in-
duction into the use of the various components.  We have booked him a
ticket on a train leaving at 5.30; perhaps you can call him a taxi if
it gets too late for him to reach the station by public transport.


Yours faithfully



R Beckett
Sales Manager
```

Scandisauna Constructors Ltd

Scandisauna House
Long Eaton
Notts

Telephone: 23897

Your Ref Order No 1306 3 February 19--
Our Ref TRA/VB

14 February 19--

Brightside Health and Beauty Clinic
South Parade
Brightside
Suffolk

Dear Madam

Scandinavian Sauna Construction - Your Order as Quoted

Thank you for your order for the construction of three (3) of our
Scandinavian Sauna at your premises. This appears to conform in every
way with the preliminary negotiations conducted by our engineer Thor
Friedrickson, and we accordingly accept the order, and give notice of
our intention to commence the work on Monday 21 February 19--.

In accordance with the arrangements discussed our construction team
of three will arrive in their trailer caravan on Sunday 20 February at
about 3 pm ready to start work next day. Please ensure that a piped
water supply is available as promised, and that access to the rear
yard is available to prevent any parking difficulties.

Yours faithfully

T R Anderson
Progress Controller

Macclesfield Mechanical Handling (Langley) Ltd

Lower Town Road, Langley, Cheshire　　　　　**Telephone: 490490**

T Steadman Esq　　　　　　　　　　　Your Ref　Order No 217
Jordan Bros Ltd　　　　　　　　　　　Our Ref　PA/TD
131 Park Street
London W1　　　　　　　　　　　　　　　7 July 19--

Dear Mr Steadman

Thank you for your order to overhaul and repair three fork lift trucks
from your wharf during the August holiday period. We accept this order
and I have made arrangements to collect the three trucks as agreed on
the afternoon of 31 July.

We agree to return them on Monday 17 August, at 9 am, but if unforeseen
circumstances delay the repairs a replacement will be provided for any
truck not available at the nominal charge of £30 per week, per machine.

We very much appreciate this order, and hope that you will have a rest-
ful and enjoyable vacation.

Yours sincerely

Peter Allswell
Maintenance Supervisor

6.9　Exercises on the acknowledgment and acceptance of orders

1　Write a brief letter to S J Fraser (Kensington) Ltd acknowledging
the receipt of their order for a mini-computer. Be careful not to
accept the order, which has not yet been examined carefully, but
promise a letter about the order within a few days. Invent suitable
addresses. Your own firm is called Compulogic (London) Ltd.

2　Mycelium Ltd have received an order for bacteriological equipment from the Outback University, Alice Springs, Northern Terri-
tories, Australia. Send them a letter acknowledging receipt of the
order and promising a decision about acceptance of the order
within seven days.

3　You have received an order from A Broadbent for seeds and cut-
tings. Due to weather conditions stocks are low and you do not

want to accept the order until the supply position is clearer. Acknowledge the order and promise a letter about acceptance within 21 days. Invent suitable addresses.

4 Camside Rentacar Ltd of Thetford Road, Bradwell, Suffolk have sent you an order for intercom equipment. There are two types, Instant Contact and Page-a-Car, and they have omitted to say which they prefer, though the price indicates that it is probably a Page-a-Car device. Write to them to clarify the problem. Your firm is On Call (Luton) Ltd, 247 Downsway, Luton, Bedfordshire.

5 Bedford Jewellery Centre Ltd, of 2174 High Street, Bedford have ordered a machine used in gold-soldering. Unfortunately they quote from a catalogue so ancient that the price suggested is only about half the current price. Write to clarify the situation and enclose a current brochure. Ask them to send cash with order, as you have not dealt with them before. The device is called Gold-solder, and sells at £194.50 (including carriage and insurance).

6 The visual aids centre of Durino Technical College, Durino, Fife, Scotland has sent an order for a fibre optics copier without specifying the make. You are the agents for three such copiers. Write them a letter asking them to clarify which machine they require, and enclosing brochures about the Fibre Optic 127, the Half-Tone Specialist 42B and the Instant Copy Photo-Electronic 60. Also enclose your current price list and impress on them that an educational discount of 15 per cent is available.

7 Write to Great Easton Truck Co Ltd, accepting their order for a drilling machine, Lathex 127 at £1425.50. This order appears to be in accordance with the pre-contract negotiations conducted by the sales representative Geoffrey Skinner. Promise them delivery by road on the Monday morning of next week, and installation by an engineer, Peter Crawley. Remind them that they have agreed to provide lifting tackle and labour to move the machine to its work site and that it weighs 758 kilograms. Your firm is called Workshop Supplies (Saffron Walden) Ltd.

8 Write to Thomas Jenkins and Partners accepting an order they have placed for fireproof paints for exhibition work. Promise delivery by Road Haulage Services Ltd within three weeks. Your firm is Fire Security Services Ltd, 27 Newmarket Road, Chevington,

Suffolk. Enclose a brochure called 'Exhibition Safety' with helpful hints about fire hazards at exhibition centres.

9 Accept an order from Gerard Montier SA, 1784 Rue de Paris, Arois-sur-Aube 10700, France for knitting machinery negotiated by a foreign salesperson, Christina Carpentier. Your firm is Knitwear Machinery (Blackburn) Ltd, 2174 Church St, Blackburn, Lancashire. Delivery will be in ten days' time, by road haulage using the cross-channel ferries. Ask them to call Christina Carpentier for advice on installation and any problems that arise.

10 Write to Zimbabwe Heavy Haulage Ltd, Uhuru Street, Harare City, Zimbabwe, accepting an order for spare parts for their heavy haulage fleet. The order no. is P2145, Ministry Authorisation 264. Promise delivery by air freight within 21 days and assure them of your willingness to fulfil further orders as required. You are Heavy Haulage Supplies (Grays) Ltd, London Road, Grays, Essex, England.

6.10 Appendix on the English language: 'should' and 'would'

'Should' and 'would' are auxiliary verbs, which we have already defined as verbs that help us make the tenses of other verbs. They are the *past* form of 'shall' and 'will', and their basic function is to express futurity from the viewpoint of some past time. For example:

I explained that I should be available later in the day.

He explained that he would be available later in the day.

Both 'should' and 'would' are future with respect to the verb 'explained' — at the time of the explanation neither person was available — their availability lay in the future.

As far as simple futurity is concerned the rules are the same as 'shall' and 'will' — 'should' in the 1st person singular and plural, and 'would' in the 2nd and 3rd persons.

The reason why 'should' and 'would' are confusing is that they are also used in other ways, and we have to consider the **context** in which they are used. The context means the actual words in use at the moment. We have the following uses:

a Simple futurity — as explained above.

b Duty, or fitness for purpose. 'Should' is used for all three persons:

In these circumstances I should take command.

You should examine the machine for airworthiness.

Forty watts should be enough.

c Hesitancy or doubt. 'Should' is used for all three persons:

Should we do it, it must be before dawn.

If you should see the engineer, congratulate him for me.

d In reported speech 'should' takes the place of 'shall' and 'would' takes the place of 'will':

'I shall be available after the meeting with the sales representatives.'

I said that I should be available after the meeting with the sales representatives.

'Morgan will arrive at ten am' said the manager.

The manager declared that Morgan would arrive at ten am.

e To show custom, or habit, 'would' is used:

At New Year the traders would gather together and drink toasts to the year ahead.

f To show determination 'would' is used in all three persons:

I would go, even though the ambassador cautioned me against it.

You would do it, and now all of us must suffer.

They would resist, whatever the show of force from the police.

6.11 Exercises on 'should' and 'would'

1 Choose the correct form of each of the following sentences, and explain why it is correct:

a I (should, would) report the matter, as I am the senior member of staff present.

b Despite the presence of the customs officer the driver (should, would) not open the locked compartment.

c The Minister stated that she (should, would) be replying to the debate on the final day.

d Every month, when the moon was full, the caravan (should, would) depart to take the goods to the oasis and avoid the day-time crossing so feared by travellers.

e Exporters (should, would) respect the laws of the countries with whom they trade.

2 Report to your managing director the following statement made by an export clerk. Begin : 'The export clerk said that he . . .':

'I shall be able to deliver the goods to the freight forwarders by Friday, and they will be able to deliver them to Doha by the 26th, provided that the inspection is completed by tomorrow.'

7 The fulfilment of orders

7.1 Order data folders and management feedbacks

Every business organisation must lay down procedures for every activity that is to take place. It is the duty of each head of department to ensure that a procedure is devised for every new activity that arises, and that staff are made aware of the procedures to be followed, and trained adequately to carry them out. Often the completion of a form, or the opening of a file, is the first stage in any procedure. For the fulfilment of orders an 'order data folder' is a useful standard procedure and the type of folder illustrated in Figs 7.1 and 7.2 is reproduced by kind permission of Formecon Services Ltd, Gateway, Crewe, CW1 1YN.

The procedure starts with the opening of the order data folder to give all the details of the order in readily accessible form. The front cover of the data folder should be carefully typed or written up. Its boxes record the essential data. The page 'Considerations for Action' suggest 10 headings under which most orders can be processed, but there is plenty of room for managers to insert stages which they wish to incorporate – for regular orders needing attention on a specific matter a rubber stamp could be made and blank folders could have the extra items stamped in before they are issued for use.

The reader will note that items 1-10 cover most of the points made in Chapter 6. For example there are spaces for checking that the order agrees with the price list or quotation, the acknowledgment of the order, letters of clarification, the supply position, the acceptance of the order and so on.

The whole purpose of an order data folder is to establish a 'live' file which will be continuously reviewed until the order is completed and dispatched. The concept of the **progress-chaser** is important. A progress-chaser is a person who keeps track of the stage the firm has reached in the fulfilment of the order, and who is alerted by anyone who becomes aware of a change in the situation affecting the order. For example, if a workshop making up a special order for a customer

HOME
M A R K E T DATA FOLDER

Date	
Order via PHONE ☐	order via ☐
Completed by	

Customer's Order No.		Dated		Name & Address of Customer (Invoice)
Representative/Agent	Territory		Commission	
Receipt of Order acknowledged to Customer		Date		
Confirmed Acceptance of Order to Customer		Date		
Terms of Payment				Delivery Address
Credit Approved By		Monthly Limit £		
Method of Remittance				
Name & Address of Customer's Bank		Account No./Giro No.		Name of Customer Contact
		Branch Code		Telephone No. Ext. Telex No.
Date(s) Delivery Required	Transportation by			Cost of Delivery

EXCLUDED FROM / INCLUDED IN — SELLING PRICE

Production/Goods Description	Our Part No.	Quantity	Unit Price	Total Value

Internal Works No.	Advice Note No.	Delivery Note No.		TOTAL INVOICE ORDER VALUE

REVIEW THIS FOLDER **REGULARLY** UNTIL ORDER COMPLETE

Fig. 7.1 A 'Home Market' data folder

CONSIDERATIONS FOR ACTION

1 Check that Customer's order agrees with our price list or quotation. Acknowledge receipt of the order and refer to any discrepancies, amendments or queries as necessary. Insert acknowledgement date on front cover of folder and note here those points requiring clarification...............................	**5** Despatch date target/deadline ....
	Progress on .... NOTIFY
	Again on .... CUSTOMER IF
	Again on .... ANY CHANGE
	Again on .... OF DELIVERY
	Again on .... DATE EXPECTED
	6 Complete transport arrangements (see front)
	7 Note partial deliveries (if any) in record section provided on back cover
2 Enter on front cover details of the order and all financial particulars	**8** Note here any difficulties or problems encountered with this transaction up to time of delivery ....
3 Supply position/information.....................................	
	9 New order or repeat prospects – action taken ....
	10 Other information ....
4 Confirm acceptance of order to Customer and insert date order accepted in box on front cover	CHECK ALL DOCUMENTATION AND CORRESPONDENCE IS ENCLOSED IN POCKET OPPOSITE AND FILE THE COMPLETED FOLDER AWAY FOR FUTURE REFERENCE.

Fig. 7.2 Action procedures for fulfilling an order

is held up by a missing component, or supply of material, the foreman should at once phone the progress-chaser about the matter. The progress-chaser will not only alert the customer to the possibility of delay, but will chase-up the missing component or source of materials to ensure that the necessary item is supplied at once. Having accepted the order the firm is contractually bound to supply the goods according to the contract. Failure to keep a file 'live' and under review may lead to legal action for delay, or breach of contract.

Another concept that is important is **management feedback.** There should be a built-in feedback system so that management is kept informed of all the problems that arise. If an order is commenced, continued and completed without any difficulties using the routine procedures management will not need to be informed at all except perhaps for some signal on completion. It is when the standard procedures prove inadequate for some reason that management needs to be informed. This is often called **management by exceptions** – management only needs to know when standard procedures do *not* work.

Even where a standard procedure is satisfactory and there has been no need to alert management to a problem with an order, it is always advisable to review procedures regularly. The most appropriate moment to review procedures is at the point where an order data folder ceases to be 'live' and is about to be filed away for future reference. Section 8 on the order data folder (Fig. 7.2) gives an opportunity to review the progress of the order and the problems overcome in its fulfilment. Where these are the result of personal failings we should draw them to the attention of the person concerned, preferably in an informal way. If the matter is not one where an individual can be blamed, but is due to a change in the circumstances, an internal memo to an appropriate person is called for. Thus if experience shows that it is better to give the freight forwarder 14 days' notice, rather than the present 7 days' notice, this modification of standard procedures should be drawn to the attention of management by an internal memo.

7.2   Internal memos and procedures

A memorandum is a note to help the memory. At one time memos were regarded as 'informal' notes, and were not signed, and no doubt many trivial matters even today are scribbled on pads of scrap paper and passed to those whose memory needs to be jogged. More usual today, since the scale of business tends to be large, is for memos to be made available as pre-printed memo sets of NCR paper. NCR means 'no carbon required'. The back of the paper is specially coated and when the sender writes on the top copy, the message is repeated on the sheets below. A three-part set, in different colours, gives the sender one copy to retain as a personal record, and two to send to the addressee. The addressee then replies to the memo in the space provided, the message being copied by the NCR system on to the third copy. One copy is now returned to the sender, who thus has both the original message and the answer to it on one piece of paper. The third copy is retained by the original addressee, who knows both the original query and the reply he/she gave to it. This slightly more formal system, where the parties involved actually sign their names, is clearly a very simple and efficient method.

When fulfilling orders many memos will be passed to various departments. They may ensure that the goods are produced, or selected from warehouse stocks; transport may need to be organised; packing may need to be of a specialised type, etc. Sometimes these procedures can be started by sending copy invoices to the various departments, so that they are alerted to the need for their services — the copy invoice virtually becomes a memo. Sometimes a formal memo will be desirable and at other times an informal scrap of paper may be enough. Never let the informality of the note deteriorate to the point where the recipient is misled. 'Charlie rang' may convey much to the sender who took the call from Charlie; the recipient may know five Charlies in five continents. Give Charlie's phone number, and some indication of the subject matter, to make the memo intelligible. Examples of typical memos are given below.

SL7.1

```
Memo from: Sales Manager
To:         Factory Supervisor                7 October 19--
```

```
Copy of Order No 1256 attached.  Please proceed to manufacture these
items at once and report progress to me every Friday.  We hope to
export the goods on the 'Southern Star', sailing 12 November, South-
ampton.  Thanks,
                              Bill
```

SL7.2

```
Memo from:  Mike Thomas
To:         Mark Letchworth                      Date: 27 November 19--
_____

Message:    Roger Fryer phoned from Leavis Airframes (Cambridge) Ltd, re
Order No 1625.  He wants to modify the aileron trim wheels on the CT204
to comply with Japanese requirements.  Can you phone him urgently on
0223-01945?
Should there be any difficulties over this you can contact me as follows:

Place:  H O     Phone No: Usual     Time: Any time after 2 pm
```

SL7.3

```
Memo from:  R Fryer (Extension 218)
To:         General Manager                      Date: 27 November 19--
_____

Message:    I contacted Mike Thomas about the aileron trim wheels on
the CT204.  Mark Letchworth is coming down on Tuesday to look at the
problem - bringing two prototypes designed for similar jobs elsewhere.
Looks hopeful anyway.  Should be able to keep Osaka happy.  Will report
on Tuesday.
                                        Roger
```

SL7.4

```
                            MEMORANDUM

From:  R Metcalf (Stores)                Extension:  179
To:    J Fisher (Sales)                  Date:  17 October 19--
_____
Re Order No 1256 - final stage of manufacture.  Request from Production
Dept for heavy gauge brass sheeting cannot be fulfilled due to trans-
port problems up north.  Will medium gauge sheeting do?  Please check
this out.  If not please contact Buying Dept about the possibility of a
local purchase - we did get some once from the Generating Board (as a
special favour).  Could be worth a try.  We are ahead of schedule - but
please treat this as urgent.
                            Ron
```

MEMORANDUM

From: Richard Jones   *Extension:* 248
To: Peter Gold (Progress Chaser)   *Date:* 17 December 19--

Re Order 2785 for Doha. I see from the Journal of Commerce today that
the Silver Crescent line ferry 'Star of the Sea' was lost in the Mediterranean yesterday. She was due to handle this cargo to Doha on her
next trip. Can you get on to the agents and find out the position
please so we don't let Doha down? These units are urgently required for
their construction project. Please keep me informed of the position.

                                        Dick

7.3 Exercises on internal memos

1 Design a memo form to be produced by your in-house printing department for use by members of staff, one with another. Make sure you include spaces for the date, the time, the name of the sender, his/her department and the telephone extension. The message section should be clearly headed, and large enough to permit a detailed memo to be sent if necessary. There should be a space for the addressee and his/her department.

2 You have noticed that an order, sent to your dispatch department for immediate delivery, contains an item which cannot be delivered at once, although supplies are promised by the weekend. Write a memo to Mark Tarfor in the sales department asking him whether the order can be delayed until Monday of next week, or whether you should send what you have, and promise delivery early next week of the outstanding item. Point out that the delivery destination is at the very limit of your delivery area, so that a double delivery involves an extra cost of about £8.

3 Write a memo to Sheila Thornbury in the publicity department telling her that an order delivered this week exceeded the record for order size — 625 camera units for Japan — which is like selling refrigerators to Eskimos. Suggest it might make an item for the house magazine and tell her the salesman, Peter Ellis, is available until next Friday on Extension 2147.

4 A major order — called 'The New Zealand Project' — is awaiting final approval from Wellington. Send a memo to Giles Kennedy, the factory manager, telling him that Wellington have sent a telex reading 'Project approved for payment — start to manufacture at once'. Ask him to proceed at once as planned, and make arrangements to implement the double-shift system already approved by the Joint Planning Committee.

5 Send a memo to Peta Lorenzo in the stores department asking her to check supplies of 3 mm and 4 mm aluminium rivets as large quantities will be needed in the near future for Order 1568. Suggest she ensures at least 10 000 of each are available.

6 Write a memo to the general manager telling her that Umo Eyo, the Lagos representative, sold 100 000 garments last month to clients in the Lagos area. Ask her if she finds it interesting in view of her speech to African representatives at the sales conference next Friday.

7.4 The frustration of contracts

Inevitably occasions arise when it is impossible to fulfil an order by the agreed date or in the agreed way. Provided the circumstances are not the result of your own fault, but are due to matters quite outside your control, the other party to the contract must accept the new situation. The contract is said to be **frustrated**. Thus where it becomes illegal to trade in a particular article, a contract to supply the article will be frustrated by supervening illegality. If the subject-matter of the contract is destroyed, as where a prize bull dies before it can be delivered to the purchaser, the contract is frustrated.

In many cases contracts will not be frustrated, but their fulfilment may be delayed, or the exact specifications can no longer be achieved and you may need to persuade the customer to modify the specifications to make fulfilment of the order possible. Such matters must be the subject of immediate correspondence to resolve the difficulty.

ELECTROFITTERS (Beeston) Ltd

Unit 27, Tennis Street Trading Estate, Beeston

Telephone: 37456

Your Ref: GW/KT
Our Ref: Order 1287

Date   21 October 19--

Goodwood, Harthouse (Sheffield) Ltd
Hallam Grange Road
Upper Fulwood
Sheffield 10

Dear Sirs

Installation of Power Units - 28 October 19--

We regret to inform you that due to the death of an installation fitter
in the recent oil rig disaster we shall be unable to commence the work
planned at your factory until 9 November. We have two fitters returning from a job in the Middle East on 7 November and they have agreed
to postpone the leave due to them and work together on your
installation.

Although this delay in the commencement of the work is an inconvenience
this co-operation enables us to say that the final completion date
should still be met, and the start-up procedure commence on 7 December
as planned. Please may we have your confirmation that these revised
arrangements are acceptable to you.

Yours faithfully

George Walker
Contracts Manager

BOWMAN ELECTRONICS LTD

2027 CANTON HILL, HERTFORD
Tel. Hertford 019576

Your Ref: Order 2596
Our Ref: SA/PT

27 February 19--

Benzinger A G
Ch 127884
Via St Gothardo
Locarno
Switzerland

Dear Sirs

<u>Delay due to Sinking of Cross-Channel Ferry</u>

I refer to the completion of this order which we telexed you to say
would be achieved by delivery to your warehouse last Saturday. I am
sure you will have heard of the loss of the ferry 'Tricolour' last
Thursday; I regret to say that the road haulage vehicle containing the
remaining crates was lost in the collision. Our driver was among those
saved, and he had the documents on his person so we have had no
difficulty in claiming for the loss.

We have instituted a crash programme to manufacture the specialist
parts you require, and are assembling the stock parts which also form
part of the order. The test engineers nominated by you have agreed to
carry out a repeat of their tests at 24 hours notice, and we therefore
have every expectation of getting a replacement set of parts to you by
about Wednesday 9 March.

We are sending this letter by Air Courier Services Ltd, and would
appreciate a telex in reply confirming that you agree to these proposals, and are prepared to honour the original agreement.

Yours sincerely

S Archibald
Sales Manager

Miller-Lansdowne Associates (Blackburn) Ltd

Public Relations Consultants

High Tor House, Mintsfeet Street, Kendal, Cumbria
Telephone: Kendal 51124

```
Your Reference:   Order No 2578
Our Reference:    KM/ST

3 April 19--


The Head Teacher
The Haymakers' Trade School
Crescent Road
Cambridge
CB4 1PQ


Dear Sir

With reference to the delay caused to your order by the difficulties
of our suppliers on the continent, we are now able to confirm that the
public relations equipment you require has been dispatched from Hamburg
direct to your school, and should reach you by Friday, 12 April.  We
very much regret that this will still be too late for the function you
are holding on 10 April.

In confirmation of our telephone conversation today I have made
arrangements for a representative of Public Events Ltd, Grantchester
to call on you.  They will provide full coverage of your function using
a similar public address system, and will invoice the charge direct to
us.  I hope this will compensate you for the inconvenience you have
suffered, and that you will have a very successful day.

Yours sincerely




Kenneth Miller
Consultant
```

ORIENTAL PETROLEUMS

1439 Chung Shan, 3rd Road, Kaohsuing, China

Sheldrake (Norfolk) Ltd   Your Ref: JKL/SD
2074 Morley Road   Our Ref: TM/SA
Wymondham
Norfolk   4 October 19--

Dear Mr Lawrence

Frustrated Contract 2187

Thank you for your letter dated 27 September. We are very surprised
to hear that you intend to hold us personally responsible for our
failure to supply the plastic materials agreed under Contract 2187.
We have already informed you that the supply of these materials has
been made illegal by an order from the Ministry of Trade in Shanghai,
and we are quite unable to influence this decision.

We wish to remind you that under the terms of the contract this trading
relationship was agreed to be subject to the laws of the People's
Republic of China (Clause 19). Even if you bring action against us in
the English courts, which may or may not have jurisdiction in the
matter, they will certainly insist on trying the case by the law nominated in Clause 19, and this will involve very costly expert witnesses
being called in London. We doubt whether you could win your case even
if such legal experts could be persuaded to travel to London. This is
in our view a clear case of frustration by supervening illegality.

We are naturally distressed to be unable to help you in this way. May
we suggest that you approach a very good customer of ours, Hon Kuing
Wong, of Palace Road, Krung Thep, Thailand. He is in the Telex
Directory, and recently purchased a very large consignment of this
plastic material which we shipped two days before the embargo. He may
be willing to make some available to you.

We hope we may resume trading with you one day, when the present short-
ages of this material have been overcome.

Yours sincerely

Thomas Mann
General Manager

7.6 The completion of an order

When an order has been completed it is usual to notify the firm concerned. Frequently goods will be sent to branches remote from head office, where the accounts department is usually situated. Similarly work may be performed at sites other than the head office, and unless a formal notification is sent that the work is complete and payment is due no attempt will be made by the customer to settle the account. A letter about the completion of an order will often have the account enclosed, and will trigger off the mechanism to confirm that the goods have arrived, or the work has been completed to the customer's satisfaction. Payment of the account will then be arranged.

Study the specimen letters in section 7.7 below, and then attempt some of the questions in section 7.8.

7.7 Letters after completion of an order

SL7.10

Conservaspace Ltd

24 Tileway Estate, Royston, Herts. Tel: 72910

Your Ref: Order No 2146   *Our Ref:* GRT/STC   7 January 19--

Cox and Co Ltd
Station Road
Willingham Junction
Herts

Dear Sirs

I have much pleasure in confirming that your order for six conservaspace filing cabinets was completed today with delivery to your offices. We hope you will find the cabinets and fittings satisfactory and experience a real improvement in both work-convenience and security.

Naturally we hope that this will not be the last order we fulfil for you. We shall, with your permission, send you details of any new lines we introduce, and our catalogues as they appear.

Our account is enclosed, and we hope you will pass it to your Accounts Department for payment.

Yours faithfully

G R Trainier
Sales Manager

MOYLAN FUELS LTD
REFINERY ROAD
CANVEY ISLAND
ESSEX

Tel: 736900   Telex: 97452

Your Ref: Order No 1758
Our Ref: ST/VB/95

17 September 19--

J R Whiteside
Make and Mend (Thaxted) Ltd
2175 Walden Way
Thaxted
Essex

Dear Mr Whiteside

Completion of Installation and Supply of Fuel

We are happy to report that the installation undertaken at your
Thameswharf Depot is now complete and your engineer has sent us his
letter of acceptance confirming that the heating equipment is operational. I see he has copied this letter to you and trust this
confirmation has reached your department.

As arranged our Delivery Department will deliver fuel supplies on the
last Monday of each month, and the quantity supplied will be invoiced
to you the same week.

Our account for the installation work is enclosed.

May we thank you for this order, which has been completed without any
difficulties on either side. Our fitting engineers have particularly
referred to the cooperation they have received from your staff, and
we should be grateful if you would convey to them our sincere thanks
for this helpful approach.

Yours very sincerely

S Taylor
Installation Engineer

Enc

Cottage to Castle Ltd
**2424 Scotland Road
Newcastle upon Tyne
Tel: 789345**

Your Ref: Order No 1458
Our Ref: TD/SA/C1
24 March 19--

The Estate Manager
Tyneside Stately Homes Ltd
Alwinston
Tyne and Wear

Dear Sir

We confirm that the renovation work and cleaning undertaken under this
Order No 1458 have now been completed to the satisfaction of the house-
keeper at the Hall, and we hope that upon inspection you will find
everything to your satisfaction.

The work has proceeded smoothly considering that it is the largest
commission we have tackled to date, and we are grateful for the
opportunity. Should you wish similar work to be carried out at any of
your other properties we should be most happy to undertake it. Our
account will reach you within a few days; we should appreciate payment
as soon as possible.

Yours faithfully

T Donaldson
Contract Foreman

7.8   Exercises about the fulfilment of orders

1 As order clerk for Cork Products (Suffolk) Ltd, 24 Mildenhall Way,
Ipswich you are dealing with an order for table mats from Tourist
Souvenirs (Cambridge) Ltd, of 245 Trinity Street, Cambridge. The
order requires illustrated mats of a certain design on 3 mm cork,
but the only mats of this design are on 4 mm cork. You have
plenty of illustrated mats on 3 mm cork but not this design. Write
to clarify the situation.

2 An order from Shopfitters Ltd, 24 Roydon Way, Waltham Cross
includes an item entitled 'guard rail to surround floor well' in oak

or walnut. Write in your capacity as sales manager for Safety Devices (Southampton) Ltd to say that wooden guard rails for such features are not advisable since many insurance companies insist on metal fittings. These are available in steel or brass, and some of the steel units are available in light oak or teak finishes. Ask for clarification of the order. Your address is 1727 Western Esplanade, Southampton, Hants.

3 An order from Joliblouse (Totton) Ltd, 2384 Ilford Lane, Totton, Southampton for four sewing machines fails to state whether new machines or factory re-built models are required. In your capacity as industrial machines manager of Gosport Sewing Machines Ltd, Gosport, Hants, write to inquire which is required, pointing out that there is a difference of £78.50 in the price of each machine.

4 A customer, Harry White, of Fleming Way, Crawley, West Sussex, has ordered a garden shed in cedar, but has quoted the price of a soft-wood shed which is £23.00 cheaper. He has also referred to 'free delivery and erection' although in fact he lives outside the free delivery area and there is a charge of £15 for the extra mileage. Write in your capacity as dispatch clerk for Domestic Sheds (Titchfield) Ltd, of Segensworth Road, Titchfield, Hants seeking clarification of the customer's order and willingness to pay the full charges.

5 You have just completed an installation job for industrial machinery at the Arrowsmith Electrical Manufacturing Co (Durham) Ltd, whose head office is at Framwellgate, Durham City. The site of the installation was the Ponteland Industrial Centre, and the site engineer has confirmed his acceptance of the work done in a Site Office Memo 216 which has been copied to Head Office. Write to them enclosing your account for £384.50, referring to the memo mentioned above and expressing your willingness to undertake similar work at any time.

6 You have just completed an order to fly four parties of geologists over Pennine hill sites for the purpose of spotting locations for industrial premises. The work is to be charged to Pennine Surveys (Matlock) Ltd, Quarry Lane, Matlock. Write as manager, Hovercopter (Castleton) Ltd, Castleton Airport, South Yorkshire. Write enclosing your account and seeking further employment on any similar survey work in the area.

7.9 Appendix on the English language: agreement between nouns and pronouns

A **noun** is the name of a person, place or thing. A **pronoun** is a word which is used in place of a noun, to save repetition. It usually refers to a noun that has already been mentioned, which is therefore called the antecedent noun.

When using a pronoun it must agree with the noun it replaces in:

a number, i.e. singular or plural
b gender, i.e. masculine or feminine
c person, i.e. first, (I, me, my, mine, etc.)
               second (you, your, yours, etc.)
               third (he, she, it, his, her, its, etc.)

For example it would be wrong to say 'The *boy* took off *her* hat' as the noun 'boy' is masculine, whereas the possessive pronoun 'her' is feminine. The sentence should say 'The *boy* took off *his* hat' as the pronoun now agrees in number (singular), gender (masculine) and person (third).

Similarly: 'The lecturer expects every student to produce *your* assignment.' Here it is the 'person' that is wrong. The word 'person' refers to three possibilities: the first person is the speaker, the second person is the one spoken to, and the third person is the one spoken about. In the sentence above the antecedent noun is 'student', which is the third person, the one who is being spoken about. 'Your' is a possessive pronoun referring to the second person, and is only used for the person actually being spoken to — as for example in the sentence 'Where is *your* assignment, Smith?' Clearly, the lecturer does not expect every student to produce *your* assignment. It is not sensible. What the lecturer does expect is that every student will produce an assignment. Since students may be either male or female, the correct sentence would read:

> The lecturer expects every student to produce his (or her) assignment.

If mistakes of 'gender' and 'person' are fairly obvious, mistakes of 'number' are not so easily appreciated. Thus many students would write:

> The lecturer expects every student to produce *their* assignment.

This is incorrect, because 'every student' refers to every single one, and 'their' is plural, so the number is incorrect. Suppose the sentence had read:

The lecturer expects all students to produce their assignments.

Is this correct for number? Yes, because 'students' is plural, and so 'their' is correct, and of course the word 'assignments' is plural too.

7.10 Exercises on agreement between nouns and pronouns

1 Which of the words in brackets is correct in each of the sentences below? Write out the sentence in its correct form.
   a The injured boy dried (her, his) eyes.
   b If anyone objects let (him, them) leave the room.
   c Schubert is one of the composers who sing to (his, their) audiences.
   d The team seeking promotion lost (their, its) final match of the season.
   e The court gave (its, their) ruling.

2 Write two column headings on a sheet of paper: 'Antecedent noun' and 'Correct pronoun'. From each of the sentences which follow select the correct pronoun and the antecedent noun to which it refers:
   a The actress forgot (his, her) lines.
   b We enjoy collecting coloured postcards because (they, it) are attractive.
   c The statues are packed in (its, their) cases.
   d The car was noisy as (her, it) came round the corner.
   e I won't attend student union functions because (it, they) interfere with my studies.
   f You will find (you, your) bags in the corner.
   g If anyone steals from the shop we prosecute (him, them).
   h The boy (which, who) came top was applauded.
   i When (they, she) saw the team, the spectators applauded.
   j The boat had suffered damage to (its, their) steering gear in the storm.

8 Complaints and their adjustment

8.1 The nature of complaints

We have seen that business relationships are largely a matter of contractual links between two parties: the customer being the buyer of goods or services, and the supplier being the seller of goods or the provider of services. All contractual arrangements must be mutually beneficial or business will cease. The buyer must receive goods or services of the kind or quality he anticipated; the seller must receive the price of the goods, or payment for the services. Failure to achieve either of these aims will lead to complaints, but in this chapter we are dealing with complaints by the customer. The customer may of course be a retail customer, or a person in business who is dissatisfied with goods or services supplied. Either way the making of complaints is an unpleasant business and needs to be well-prepared and well-documented. Failure to make a complaint effective usually occurs as a result of inadequate presentation of the complaint. A vague complaint will almost always fail, for to give satisfaction over any complaint almost certainly reduces the profit on a transaction to zero, and if every vague grievance were to be compensated business would become unprofitable and pointless.

The position in contract law is interesting, and since the ultimate sanction in any complaint is to take legal action it is helpful to understand the position. In English law there are two kinds of undertakings entered into in every contract. The more important of the two is called a **condition**. A condition of a contract goes to the root of the contract. To break a condition is to break the contract and leads to an action for breach of contract. Thus if a bridge is to be made of steel, and in fact it is made of iron, or some less satisfactory material than steel, this would be a breach of a condition of the contract. If I wanted a crimson car and it proved to be maroon in colour this might, or might not, amount to such a serious difference that it amounted to a breach of the whole contract. The less important type of undertaking is called a warranty. A warranty does not go to the root of the contract, so I cannot claim breach of contract, but it does entitle me to compensation for breach of warranty. These undertakings do not actually need to be stated in so many words; they may be implied by law. The Sale of Goods Act states quite clearly that in any sale of goods there are a number of 'implied conditions' and 'implied warranties' which are understood to be part of the contract of sale even if these undertakings were never actually mentioned. If it were not so, we should complicate life very much, for every time we purchased a bar of chocolate the shopkeeper would need to say 'I warrant that you shall find this bar of chocolate fit for the purpose for which it was intended', etc.

If we wish to complain, and the basis of our complaint is that goods or services did not fulfil the contract in some vital way, and amounted to a breach of condition, or a breach of warranty, then we should say so, and prove it by a detailed presentation of the facts. This will leave the supplier very little alternative to compensation, if he/she wishes to avoid legal action.

Complaints should be made in a restrained and tactful way so that future business relationships are not jeopardised. A reference to an earlier course of business which has been untroubled and mutually beneficial will often lead to a more generous consideration of the complaint, and will arouse in the supplier concern for the preservation of the customer's goodwill. Redress of the grievance should be requested firmly. Most reputable firms will of their own accord propose an acceptable solution to the complaint, which may include some compensation for the trouble and inconvenience. Abusive language should never be used, of course.

The essential parts of a letter of complaint may be listed as follows:

a A subject heading which will draw attention to the nature of the complaint.
b An introduction which, without being apologetic, refers to the hesitation the writer feels in making the complaint in view of the value placed upon the business connection.
c A detailed explanation of the complaint, with such evidence as is available.
d A request for corrective action appropriate in the circumstances.

These key points are illustrated in various circumstances in the specimen letters of complaint below.

Stone and Simpson Ltd

24 Darby Street, Salisbury, Wilts

Telephone: 0722 47942

Your ref: Order 1257
Our ref: JD/RS

Date: 12 December 19--

Belfairs Decoration and Design
(Southampton) Ltd
Downs Way Estate
Chandlers Ford
Hants

Dear Sirs

Discolouration of Ceiling

You will remember that the work you recently performed at these
premises included the redecoration of the Boardroom on the top floor.
I regret to inform you that a serious discolouration of the ceiling
has occurred in one particular area which is extremely unsightly. Our
Chairman has asked me to draw this to your attention and request you
to put the matter right.

We do hope that any correction to this ceiling can be made without
damage to the expensive furnishings and carpets which have recently
been installed. Please make it clear to your staff that no actual
work is to be carried out without full consultation with myself. Our
next function is on 22 December, so perhaps you could inspect the
problem without delay.

Yours faithfully

J Danvers
General Administration Officer

Hilbury Garden Centres Ltd

247 Romsey Road, Westchester, Hants. Tel. 23455

```
Your Reference: J Wilkins, Salesman
Our Reference: Order No 1278
```

27 February 19--

Hollowbourne Nursery
Winterbourne Crescent
Hamble
Southampton

Dear Sirs

<u>Immature Spring Pot Plants</u>

I regret very much that it is necessary to complain about the immaturity of the spring pot plants delivered by your driver today, at a time when there was no-one available to take delivery or reject the plants out of hand. We have been dealing with your nursery for seven years, and this is only the second time that I have ever had to complain.

Your representative Mr Wilkins promised that the plants ordered would be well-grown and approaching flowering point, and should reach flower before Easter week-end, which as you know is early this year. He actually wrote on the order, a copy of which he left for me - 'approaching flower for Easter', so there can be no question that this requirement was a condition of the contract. I am therefore extremely disappointed with the plants that have been delivered, and even more with the manner of delivery. Your driver knows well enough that I never allow him to unload until I have inspected the plants, and he can only have chosen this time for delivery because of the extreme probability that he would be able to unload without the presence of myself or Mr Timms.

If I am to dispose of these plants I must cut the prices by at least 20 per cent, and I should be grateful if you will send me a credit note for the same amount on the full value of the order. What I am to do for my more valued customers I cannot imagine, but if you do have, or can obtain for me, a selection of 'point of bloom' plants I would greatly appreciate it. This would be taken as a gesture of your desire to preserve my goodwill, which has suffered considerably by this little incident.

Yours faithfully

T Hilbury
Managing Director

Auckland Pulp and Paper Co Ltd

Walmer Road, Octapipi, Auckland

Your Ref: --
Our Ref: TSH/DA

14 October 19--

Combined Transport Operators Public Limited Co
Netley Road Depot
Southampton
England

Dear Sirs

Claim on Container No NZ17585

We wish to draw to your personal attention the claims which we have
lodged with your agents here in Auckland about the damage done to our
goods. A copy of this claim is enclosed.

You will notice that the engine and pump supplied by Crown Pumps
(Gloucester) Ltd was insecurely bolted to the restraining frames when
the container was packed, and broke loose - presumably in heavy
weather. It did considerable damage to the other goods in the container, and also to itself.

Our insurance policy requires us to notify all claims at once to those
likely to be liable for the damage, and we have accordingly lodged a
claim as stated. Since the contract of carriage was made under the
Uniform Rules for a Combined Transport Document it seems likely you
will hear from our insurers in due course.

Yours faithfully

T S Hartford
Import Controller

Enclosure: Claim on Auckland Freight Agency Ltd

The Invalid Car Public Company (Chelmsford) Ltd

2047 Moulsham Way, Chelmsford, Essex
Telephone: Chelmsford 38992

Your Reference   Order No 745
Our Reference   TR/DC

17 May 19--

Industrial Fabrics Ltd
2765 Southgates
Kings Lynn
Norfolk

Dear Sir

Inferior Quality - Seat Material

With reference to the delivery of seat material yesterday we have to
notify you at once that this material is quite unusable as far as we
are concerned. We have been buying the material for our invalid cars
from you since 1954, and have never previously been supplied with the
wrong quality. It appears that the recent take-over of your company
has placed someone in charge who does not understand our needs or
realise that we are a valued customer.

The seating of invalid cars is subject to extremely heavy wear because
the occupant of the car is disabled and must move his/her body by arm
leverage. It is also necessary to lift an awkward chair in and out of
the passenger compartment. We must comply with a Board of Trade standard on the material used and the quality of material sent to us just
will not do. Will you please enquire into this matter at once and
send us proper supplies, arranging at the same time to collect this
unsuitable material. We will help re-load it at this end, but otherwise can take no responsibility for it since it is not a class of
material we usually handle and we have no experience of its qualities
at all.

Our supplies of seat material are now down to two weeks' stock, so it
is essential that we receive a special delivery of our material
immediately.

Yours faithfully

T Robertson
Production Manager

8.3 Conciliatory responses to letters of complaint

The response to a letter of complaint is often a delicate exercise. In business correspondence we find that an attitude of 'the customer is always right' will usually reduce tension, preserve goodwill and be no more expensive than a lengthy recrimination and legal consequences. Of course there may be circumstances where a customer is being unfair, and taking advantage of a situation. In such a case we shall stand on our business and legal rights in the matter, as explained in section 8.5 below. The majority of complaints probably have some justification. If we are at fault we shall come out of the situation best if we admit the fault, apologise and offer suitable redress of the grievance. If it is not our fault, but we are in some way the medium through which the customer suffered the fault, we shall preserve goodwill if we do what is best for the customer in the circumstances. Thus where a manufactured article has a manifest fault, which only reached the customer because we supplied the appliance, it is better to replace the item and take the matter up with the manufacturer. To some extent this sort of situation is affected by the custom of a particular trade, and we would then be guided by the recommendations of our trade association and the **Code of Practice** laid down by them.

A conciliatory response to a complaint might therefore take the following form:

a An apology for the error or fault, or an expression of regret if this is more appropriate.
b A short explanation of the circumstances without too obvious an attempt to justify the failure. It is better to leave it to the customer to decide whether the explanation is valid.
c A proposal for settling the difficulty in some fair way, without too great an expense being incurred. An offer to take the goods back, or to replace them, may involve considerable expense, whereas a customer might be quite satisfied with a small cash adjustment. For example where goods were the wrong colour, they may still be quite acceptable and a small discount may be all the compensation that is required.
d A concluding paragraph aimed at retaining the goodwill of the customer. It is unwise to state positively that the same mistake will not occur again, but we may declare that every effort will be made to avoid a repetition.

8.4   Specimen conciliatory responses

SL8.5 (Response to SL8.3)

Combined Transport Operators Ltd

Netley Road Depot, Southampton, Hants, England

Tel: Southampton 89895

Your ref: TSH/DA
Our ref: NZ1/TB/RTC

Date: 21 October 19--

Auckland Pulp and Paper Co Ltd
Walmer Road
Octapipi
Auckland
New Zealand

Dear Sirs

Container No NZ 17585

Thank you for the copy claim you sent us. We are sorry for the
damage and inconvenience you have suffered. The weather seems to
have been particularly severe, since we have received nine other
claims, compared with only three since the service started 15 months
ago.

We have passed your letter to our Claims Department who will deal with
the matter through our insurers. We trust this unfortunate incident
will not prevent your suppliers from making use of our services in the
future. A typhoon in this particularly area is a rare event and
clearly one for which we were in no way responsible, even though we
may be liable as the combined transport operator as far as you
personally are concerned.

Yours faithfully

Thomas Brown
Operations Manager

HOLLOWBOURNE NURSERY

Winterbourne Crescent, Hamble, Southampton, Hants

Tel: (0703) 46590

T Hilbury Esq
Hilbury Garden Centres Ltd
247 Ramsey Road
Westchester
Hants

Your Ref: Order No 1278
Our Ref: HH/AB

28 February 19--

Dear Mr Hilbury

I must apologise most sincerely for the unfortunate mistake which
occurred yesterday when my driver delivered to you in error a consignment of immature pot plants, instead of your 'point-of-bloom' plants.
We have a new customer at Fareham whose plants you have received and
he has received your order. I was rather puzzled when he phoned me
yesterday to express his delight with the plants delivered to him, but
I can quite understand now why he was so pleased with them.

It appears that my driver was diverted away from Hamble by police
warning signs, and that he noticed that the diversion route would take
him half way to Fareham. He therefore decided to deliver the Fareham
order first, but unfortunately muddled the orders.

We have plenty of 'point-of-bloom' plants and I am accordingly sending
you a repeat order with this letter, which the driver will deliver by
hand. It is kind of you to agree to keep the immature plants and sell
them off as and when you can. I think a reduction of 35 per cent
would be more appropriate, and payment may be delayed until April to
give you opportunity to sell them in the meantime. I enclose therefore
a credit note for £38.50.

I trust that these arrangements restore your confidence and re-establish
our goodwill. I am sure you appreciate that the driver's arrival at
lunch time was solely the result of the diversion and the other delivery,
and was not in any way deliberate. It did not occur to him that the
order was likely to be unsatisfactory, and he hesitated to disturb you
with what was clearly an order that was immature, and therefore not
likely to be past its best and unsatisfactory for that reason.

Yours very sincerely

H Hollowbourne
Proprietor

Enc: Credit note

INDUSTRIAL FABRICS LTD

2765 Southgates
Kings Lynn
Norfolk

Telephone: 55766

Your Ref: TR/DC
Our Ref: Order No 745 RLH/DC

19 May 19--

T Robertson Esq
The Invalid Car Public Company
(Chelmsford) Ltd
2047 Moulsham Way
Chelmsford
Essex

Dear Mr Robertson

Inferior Material - Exchange Arrangements

I must apologise for the incorrect material sent to you on 17 May.
As you may have heard Mr Scott who has handled your orders for many
years opted to take severance pay on the occasion of the recent take-
over to which you referred in your letter. Unfortunately he was
rather upset at the change in arrangements and therefore uncooperative
during the transition period. We failed to appreciate the special
nature of your needs and so the order was not marked up correctly.

In order to meet your supply position we propose to send a lorry down
next Friday, 23 May, reaching you about 11.00 am with your correct
order. It is kind of you to offer to help our driver reload with the
unsatisfactory material. This is a fairly lengthy task for one man
and it will enable him to return here in reasonable time.

Once again our sincere apologies for this incident; we hope to retain
your custom and continue to supply you for many years to come.

Yours sincerely

R Lance Herries
Sales Manager

8.5 Letters rejecting complaints

However considerate we may wish to be to the claims of our customers we cannot assume responsibility for errors which we did not make, or offer compensation where no compensation is due. To do so would simply invite business failure, for businessmen and the public generally are quick to take advantage of an accommodating supplier. It follows that there will be many occasions when we are forced to rebut the claims made upon us and place the responsibility squarely upon the individual or firm concerned. Such a letter of rebuttal needs to be well presented, stating firmly that we reject the complaint, and giving the reasons why we reject it. It is often the case that the matter complained about is clearly stated in our 'Terms and Conditions of Sale' as being one for which we will not accept responsibility. Clear reference in the negotiations leading up to a contract to the existence of such 'Standard Conditions' entitles us at a later date to use them to reject complaints which are covered by them.

At the same time as we harden our hearts to reject an unjustified claim we must bear in mind that goodwill is important in all business activities and we would hesitate to reject out of hand a complaint from a trusted and valued customer even if he/she was in technical breach of our standard conditions. The case is quite different when we feel instinctively that we are being imposed upon. Where a fault either does not exist, or manifestly is the result of some other party's misbehaviour or carelessness, we reject all responsibility.

The general layout of a letter rejecting a complaint is as follows:

a An expression of regret at the dissatisfaction, which goes on to reject any responsibility for the complaint.
b A detailed explanation of our reasons for rejecting responsibility.
c If the plaintiff is responsible, some attempt to preserve goodwill while recognising that nothing can be done in the present circumstances.
d If a third party is to blame, or is liable (for instance an insurance company may be liable for compensation if an Act of God caused the damage complained of) we should direct the plaintiff to seek redress in that direction, while preserving their goodwill to us.

These suggestions are used in the specimen letters of rebuttal below.

Ruston Saddlery Company

Ruston Woods, Near Sandy, Beds.

Telephone: 0767 - 658921

```
Your Reference   TH/DG  21 February 19--
Our Reference    ST/RBG
24 February 19--
```

West Country Rodeos (Braunton) Ltd
247 High Street
Braunton
Devon

Dear Sirs

I must confess to feeling extremely indignant at the tone of your
letter earlier this week about the quality of the workmanship on the
six saddles and other tack we made for you last year. We never use
anything but the finest materials in our work and I have never had a
similar complaint in twenty-five years of making equipment for some of
the most famous names in show jumping.

What has happened is quite clear. The items you returned to me have
been dyed or painted for some reason, perhaps to give a more glamorous
appearance to the rodeo - I would not know. This paint or dye has
then been removed by the use of a chemical cleaner of some sort which
has attacked the stitching and caused it to break up. You can see the
chemical erosion quite clearly under the microscope.

Naturally in these circumstances we are not prepared to offer any compensation, and I would not even like to do repairs for payment. There
is plenty of cheap, mass-produced tack about which would be less
expensive than repairs to these items, and more appropriate to the kind
of treatment to which - I suppose - rodeo tack must be subjected.

I am returning the items you sent me by recorded delivery.

Yours faithfully

S Tibbotson
Saddler-in-chief

Belfairs Decoration and Design (Southampton) Ltd

Downs Way Estate, Chandlers Ford, Hants.
Tel: 675990

Your Ref   JD/RS/12 December 19--
Our Ref   RB/ac

14 December 19--

J Danvers Esq
Stone and Simpson Ltd
24 Darby Street
Salisbury
Wilts

Dear Mr Danvers

<u>Discolouration of Ceiling</u>

I have inspected the ceiling with your assistant Mr Parker, and I am
sure you will know we found that the discolouration was caused by the
fracture of a tile in the roof above the north-west corner of the room.
The damage was obviously caused by a large firework, a rocket which
looks as if it was one of those used in the town's firework display on
5 November. You will remember that we handed over the decorations to
you on 2 November, before this incident occurred.

You will appreciate that in these circumstances we cannot accept
responsibility, and must charge you for the repair, but I take it that
you will want the work put in hand at once and have already sent my
roofing expert round to replace the tile and make quite sure the roof
is sound. Your assistant has agreed to see that a drier which we will
supply is placed in the loft below the roof to dry out the area before
we do the repairs next Monday. I shall attend the start of the work
personally to ensure the adequacy of all protective shrouds etc so
that your furnishings and carpets are not damaged. I will liaise with
you at that time.

I notice from our own insurance policy that accidental damage of this
sort is quite clearly covered, and presumably you would find the same
on your premises. Would you please let me have an official order for
this work to be done, and I should greatly appreciate it if you would
explain what happened to your Chairman, since he originally raised the
complaint. I should like to feel that he was aware that the discolouration was in no way due to faulty workmanship on our part.

Yours sincerely

Robert Belfairs
Director

Nationwide Transport (Histon) Ltd

2471 Cambridge Road, Histon, Cambs
Telephone: (022 023) 6988/9

```
Your Reference   Claim No 217
Our Reference    TS/DJ
17 March 19--
```

```
R Thomas (King's Lynn) Ltd
84 Station Road
King's Lynn
Norfolk
```

Dear Sirs

Thank you for the claim you have submitted for damage to two jars of sulphuric acid consigned by you to your depot in London. It provides us with the exact evidence we need to sue you for damages to our vehicle, and also to the goods of eight customers who have claimed against us for damage by acid contamination.

We refer you to our Standard Terms and Conditions, a copy of which was sent to you on 12 February last, and a further copy of which is enclosed. You will see that under Clause 4 headed 'Dangerous Goods' you are required to compensate us for all damage caused by the carriage of dangerous goods whether declared as such or not. You did not declare that your package included dangerous goods, or give us any opportunity to refuse to carry them, and accordingly we hold you liable for all the loss, damage or injury suffered as a result.

We reject your claim outright. Instead you will receive our claim as soon as our lawyers have sorted out and paid the various claims made upon us, all of which you are bound to indemnify us for, as well as for the damage to our vehicle, compensation for loss of its use and the legal expenses involved.

Please do not ask us to carry any goods for you in the future. We shall report these facts to our trade association so that other carriers may know of your conduct.

Yours faithfully

```
T Sorenson
Freight Director
```

8.7 Exercises on the adjustment of complaints

1 Tanner and Rigmore (Derby) Ltd of 1227 Hailsham Street, Derby, have received a consignment of cloth from Mellor's Mills (Bradford) Ltd. The quality is very inferior to the sample supplied by their representative Tom Jenkinson. As manager you write to say that you must have material of the quality promised and ask them to make a delivery at once, collecting the present unsatisfactory goods at the same time. Their address is 215 Gritstone Way, Bradford. (See Question 4 below.)

2 Your educational establishment writes to the Autotype Word Processing Co (Hong Kong) Ltd to complain that service by their local agents, Speediserve Ltd, is unsatisfactory. Delays of two or three days occur when the equipment is out of use and student programmes are being interfered with. Use your own signature, but describe yourself as 'Head of Word Processing Department'. The Autotype address is 20174 Tan Shui Road, Hong Kong. (See Question 5 below.)

3 The managing director of Henry Baxter and Sons, 2174 High Street, Luton asks you to write to complain to the suppliers Excelsior Trading Co (Nottingham) Ltd, of 214 Melton Road, Nottingham about goods which have been stored for you during alterations to your display rooms. These have been damaged by damp. You maintain that as payment (£350) was made for storage, the Excelsior Trading Co is liable for the damage. You ask the company to arrange for an immediate inspection. (See Question 6 below.)

4 (In reply to Question 1 above.) Mellor's Mills reply in conciliatory tones to the letter of complaint from Tanner and Rigmore (Derby) Ltd. They regret the error, which is due to careless stock control, and plentiful supplies of the superior quality are available. They propose to deliver on Friday next, and collect the incorrect goods at the same time. They trust this prompt correction of the mistake will restore their goodwill.

5 (In response to Question 2 above.) You receive a letter from Speediserve Ltd, of 214 Market Street in your own home town referring to your letter to Hong Kong. Urgent telex messages have

been passing between Hong Kong and Speediserve Ltd, who are now fully aware of your dissatisfaction. They promise 'same-day' investigation of all faults in future and state that their best mechanic Peter Spiers has been designated to service your installations as a priority. His home telephone number is supplied to you, for instant call-out during evening sessions, if this is necessary. Compose such a letter.

6 (In response to Question 3 above.) The Excelsior Trading Co (Nottingham) Ltd having inspected the goods supplied to Messrs Henry Baxter and Sons agree that a certain amount of deterioration has occurred during storage but that this is inevitable. They disclaim liability but express their willingness, in view of their long association, to make a gratuitous payment of £— towards covering the loss.

7 Write as the managing director of Alpha Electronic Components Ltd to reject the complaint of Moderntoys (Maidstone) Ltd, 247 Chatham Way, Bluebell Hill, Maidstone, Kent, about the quality of components supplied to them the previous year. Laboratory tests show that the defects are caused by a liquid glue, sold under the trade name of Gluquick. No such product has ever been used in your factory and the delivery note signed when the goods were delivered bears the words 'Received in good order and condition' and the signature M. Wyatt. It also bears wording to the effect that all defects discovered after delivery must be notified by 'recorded delivery' letter within seven days. Your address is 1374 Clifton Road, Bowers Gifford, Basildon, Essex.

8 Write as the chief engineer of Solar Panels (Royston) Ltd to reject the complaint of Energyconscious (Ampthill) Ltd regarding the ineffective operation of the solar panels installed eighteen months previously. On inspection of the site you discover that a huge block of offices has been erected next to the site which effectively screens the panels for most of the working day. The consequent output is greatly reduced. Suggest to them that one corner of their site is still free from this shielding effect, and a solar panel of a new type could be installed at this point to feed energy into the existing system. Your address is 1258 Dunford Way, Royston, Herts. Theirs is 2157 Pedlars Way, Ampthill, Beds.

8.8 Appendix on the English language: more about sentences in business correspondence

Business correspondence must always be direct and clear in its meaning. It need not be too literary in style, with long, complex sentences. Students frequently write sentences that are too involved, and therefore difficult for the reader to take in. The matter is made worse by the failure of many students to read their work through afterwards. Never put a full stop and fling your pen down, or leave your typewriter with a muttered 'Finished'. Go back and read the work again. You will frequently find that what you have written is unclear, or that some sentences have too many ideas in them. To turn a long sentence into two shorter ones will frequently improve the presentation. Short sentences are most useful:

a To give a systematic account of a sequence of events or procedures.
b To sum up an argument, or drive home points of importance.
c To make recommendations.
d In definitions.
e As a matter of literary style, they help to convey an impression of tension and rapidity of events.

The report of a committee set up to review safety procedures after a terrorist incident included the following description of events.

> The first explosion at the Harold Wood Terminal occurred at 3.30 am. Assistance was immediately summoned by the night security staff. The police and fire services arrived within three minutes. It was decided to evacuate buildings close by. This was completed by 4.10 am. The second explosion occurred at 4.15 am.

The short sentences provide a clear record of events, as well as conveying the urgency of the situation.

A more restrained passage of the same report reads as follows:

> It does not appear that adequate supervision exists over casual visitors at a terminal as potentially hazardous as the Harold Wood terminal. Even if superficially satisfactory passes or letters of introduction are presented at the security gate there is a strong case for escorting visitors to the actual interview room or other site within the terminal. Such visitors should be

invited to walk ahead of the escort, not to follow behind, and escorts should remain with the visitor until he/she is actually handed over to the person they have asked to see. All staff receiving visitors must similarly have them escorted back to the security gate by a member of their department, or by a security guard called to the department for this purpose.

Here the sentences are longer, and present a reasoned argument and detailed proposals for improving security.

It is important to remember that a writer should aim at a balance of sentence length and structure, as repeated use of short sentences may become monotonous, while use of long, involved sentences may obscure the meaning of the communication.

8.9 Exercises on sentences in business correspondence

1 Define in short, clear sentences:
   a a typewriter
   b a photocopying machine
   c a telephone switchboard.

2 Write a reasoned explanation, in longer sentences, of the role of a security officer in a large organisation.

3 Using a mixture of long and short sentences write a report on a breakdown of a factory machine and the action to be taken to compensate for it.

9 Semi-blocked and indented styles of business correspondence

9.1 Alternative styles in business correspondence

The vast majority of business houses today use the fully blocked style of letter, which achieves economies in typing time. It does however have one disadvantage. When filed, the significant details, particularly the references, the date and the signature block, are on the extreme left of the page and therefore slightly more difficult to see for easy abstraction of a particular letter. Some houses therefore use a **semi-blocked style**, bringing over to the right-hand side of the page those features which, in that particular firm, are the most helpful to filing clerks searching for items of correspondence.

Other business houses dislike letters which are not fully punctuated, and produce correspondence in a more traditional style. In such a **fully displayed style** the letter is fully punctuated and the secretary centres such items as the subject heading. This involves a considerable amount of extra work for a secretary who does not have a **word processing** typewriter.

A semi-blocked style and the fully displayed style are described in sections 9.2 and 9.3 below, and illustrated in Figs 9.1 and 9.2 respectively. Although the student is recommended to use the fully blocked style unless otherwise instructed it is essential to practise the typing of business correspondence in these alternative styles, and from this chapter onwards some of the exercises will include an instruction to use the semi-blocked style, or the fully displayed style.

9.2 Semi-blocked letters

Since the semi-blocked letter is essentially a form of 'house style' the actual layout in a particular firm will depend upon discussions between the Head of Secretarial Services and other senior members of staff. The style will then be prescribed for all secretaries and a new member of staff would be shown the layout as part of the induction procedure. In the illustration (Fig. 9.1) note the following points:

Tyzack & Partners Ltd.

P. T. Prentice

R. T. Addis	A. Longland
A. Barker	C. A. Riley
D. A. O. Davies	J. L. Rogers
J. E. B. Drake	K. R. C. Slater
G. W. Elms	J. B. Tonkinson
N. C. Humphreys	Dr. R. F. Tuckett
P. A. R. Lindsay	Sir Peter Youens

Scotland

P. Craigie   B. N. Innes-Will

J. A. Sturrock

10 Hallam Street,
London, W1N 6DJ
Tel. 01-580 2924/7
Cables TYZACKLON LONDON

and at

21 Ainslie Place
Edinburgh, EH3 6AJ
Tel. 031-226 6112/3

4 November 19--
Our Ref RTA:jb

The Advertising Department
The Economist Newspaper Ltd
25 St James's Street
London
SW1A 1HG

Dear Sirs

This is to confirm that we wish to reserve a half page in the £15 000 +
section of the recruitment advertising on Saturday 22 November.

You will be receiving the block from our advertising agency in due
course, but I enclose a copy of the text for your information.

Yours sincerely

R T Addis
Partner

Directors: Sir Harold Atcherley (Chairman), P. T. Prentice MBE (Managing Partner)
Secretary: Miss B. G. Betts ACIS
Licensed by the Department of Employment (Licence No. SE (A) 1528)
Registered Office: 15/17 Eldon Street, London EC2M 7LJ. Registration: London—628523
Associates in Hong Kong, New York, Brussels and throughout Australasia

Fig. 9.1 A semi-blocked letter

a The style is still very similar to the fully blocked letter.

b The references and the date have been brought over to the extreme right-hand side of the page, where they are readily accessible to filing clerks searching through a file of correspondence.

c The signature block commences at a tabular point approximately half-way across the typing line, and is fully blocked at this point.

9.3 Fully displayed letters

The advantage of the fully displayed letter is that it gives an open, centralised display which some executives find more attractive and aesthetically satisfying. It is also fully punctuated, which many consider a desirable feature in correspondence. The disadvantages are that it is more time-consuming and more tiring to type, because it is not related to the technology in use (the typewriter), which in most machines returns the carriage to the same point when the carriage return key, or the carriage return lever, is used. The latest word processing typewriters can overcome this difficulty. In the illustration (Fig. 9.2) note the following points:

a The date is typed on the right-hand side to finish close to the right-hand margin.

b References are often included in the letterhead. If not they are typed above the date on the right-hand side.

c The attention line (if any) and the subject heading are typed in lower case with initial capitals and underscore.

d The subject heading is centred on the typing line.

e The paragraphs are indented.

f The complimentary close starts at the centre of the typing line, with all the other following lines centred around it.

g Any reference to enclosures is in fully blocked style.

9.4 Exercises on alternative styles in business correspondence

1 Lightwise (Burnley) Ltd, of 2742 Nelson Road, Burnley, Lancashire write to Mrs K Templer, of 1716 Claremont Avenue, Morecambe, Lancs to arrange an appointment for a representative Ken Stevens to discuss lighting fixtures and electrical layouts at the premises she has just purchased. Offer alternative dates on Monday and Tuesday of next week, and enclose a stamped addressed postcard for her use in replying. Write or type this letter, in semi-blocked style.

THE VYNER GROUP

INTERNATIONAL DISTRIBUTORS **SIMPLEX** **SPECIALISED ACCOUNT BOOKS**

GEORGE VYNER LTD   **GEORGE VYNER** (EXPORTS) **LTD**   **GEORGE VYNER** (DISTRIBUTORS) **LTD**

P.O. BOX No. 1
HOLMFIRTH
HUDDERSFIELD HD7 2RP

Our ref: BS/AB

TEL. No. HOLMFIRTH
(STD 048489) 5221
CABLES VYNER HUDDERSFIELD

Your ref: Letter dated 30.9.19--

3rd October, 19--

Mrs. R. J. Green,
2194 Harbour Way,
Felixstowe,
Suffolk.

Dear Mrs. Green,

<u>Simplex Teachers' Record Book Series</u>

Thank you for your comments on the Class Teacher's Lesson Preparation
Book. We are delighted that you have found it helpful over your first term.
In our experience by the end of the year you will find that countless useful
notes will have been accumulated in it, making the work of writing reports,
dealing with parents' enquiries and - above all - preparing next year's lesson
programme, much simpler.

Unfortunately it is very difficult to incorporate amendments into these
books quickly - there are such long production runs to keep costs down - but
I have passed your comments to our designer for consideration.

I enclose with my compliments our latest product, (Booklet E.S.1.),
<u>Arithmetical Tables for Junior, Middle and Secondary Schools</u>. It is designed
for class use by schools such as your own, and is relatively economical in
price. Perhaps you would like to try it out.

Yours sincerely,

B. Senior
General Manager

Enclosure: E.S.1.

Fig. 9.2 A fully displayed letter

2 Pre-fitted (Darwen) Ltd, of Pennine Mills, Bolton Way, Darwen, Lancashire write in fully displayed style to Mrs R Lowland, of 2174 Keswick Way, Wythburn, Cumbria. They regret the error in length made in the order for curtains, and inform her that a replacement set is on its way by British Roadline. They also enclose a stamped, addressed label which they ask her to use in returning the incorrect curtains by parcel post, and thank her for her cooperation in re-packing them. Write or type this letter.

3 Thomas Gialzemo (Gwelo) Ltd, of 3142 Bulawayo Road, Gwelo, Zimbabwe, write to the Rutland Polytechnic, Oakham, England about the placement of a sponsored student on their agricultural and animal husbandry course. He is Isaac Selukwe, aged 18. They enclose photocopies of his educational qualifications, including 'A' levels in English, Pure Mathematics and Physics. They promise adequate financial support, which has been cleared by the Central Bank of Zimbabwe, subject to the Polytechnic appointing a custodian to receive the money and pay it at monthly intervals to the student. Clearance has also been granted for the course fees and educational materials. An air mail reply is requested. Write or type this letter, in semi-blocked style.

4 F Brea-Nieves, of 2174 Calle San Juan, Ortiz, Venezuela writes to the International Omnibus Company (Southampton) Ltd about a possible purchase of ten buses for the transport of plantation workers. Six-wheel drive is essential, with wooden slatted seats and no windows in the passenger section because maximum ventilation is essential. The letter is in fully displayed style and lays particular emphasis on the fact that it will be necessary to obtain government sanction for the purchase. This is subject to a three months' delay, but can only be arranged on the basis of a firm quotation in Venezuelan bolivars. Write or type this letter.

5 Elfreda (Hornsey) Ltd, of 2749 Colney Hatch Lane, Muswell Hill, London, N10 write to George Vyner Ltd, Mytholmbridge Mills, Holmfirth, Huddersfield, HD7 2RP asking them to quote prices for the supply of 'Simplex' Account Books for sale in their stationery store. Refer particularly to the Simplex D Account Book and the Simplex VAT Record Book, but also ask what other titles are available in the series. Write or type this letter in fully displayed style.

9.5 Appendix on the English language: punctuation

The general view of punctuation today, especially in business correspondence, is that punctuation is essential for clear communication. The *sole aim of punctuation in business correspondence is to bring out more clearly the thoughts of the writer*. If a punctuation mark clarifies the text it must be used, if not it should be omitted; this style is often called informal or open punctuation. It leaves out punctuation marks which only serve a formal purpose, adhering to traditional rules, but includes those punctuation marks required if we are to communicate intelligibly.

As we have seen, the basic organisation of formal business language is in sentences. It is important that students do not confuse the use of the full stop (or period) and the comma.

The full stop (or period)
This is used to mark the end of a statement sentence:

> The development of containerisation was the most important advance in cargo handling this century.

The comma
The comma is used *within a sentence* to separate additional information from the main part of the sentence:

> The lorry, *which had shed its load of steel,* returned to the depot last night.

In this case the clause in italics contains additional information, and is therefore separated from the main body of the sentence by commas.

Other important punctuation marks for sentence punctuation include:

The question mark
The question mark is placed at the end of a sentence which asks a question:

a Was the consignment delivered on time?
b When will the new manager take over?

The exclamation mark
This is used at the end of a sentence which expresses strong feeling:

a Your account must be settled by the end of the month!
b Please send my congratulations to all members of the firm!

The semi-colon

This is a useful punctuation mark as it emphasises the connection in meaning between two sentences. It is used in place of a full stop, and makes the reader aware of the connection in meaning:

a Please send the replacement part at once; it is essential to the success of the programme.

b Unfortunately we will not receive payment; the firm has gone bankrupt.

The semi-colon is also used to separate subjects in a long list:

c While on his visit to France, the buyer visited: the salons in Paris; the recently opened fabrics factory in Orleans; the Head Office of the European advertising agency in Lille; and the shop outlets in Paris, Lille, Rouen, Cholet and Marseilles.

The colon

This is chiefly a signal that the next passage will explain or amplify what has gone before:

There are three types: the manual, the electric and the electronic.

9.6 Exercises on punctuation

1 Copy out these sentences, adding full stops, question marks, colons, semi-colons, exclamation marks and commas where necessary.

a We shall commence delivery on 28 May

b The temperature in the factory which is governed strictly by regulations had risen to 70° F

c Have there been any phone calls from New York

d The newspaper report was lies

e As the machine operator who had been ill for some days was not available the committee conducting the inquiry was unable to confirm the reports

f The Board has rejected the take-over bid the situation now seems to be more secure

g Where was the money it had been left in the cash box

h During his career he has worked for several large firms all of them have given him excellent references while in the Middle East he worked for an oil company and travelled extensively visiting much of the area He has been involved in personnel management office organisation and sales.

10 The settlement of accounts

10.1 Statements and the presentation of an account

In business dealings with a regular customer it is usual to send the customer a **statement** of account once a month. Traditionally this was done at the end of the month, and caused enormous pressure of work at that time both within a firm and in the Post Office system. Many firms today use a system of 'cyclical billing' in which about five per cent of accounts are sent out every working day, so that the work is evenly distributed.

A statement is a business document which reminds a debtor of the amount that is owed. It may have the words 'To a/c rendered', followed by the amount due, or it may show all the transactions for the month in full. This would include the invoices for goods or services supplied, the credit notes issued for returns, the sums received in payment during the month, etc. Such a detailed statement would be a mechanical or computerised statement.

With a single transaction the **invoice** (the document that is made out whenever one person supplies goods or services to another) frequently acts as a statement of account, and bears a request 'Please pay on this invoice by detaching the **remittance advice note**, as a separate statement will not be sent'. As its name implies the tear-off portion which is the 'remittance advice note' accompanies the remittance to enable the supplier to know which invoice is being paid.

Frequently the statement of account is sent through the post in a window envelope, with the statement folded in such a way as to show the address through the 'window'. There will be no need to attach a compliments slip or write a covering letter.

In some situations, for example when rendering the account for a fairly extensive piece of work, to a customer whose goodwill is particularly important, a brief covering letter may be appropriate. Examples are given in section 10.2 below.

Interior Designs (Redditch) Ltd

Green Gables
Orchard Road
Redditch
Worcs
Telephone: 78945

Our reference   TD/SJ

1 March 19--

Mrs K Boulding
The Manor House
Yateley-under-Wenlock
Salop

Dear Madam

The enclosed account covers the work performed at the Manor House to
31 January last, as agreed with your quantity surveyors Hart and
Hambleside.

We have received an enquiry from Mrs Fortescue, who approached us on
your recommendation, and incidentally mentioned how pleased you were
with the alterations. We are most grateful for this reference, and
hope you will be just as satisfied with the remainder of the work.

Yours faithfully

T Doncaster
Design Director

The Surgery

Fragrance Avenue, Whitchurchstone,
Gloucester. Telephone 5243

Our Reference A/c No 125

4 April 19--

The Rev B Palmer
The Rectory
Whitchurchstone

Dear Rector

Mr Whitchurch has asked me to say how pleased he is to hear of your
rapid recovery since the operation two weeks ago. Dr Temple speaks
very highly of you - his least troublesome patient ever!

The enclosed account is for consultancy services, and includes any
further consultations you may feel are necessary in the post-operative
period. Please do not hesitate to phone for an appointment at any
time.

Yours sincerely

Susan Lowndes
pp Mr R Whitchurch
Appointments Bureau

10.3 Disputing an account

When an account is received by the debtor it should always be
checked against the debtor's records. Any disparity should be examined carefully to discover the cause — a typing error, error in calcu-
lation, omission of a document, etc. Note that it is not good business
practice to let an error go without remark just because it happens to
favour you. In one recent lawsuit a judge held that it was fraudulent
not to notify a supplier who had failed to charge for goods supplied.
It is certainly unkind — the rule is 'Do as you would be done by.'

In some cases an error is best corrected on the remittance advice
note, or the statement itself if it is being used to accompany the
remittance. A covering letter may, or may not, be necessary. In other
cases a letter will be essential to clarify the matter in hand.

Lawley and Harker (Glasgow) Ltd

2147 Greenock Road
Paisley
Scotland
Telephone: 31476/7/8

Your Ref: a/c 1204
Our Ref: RL/TS

1 March 19--

Lift-off (Renfrew) Ltd
The Airport
Renfrew

Dear Sirs

Error on Statement

As you will see from the attached statement and the remittance
enclosed we have deducted from your account the sum of £134.50 which
was charged for a trip to the oil production platform site at Loch
Striven. We have no connections with the oil industry at all and it
so happens that on the day in question Mr Harker and I were attending
a seminar on Health and Safety at Work in Edinburgh.

Clearly this charge refers to some other customer and I trust you
will clarify the matter and clear our account forthwith.

Yours faithfully

R Lawley
Director

J T MACKIE (Golspie) Ltd

2147 Coastal Road, Golspie, Sutherland

Telephone: (0408) 49049

Your Ref: A/c M215

Our Ref: JTM/SA

27 April 19--

Factory Fittings (Glasgow) Ltd
2472 Auld Way
Pollockshields
Glasgow

Dear Sirs

With reference to your statement returned herewith, together with a
cheque for £1236.50 will you please note the following facts:

(a) Our contract specifies that no sums are payable on this installation until 30 days after the quantity completed has been notified to
us by our quantity surveyors D H Reece and Co of Wick. The latest
report from them, dated 24 March, certifies work completed to the
value of our cheque enclosed.

(b) In any case a bill for the full contract price (£3000) is quite
inappropriate, since we are entitled to retention money of 20% until
after the running-in period, which is three months from the date
certified by D H Reece and Co as being completion date.

Would you please make these arrangements clear to your accounting
staff.

Yours faithfully

J T Mackie
Managing Director

10.5 Failure to pay

Failure of debtors to pay accounts is always unsatisfactory for the creditor, who has to meet his/her own business commitments. It is not a new problem — one early Dutch business letter ends with a plaintive 'Bethink you of my own poor honesty.' In recent years the problem has been getting worse, because in inflationary times the longer payment is postponed the more worthless the money repaid. Also many large firms deliberately postpone payment, often by querying an account when they know there is nothing wrong. This enables them in effect to use the working capital of their suppliers. It has led to some Members of Parliament suggesting that it should be made lawful to add a penal rate of interest to all overdue accounts.

As a result of such unfair practices it is now unusual to allow too long a time to pass before taking legal action on overdue accounts. A series of letters, gradually getting more firm in tone, is now too dilatory a process and much too expensive. The chain of events is rather shorter today, as follows:

a Statement sent, with a clear deadline for payment.
b Failure to pay by this deadline leads to a letter requesting payment at once, and threatening to refuse to supply any further goods. This would be accompanied by a duplicate statement.
c Failure to pay within — say — seven days calls for direct action to stop all future credit. Sales department must be told not to accept any more orders, but to refer them to the accounts department. A letter explaining the action taken should then be sent to the debtor, requesting payment at once or legal action will be taken.
d If there is no response, pass the account to a solicitor, and ask him/her to collect the debt for you, or issue a writ on your behalf. Note that the issue of a writ does not commit you to the full costs of a legal action. The writ can be withdrawn at any time. What it does do is put pressure on the debtor, and make it more likely that you will be paid — but someone else who has not been so quick to sue may suffer instead.

Some of these letters could be in a standard form, as for example SL10.5 and SL10.6 below.

Many customers who are in genuine difficulties will respond promptly to a request for payment, asking for further time to pay. Each such request must be treated on its merits.

10.6 Specimen letters on failure to pay

SL10.5 (Form letter for unpaid accounts: I)

Hotvenda Office Supplies (Harlow) Ltd
2047 Hertford Way
Harlow
Essex
Tel: Harlow 72390

Your Ref:

Our Ref:

Date

(Space for
 Debtor's
 Address)

Dear

Overdue Account

We have to draw your attention to the overdue state of your account.
Our statement, a copy of which is enclosed, was originally sent to you
on .... Our terms of trade specifically state that
payment must be made within 30 days, as we operate on very small profit
margins. We must accordingly ask you to send us a remittance in full
settlement within seven days, or we shall be forced to suspend supplies.

Yours sincerely

Chief Accountant

Hotvenda Office Supplies (Harlow) Ltd

2047 Hertford Way
Harlow
Essex

Tel: Harlow 72390

Your Ref:

Our Ref:

Date

(Space for
 Debtor's
 Address)

Dear

Overdue Account: Second and Final Request for Payment

Our letter of .... requesting immediate payment of the
account rendered to you on ...., a copy of which is
enclosed, has brought no response, and we must therefore assume you are
unable to pay. We have accordingly instructed our delivery service to
suspend weekly deliveries of supplies to your premises, and our maintenance service to suspend maintenance of vending machines should they
become unserviceable.

These services can of course be resumed as soon as your account is paid
in full, but if payment is not received within fourteen days of the
date of this letter we shall pass the account to our solicitors for
collection. We regret the necessity of taking this action, but we did
make our terms of sale very clear when the original contract was
negotiated.

Yours sincerely

Chief Accountant

D H Howe (Royston) Ltd

2746 Crofts Way Crescent, Bar Hill, Cambridge
Telephone 896745

Your Ref: Customer No 214/ST/RT

Our Ref: DHH/TD

27 June 19--

Hotvenda Office Supplies (Harlow) Ltd
2047 Hertford Way
Harlow
Essex

Dear Sirs

We very much regret the inconvenience caused by this overdue
account. The failure of one of our major foreign debtors has
placed us in considerable temporary difficulties and we have been
forced to delay some payments. Fortunately the difficulty seems
likely to be resolved as a result of the Export Credit Guarantees
Department which has this week conceded that we are entitled to
compensation under our insurance policy, and 90% of the outstanding
invoice prices will be paid on 10 July next.

We are sending you £50 on account, and will pay the balance by 12
July next, or earlier if our bankers sanction an overdraft against
the security of the ECGD promise to indemnify us.

With sincere apologies

D H Howe
Managing Director

Hotvenda Office Supplies (Harlow) Ltd

2047 Hertford Way
Harlow
Essex
Tel: Harlow 72390

Our Ref:

Date:

Basingstoke, Granville and Co
2473 The High
Harlow
Essex

Dear Sirs

I enclose a copy of my correspondence with . . . .
from which you will see that repeated attempts to obtain payment of
their account have failed. Would you please approach them for payment
and try to discover their financial position.

If the situation cannot be resolved we shall probably use your
services to sue them for the outstanding amount.

Yours faithfully

Chief Accountant

Basingstoke, Granville and Co

Solicitors

2473 The High, Harlow, Essex.

Telephone: 0279 63466 (2 lines)

```
Your Reference   TRD/SM
Our Reference    DC/TD

31 October 19--


The Chief Accountant
Hotvenda Office Supplies (Harlow) Ltd
2047 Hertford Way
Harlow
Essex


Dear Sir

Unpaid Account - Green and Co

After pressing Messrs Green and Co for an early settlement I regret
to report that the position is highly unsatisfactory.  Their replies
to my questions were most evasive, and I have strong reasons for
believing that their embarrassment is greater than they admit.  Their
commitments throughout the town are heavy, and a feeling of uneasiness
is beginning to spread among their creditors.

There is one slightly optimistic point; it does appear quite certain
that a recovery in their industry has begun and they appear to be quite
well-placed to take advantage of it - having slimmed their labour force
down.

Perhaps you would advise us whether you wish to sue, or give the
situation time to clarify itself.

Yours faithfully



D Carver
Basingstoke, Granville and Co
```

Basingstoke, Granville and Co

Solicitors

2473 The High, Harlow, Essex.

Telephone: 0279 63466 (2 lines)

Your Reference   TRD/SM
Our Reference   DC/TD

26 November 19--

The Chief Accountant
Hotvenda Office Supplies (Harlow) Ltd
2047 Hertford Way
Harlow
Essex

Dear Sir

Following your instructions of 16 November, I have once more attempted
to obtain information from Messrs Green & Co about their outstanding
balance. Unfortunately there is little to report, beyond their
repeated claims to be solvent - provided we do not drain their working
capital sufficiently to stop them taking advantage of the revival in
their trade. They frankly admit their inability to settle in full at
this stage, but they seem confident that a few months of good trading
will make their position perfectly secure.

As my survey of the local market seems to bear out their statements,
I suggest that it would pay us to adopt a waiting policy rather than
sue them for what we can obtain. Perhaps you would let me know what
your decision is.

Yours faithfully

D Carver
Basingstoke, Granville & Co

10.7 Exercises on the settlement of accounts

1 After a considerable amount of work landscaping and laying out the grounds around the new buildings of Whitelanes, Moor and Co, Ambleside, Cumbria, you write as chief cashier of Landscaping (Kendal) Ltd, 2017 High Rigg, Kendal, Cumbria to enclose your account. Refer in your letter to the increase of 10 per cent in the agreed contract price of £1850, as provided for in Clause 9 of the contract. Express the hope that they are pleased with the layout, and remind them that the full effect will take some years to realise, as plants and trees come to maturity.

2 Send your account, as chief accountant of Langdyke Engineering Ltd, Beck Lane, Wirksworth, Nottingham to your customer Milk Processors Co, Hemington Vale Dairy, Derby. Refer to the fact that it is for payment of the work certified as completed at their new factory by their quantity surveyors Glover & Buxton of Mansfield.

3 W A Candler Ltd, of Low Farm, Chandlers Ferry, Hants have not paid an account for manure delivered during the winter months. Write as manager of New-Eggs Poultry Farms Ltd, Great Grendon, Hants to request immediate payment of the account.

4 An account rendered to you as accountant for Mellowmead Manufacturing (Wilton) Ltd, 24 Barford Rd, Wilton, Hants by the Ironmakers of Kirkby Lonsdale Ltd, Kirkby Lonsdale, Cumbria contains two errors. One is a miscalculation, where $12 \times £165 = £1920$. The other is the inclusion of an item for £340 which does not appear to be anything to do with your firm. The total of the account as rendered is £3340. Write enclosing a cheque for the amount you consider payable, and asking them to clarify the position about the item for £340.

5 Prontoprint (Brockenhurst) Ltd, 24 Shirley Way, Brockenhurst, Hants dispute the amount payable on a statement from Crescent Paper Mills, Chorley Road, Bolton, Lancs. The cause of the dispute is that paper of an inferior quality was supplied, and an oral promise was made over the telephone to reduce the charge of £840 by £300. This has not been adhered to in the statement. As the accountant of Prontoprint write to protest, and enclose a cheque for what you deem to be the correct sum payable, less a further 5 per cent cash discount.

6 *a* Messrs Harcourt & Co, Maddeley Road, Slough have sent a statement of account to Messrs Brayton & Co, Exeter, showing a balance of £357 for goods supplied during the month of May. Write as the accountant of Messrs Brayton & Co, to point out that you have not been credited for returns made on 11 May and ask to have this return adjusted before the account is paid.

b Messrs Harcourt express their regret at having overlooked this return and enclose a credit note for £27, and an amended statement of account. Write this letter in your capacity as chief clerk to Harcourt & Co.

7 You are the head book-keeper of a small firm, Chase Bros, of Preston Old Road, Blackburn, Lancs. You are being pressed by a creditor, Brassware (Clitheroe) Ltd, of 2475 York Way, Clitheroe for payment of an account for raw materials. Explain to them that because of transport problems in a recent strike you were unable to deliver orders for five weeks although your general financial situation is sound. Ask them to accept a cheque for £100 on account, the balance to be payable on the same date next month.

8 George Vyner Ltd, of Mytholmbridge Mills, Huddersfield, HD7 2RP obliged a customer, George Burns, 2205 Orchard Avenue, Bolton by sending a telephoned order for accounts books by post in advance of payment — against their usual practice. Write as their credit controller to express your dissatisfaction at the non-payment of the account despite an express promise to pay by return of post. Make it clear that you will place the matter in the hands of your solicitor if payment is not received within seven days.

9 Write in answer to the letter in Question 8 above to express your regrets at failing to pay the account. Express your satisfaction with the accounts books and enclose a cheque for double the amount of the invoice, asking them to repeat the previous order.

10.8 Appendix on the English language: spelling

Businessmen frequently complain that spelling is a neglected subject these days. Recent trends, encouraging self-expression in students, have sometimes been at the expense of accurate spelling. In business correspondence however, a high level of spelling is desirable, and consequently a dictionary is an important part of the office equipment.

Every secretary and executive needs a personal copy of a standard dictionary, such as the *Concise Oxford Dictionary,* and must be able to use it correctly.

A dictionary does not merely give the correct spelling and definition of a word, but also shows how its derivatives must be spelt. For example, after the entry 'acquit' we find '(p.t. acquitted)', information which explains that we must double the 't' in the past tense of the verb. Such information is readily available in the dictionary and invaluable to students whose spelling is weak. Effective use of the dictionary will come with practice, and is an important skill in business communication where incorrect spelling may create the impression of casual organisation.

Good spelling depends upon knowing the probable sequence of letters in a word, and this probability can be learned. If you have taken the trouble to look up a correct spelling in the dictionary, it is sensible to take a little longer and enter that word in a note book, perhaps the vocabulary book which we recommend in Chapter 12. Whenever you have a few spare minutes, check through those difficult spellings and test yourself. After a few tests you should have learnt those troublesome spellings which you would otherwise have had to check in the dictionary countless times.

Spelling rules

There are several spelling rules which can be learnt, but the student must bear in mind that they are generalisations only, and that to every rule there will be some exceptions.

Three spelling rules

1 *i* before *e* except after *c* when the sound is a long *ee*.

achieve, piece; and receive, receipt.

(There is an exception: seize.)

2 Verbs ending in a silent *e* drop it before taking *-ing*.

state — stating, make — making, hope — hoping, write — writing

(There are a few exceptions: seeing, shoeing, hoeing, singeing, dyeing.)

3 Words ending in a single *e* drop the *e* before *-able*, except where the *e* is needed to soften *c* or *g*.

> love − lovable, debate − debatable, refute − refutable, notice − noticeable, manage − manageable.

(There are a few exceptions: rateable, tameable, shakeable.)

10.9 Exercises on spellings

1 Learn the spellings of each of the following groups of words:

receive	achieve	receipt
received	achieved	receipted
receiver	achievement	deceit
receivable	achievable	deceitful
consign	rate	change
consignor	rateable	changeable
consignee	prove	exchange
consignment	provable	exchangeable

2 Use each of the following words in a sentence, to show that you understand the different meanings of each pair of words:

receipt	consignor	change	achievable
receiver	consignee	exchange	receivable

11 Overdrafts, loans and instalment credit

11.1 The credit market

In the early days of business, at the start of the industrial revolution, businessmen had to accumulate capital by self-denial. It was difficult to get started in business, and businesses grew only slowly as profits could be ploughed back. Today capital is much more freely available, and a wide variety of banks, building societies, finance houses and moneylenders are available to lend money to businesses and ordinary citizens. These financial institutions together form the 'credit market'.

The value of credit to both private and business customers is that almost any asset can be obtained in return for a series of payments made over a period of time. Thus private consumers may have the use of motor cars, home improvements, television sets, etc. The value to businesses is enormous, because almost everything from an electronic till to a multi-million pound oil rig can be purchased without having to pay out large sums of money.

The firms in the 'credit market' are lending money to their customers. Like any stall-holder in any other market they hope to make a profit on their activities, by earning interest on the loans they make. They must also be careful to deal with trustworthy clients only, since the loans will usually be repaid by instalments over a fairly lengthy period. To check on the trustworthiness of clients they usually check with a **credit reference agency**.

11.2 Obtaining a loan

When seeking a loan it is advisable to present the bank manager or other official with a carefully documented account of your plans, or, in the case of an expanding business, of your past development. Give careful estimates of your likely costs, and of the revenues that should flow in from your new project. These revenues will enable you to repay the loan with interest, so that they are vital information for anyone making a loan.

Other information may be helpful background; for example your own motivation in putting forward the new project, your experience in the field, etc. It will sometimes be necessary to complete an application form, and you may be asked to have an interview with the manager concerned.

11.3 Specimen letters about overdrafts or loans

SL11.1

Nottingham Brake Linings Ltd

1275 Normanton Road, Nottingham

Telephone: 37656

Your Ref:
Our Ref: JR/AB

17 March 19--

Nottingham Finance Ltd
2147 Mansfield Road
Nottingham

Dear Sirs

Would you please send me an application form for finance of £1500.

We are local manufacturers of specialist brake linings and despite the present recession in the motor vehicle industry are busy and able to expand production.

We need this capital to purchase two German machines which are essential to our expansion programme. We have previously dealt with Grimes and Grimethorpe Finance, but they recently closed their Nottingham office and we prefer to deal with a local firm.

Yours faithfully

J Rankin
Chief Accountant

The Canal Narrowboat Centre Ltd

The Cut, Mansfield, Notts.
Tel: (0623) 71489

Our Ref   TS/ST

1 February 19--

G W Smith Esq
Grimethorpe Bank Ltd
21 Highgrove Hill
Nottingham

Dear Mr Smith

Overdraft for £4000

I am hoping that you will be able to mark up an overdraft on our
account for £4000, to assist us in the next few weeks. We are not
short of working capital, and bookings are coming in well for the
new season which starts on 4 April, but it so happens that we have
a very valuable opportunity presenting itself in two weeks time.

The opportunity arises because Jarvis, Lorrie and Co of Leeds, who
operate narrowboats on the Leeds and Liverpool Canal are going into
voluntary liquidation. They are putting their fleet of seven boats
up for auction on 17 February at Leeds. It is estimated that the
boats will fetch between £1300 and £1500 each. We would very much
like to obtain two or three more boats, which we could easily handle
under our present working arrangements. We would expect to let these
boats at about £50 per week each, for about 26 weeks each season.

This is a great opportunity for us to expand our fleet with vessels
we know to be in good condition, so I hope you can agree to this
request.

Yours sincerely

Ted Syston
Director

ANODISERS (Thetford) Ltd
3724 Brandon Road, Thetford, Norfolk.

Telephone Thetford (0842) 54902

Your Ref A/c 12784095
Our Ref PT/SAP

14 November 19--

The Manager
Trustus Bank Ltd
2045 High Street
Thetford
Norfolk

Dear Sir

Loan for £2500, Repayable over 2 Years

We wish to obtain long term finance of £2500 to enable us to replace
a defective electroplating machine. The modern machines are so much
more productive than the existing machine that repair is hardly worthwhile and we shall be able to meet the repayments easily from the
increased turnover.

Some relevant figures for the last few years, which can be substanti-
ated from our books, are as follows:

Business established 19--	Turnover £	Gross Profit £	Net Profit £
Year 1	26 000	9 250	6 540
Year 2	48 000	16 780	11 560
Year 3	72 000	24 550	18 270
Current year (10 months only)	73 500	-	-

We estimate our turnover this year will approach £84 000, and our net
profit will exceed £22 000.

Perhaps we could call and discuss this and if you are prepared to
sanction the loan we could sign an agreement immediately.

Yours faithfully

P Thompson
Accountant and Director

Nottingham Finance Ltd

2147 Mansfield Road, Nottingham.

Telephone: Nottingham 42837

Your reference   JR/AB
Our reference   Enquiry 1054

19 March 19--

J Rankin Esq
Nottingham Brake Linings Ltd
1275 Normanton Road
Nottingham

Dear Mr Rankin

Thank you for your letter of 17 March. I enclose an application form
as requested. Please read our 'Terms and Conditions for Granting
Credit' which are printed on the back of the form. They are the standard terms and conditions recommended by our Trade Association and
have been drawn up in consultation with the Director General of Fair
Trading's representatives.

Naturally we hope very much that we can help you, but must emphasise
at this stage that we shall require a banker's reference, and shall
also conduct a search at Company House so that we can evaluate your
business properly. If it proves necessary to link any loan with a
personal guarantee from the directors we shall need to consult a
credit reference agency about your credit record.

All these matters are purely routine for loans of this type, as I am
sure you are aware. We are in business to help firms like your own,
and we look forward to assisting you, both on this occasion and for
the future.

Yours sincerely

Peter Rudd
Credit Controller

Grimethorpe Bank Ltd

21 Highgrove Hill
Nottingham
Tel: 833900

Your Ref: TS/ST
Our Ref: A/c No 21749846

3 February 19--

E Syston Esq
The Canal Narrowboat Centre Ltd
The Cut
Mansfield
Notts

Dear Mr Syston

Loan (£4000) for Purchase of Narrowboats

Thank you for coming to see me today in response to my telephone
call. It was interesting to discuss this proposal with you and find
out a little more about your business.

I hope you understand our reasons for suggesting that in these circumstances a loan is preferable to an overdraft. From the bank's point
of view a loan has a fixed arrangement for repayments, and is therefore more easy to finance, since we know how long we are committed to
lending you the money. From your point of view a loan carries automatic life assurance, and in the event of your death would be settled
by our insurance department.

I hope also that you appreciate the loan must be a personal loan to
you - we could not possibly lend £4000 to a company which is only a
£500 company.

The agreement will be ready by 8 February, and if you will call in at
the bank, bringing with you the deeds of your house on which the
mortgage is to be drawn up, the money can be transferred as soon as
the agreement is signed. The mortgage will take a little longer to
arrange, but you will be given a receipt for the deeds.

I hope you will be able to buy the narrowboats at a reasonable price
when the auction takes place.

Yours sincerely

G W Smith
Manager

11.4 Block discounting and leasing

While overdrafts and loans are established methods of borrowing from banks and finance companies, the biggest developments in the 'credit market' in recent years are more sophisticated. In particular 'block discounting' and 'equipment leasing' have developed into multi-million-pound activities.

Block discounting is the purchase of a firm's entire debtors' ledger or hire purchase debtors' ledger, at regular intervals – usually on a monthly basis. The effect is that a trader receives cash for all the goods sold, though he/she may lose a small percentage of the selling price. The customer may continue to pay the account, or the instalments, to the trader, but the trader simply banks them in the finance company's account. The trader has received his/her payment already, and has no further worries about non-payment by the debtor. If the debtor fails to pay, the finance company will pursue the debtor to obtain payment.

Equipment leasing is a way of acquiring capital assets without using one's own capital. If a trader or manufacturer wishes to buy equipment he/she approaches a finance house, who will purchase the item needed and make it available to the trader for a monthly payment called the 'rent'. The finance company retains ownership of the equipment and it does not become an asset of the company which is using it. In this way firms have the use of capital equipment at once, and only pay for it as a 'rental', using income they have earned by the use of the equipment.

Both these types of arrangement require correspondence and the drawing-up of contracts so that both parties know exactly what the terms of the contract are.

Cottenham Electrical (Cambridge) Ltd

1874 Histon Road
Cottenham
Cambs
Telephone: 23498

Our Ref: TS/DP

4 April 19--

The Manager
Cambridge Finance Co Ltd
2138 Market Hill
Cambridge
CB2 1RD

Dear Sir

We are an expanding electrical and electronic supply stores selling
at discount prices to a wide range of retailers in the area and also
on hire purchase terms to ordinary consumers. Our expansion is being
held up at present by a lack of finance. The difficulty is that while
our trade customers pay within 30 days and give very little trouble
as far as finance is concerned, our hire purchase customers tend to
spread payments over 2 or even 3 years.

Is there any way in which you can assist us with finance on this side
of our business, and what would be the terms and arrangements if we
did ask you to assist us?

Yours faithfully

T Johnson
Director

CAMBRIDGE FINANCE CO LTD

2138 Market Hill, Cambridge CB2 1RD

Tel. 0223-01567

Your ref: TS/DP 4 April 19--
Our ref: File 1274   6 April 19--

T Johnson Esq
Cottenham Electrical (Cambridge) Ltd
1874 Histon Road
Cottenham, Cambs

Dear Mr Johnson

Thank you for your enquiry about finance. I think the best arrangement
in your case is for us to arrange block discounting of all your hire
purchase business. Under this system your customers deal with you
direct, both in the drawing-up of the HP agreement and in the payments
of the accounts as the instalments become due. Effectively you sell
all your HP debts to us, receiving in return a prompt payment for
their discounted value, on an agreed day in the month.

The instalments that customers pay to you are kept separate from your
other takings and are banked to the credit of our bank account since we
are now the creditors of the customers. Your customers do not even need
to know that you have passed their debts on to us, but if they fail to
pay we shall approach them ourselves for payment, or in extreme cases
apply for repossession to the courts.

There is one point we must emphasise if such an arrangement is to commence. It is essential for the trader (yourself) to bear in mind that
instalment credit, while it is undoubtedly a great boon when sensibly
used, can also bring real problems if it is extended unwisely to customers who are already heavily committed. There is a temptation in these
circumstances, since the trader is not personally going to have to pursue the bad debtor, to be lax about granting credit to customers. We
have a clause in our agreement entitling us to cancel the arrangement
if your record in this respect proves unsatisfactory. Of course we
inevitably face the odd bad debt from a customer whose circumstances
change suddenly. We do not want to be discounting debts which have a
higher chance than average of being bad debts. It is easy for finance
houses to get a bad press in these circumstances. Please think of our
good name, as well as your own profit, when selling on hire purchase.

We clearly need to meet to discuss these arrangements. Would you please
telephone for an appointment.

Yours faithfully

B Court
Block Discount Manager

Newcastle Finance Co (Wallsend) Ltd

2175 Roman Way
Wallsend, Tyne and Wear   *Telephone* 32110

```
Your Ref:  1T/CS
Our Ref:   File No 27856


14 September 19--


R Hallam Esq
Roundhead Forge
River View
Billingham on Tees
Cleveland


Dear Mr Hallam
```

Thank you for your enquiry about the leasing to you of certain forge
equipment. We are quite prepared to consider this proposition, but
we need to have a detailed appraisal of the items required, their
likely costs, expectation of useful life etc. We should then be able
to work out a rental charge which would be fair to both parties.

You will appreciate that such equipment is not widely demanded, and if
left on our hands we might only be able to dispose of it at a considerable loss. We must therefore have your contract with us properly
signed before we proceed to place an order for the equipment. We
should also expect that you would be in a position to use the machine
for a number of years ahead - for example - if your lease on the
property was due to expire in a short while we should hesitate to
undertake the contract.

Please ring my secretary, Tina Williams, for an appointment and we
will discuss the whole matter thoroughly.

Yours sincerely

P. Collins
Newcastle Finance Co (Wallsend) Ltd

TELEPHONE ANSWERING EQUIPMENT

Agovox Limited, 4, Sydenham Road, London. SE26 5QY   Telephone: 01-778 7255

Our Ref. FW/PJO   Your Ref. AT/JM 17 Oct.   Date. 10 November 19--

Arthur Telford (Birmingham) Ltd
2022 Aston Road
Wednesbury
Staffs

Dear Sirs

Leasing Agreement: C385 Answering Machine

Thank you for your recent order for a C385 Telephone Answering Machine.
I understand from our local representative, Alan Rudman, that the machine
was installed on 22 October. I hope it is fulfilling your expectations.

I enclose the Leasing Agreement, and a direct debit mandate for the charge.
As Mr Rudman explained we will not make any demand on this direct debit
mandate other than the actual annual charge. We have entered into an
indemnity agreement with our bankers to indemnify them for any claims you
might make against them alleging unfair debiting of your account;
accordingly you need have no hesitation in completing the mandate.

If you will sign both copies of the agreement and return to us together
with the completed direct debiting mandate, we shall be happy to complete
the agreements and send you a copy forthwith.

Yours faithfully
Agovox Limited

F Webb

F Webb
Commercial Manager

Head Office: Agovox Ltd., White Lodge Estate, 353 Hall Road, Norwich. NR4 6DG. Telephone: (0803) 611016. Telegrams: BRITDICT NORWICH.

Directors: W.McCraith (Chairman) B.D.Jordan W.F.C.Symes P.W.Whiley. Regd. Office: Gothic Works, Norwich. Regd. in England No. 505010

Fig. 11.1 A covering letter for a leasing agreement

11.6 Exercises about overdrafts, loans and instalment credit

1 *a* Mrs I Lee of 2894 Community Complex, Pasir Panjang, Singapore writes to her bank manager at the local branch of the Bank of South East Asia, 2746 Port Road, Buona Vista, Singapore to ask for a loan to buy three commercial sewing machines to expand her workshops making fashion goods. The cost is 2225 Singapore dollars for each. She wants to spread the loan over three years and confidently expects that the machines will earn more than enough to pay for themselves. She refers to lucrative contracts with a major fashion house in the United Kingdom and offers to bring in details of the business done over the past four years. Write this letter.

   b Mr I Ming, the manager of the bank, replies favourably to the request. He feels the loan can certainly be arranged but requires her to bring in the correspondence as promised and also her financial records for the last three years. He asks her to phone his secretary to arrange a suitable appointment.

2 You have just started college, and have received a government grant for maintenance. You have had a current account at your local bank for six months and were told that after six months of responsible banking you would be considered for the issue of a credit card. This will enable you to borrow to a limited extent, without problems. Write to the local branch asking whether they are now prepared to issue a card. In support of your application mention that your legal guardian is prepared to act as guarantor.

3 *a* Write, as the finance director of Electrical Supplies (Winchester) Ltd, 7142 Bargate, Winchester, Hants, to the manager of Prosperity Finance Co, 2174 Ramsey Road, Winchester, Hants asking for a loan of £34 500 to purchase the business of a competitor. Explain that negotiations are secret but details will be supplied if the finance company expresses its willingness to consider the project and undertakes to keep the matter confidential.

   b Reply, as G R Tomkin, managing director of Prosperity Finance Co Ltd, stating that funds are certainly available for this type of business purchase, and enclose a form for completion as an initial stage. Give the very firmest reassurances about confidentiality, and promise prompt consideration of the project.

4 *a* Write, as general manager of Family Motoring (Chisamba) Ltd, Kabwe Road, Chisamba, Zambia to the managing director of Rufunsa Finance Co, Lusaka Rd, Rufunsa. The failure of a merchant bank which formerly covered your hire purchase contracts from an office in Lusaka has left you without finance, and you write to ask whether Rufunsa Finance Co can offer you finance and on what terms. The sum involved is likely to be about 40 000 Kwacha a month, and repayments would be made by customers direct to the Finance Co.

   b Write, as Joshua Wabenze, of the Rufunsa Finance Co offering block discounting of all accounts, with immediate payment of 75 per cent of the net price of vehicles sold (i.e. not counting the interest charged to the customer). Of the remaining 25 per cent half will be a charge for the finance made available, and the other half will be paid on the day the last instalment is collected from the customer.

5 Sigismunde Matabele, of Gwelo Road, Insize, Zimbabwe, wishes to purchase a tractor from Agroproducts (Gwelo) Ltd, Liberation Compound, Gwelo. Agroproducts recommend that instead of incurring a large debt he allows them to buy the tractor, and lease it back to him at a charge of 32 dollars per week. This charge need not be paid until harvest time, when it will be deducted from the cash due for the sale of his crop to the Agricultural Cooperative in Gwelo. Write this letter to Mr Matabele. Use your own name, as leasing manager.

11.7   Appendix on the English language: more spelling rules

a Words ending in *y* preceded by a consonant change to the plural following the rule: *change the y into i and add -es:*

   baby — babies, lady — ladies, copy — copies, body — bodies.

This rule (change *y* to *i*) also applies when verbs change their tense:

   rely — relied, reply — replied, deny — denied, apply — applied.

b Words ending in *y* preceded by a vowel are unchanged (except for a final *s*) when made plural:

monkey — monkeys, donkey — donkeys, chimney — chimneys, play — plays.

The plural of the word money is spelt *moneys,* not *monies.*

This rule applies also when tenses change, except for these exceptions shown below. Thus:

play — played, convey — conveyed, destroy — destroyed.

The exceptions are lay, pay and say:

lay — laid, pay — paid, say — said.

c Words ending in a single consonant preceded by a vowel which is stressed double the final consonant when adding *-ed, -ing, -er:*

thin — thinner, run — running, ban — banned, don — donned, refit — refitting, rebut — rebutted, admit — admitting.

d If the vowel is not stressed the consonant is not doubled:

profit — profiting, merit — merited, benefit — benefiting.

11.8   Exercises on spelling

The following business words are frequently misspelt. Memorise each group:

accept	commodity	advise
accepted	accommodate	adviser
acceptable	accommodated	advisory
acceptability	accommodating	advisability
acceptor	accommodation	advice
align	benefit	extend
aligned	benefited	extension
alignment	beneficent	question
commitment	beneficial	questionable
committee	beneficiary	questionnaire
necessary	consent	relevant
necessitate	consented	relevance
sincere	consensus	irrelevant
sincerely	occur	persevere
sincerity	occurrence	perseverance

12 Bills of exchange

12.1 What are bills of exchange?

A bill of exchange is a method of payment which may be used in both inland and overseas trade. The system works as follows:

a The person who is owed money, the **creditor**, writes out the bill. The old-fashioned word for this was 'drawing' a bill, and the term **drawer** is given to the person who writes out a bill of exchange, and signs it.

b In writing it out, he orders the debtor (usually his customer) to pay a sum of money either 'at sight' or after some specified time, for example, three months or six months. The person drawn upon in this way is called the **drawee**. The sum of money must be a fixed sum, like £3000 or £500. You cannot make out a bill ordering someone to pay 'whatever price my horse fetches at auction'. It must be a 'sum certain'.

c In the usual course of events the bill will be sent to the drawee, who will sign his name on it, and perhaps write the word 'accepted' as well. He has now accepted the obligation to honour the bill on the due date, and has become the **acceptor**. Only the drawee can become the acceptor.

d He now returns the bill to the drawer, who can do one of the following things:
  i Keep it until maturity, when the acceptor will honour the bill on the due date, in full.
  ii If the drawer does not wish to keep the bill he/she can use it to pay one of his/her debts to someone else, by endorsing the bill over to that person. **Endorsement** means that you sign your name on the back of the bill (*in dorsare* = positioned on the back). His signature on the bill, perhaps with the words 'Please pay Thomas Jones', makes the drawer the 'first endorser' of the bill. The bill now has three signatures: the acceptor has signed once, and the drawer has signed twice, once as drawer

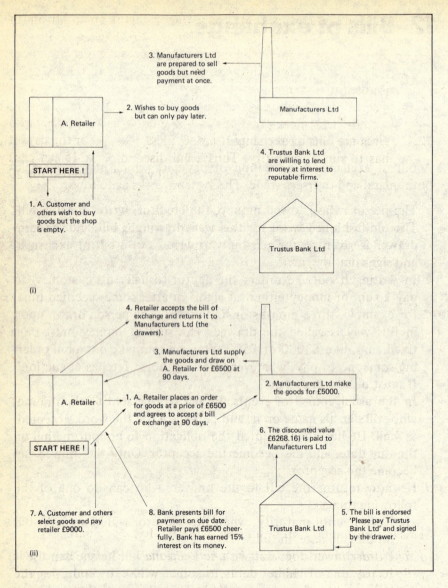

Fig. 12.1 Solving business problems by using bills of exchange

Notes: The results are:

   (i) Manufacturers Ltd have kept busy and earned profits of £1268.16

  (ii) Retailer has made profits of £2500

 (iii) The bank has earned interest of £231.84

 (iv) Customers have experienced the satisfactions of the consumer-orientated society

172

and once as endorser. Mr Jones might pass it on to Mr Smith who might pass it to Phillis Broan and Co. Each time it is endorsed it gets another signature and becomes more and more reliable, for everyone who signs a bill must honour it if he/she is asked to do so.

iii The third alternative is for the drawer to discount the bill with a bank. This means that the bill is endorsed to a banker, who gives the drawer the sum of money, less interest for the days it has to run to maturity. Thus a bill discounted at 15 per cent for 29 days would be paid at the full value less interest for 29 days at 15 per cent.

e On the due date whoever has the bill will *present it for payment.* The debtor will pay the sum due, and everyone will be happy. The advantage of this system is that the debtor (customer) who bought goods from the creditor (supplier) had a period of time – say three months – to sell them at a profit. By the time the acceptor has to honour the bill he/she has the money to do so.

All these events cannot be illustrated in one diagram but the most usual case, discounting the bill with a bank, is shown in Fig. 12.1.

12.2   Definitions of a bill of exchange and a cheque

The definition of a bill of exchange, as given by the Bills of Exchange Act, 1882, should be memorised:

A bill of exchange is an unconditional order in writing, addressed by one person to another, signed by the person giving it, requiring the person to whom it is addressed to pay on demand, or at a fixed or determinable future time, a sum certain in money to or to the order of a specified person, or to bearer.

This is a very important definition. Note the following parts.

a *The order in writing must be unconditional* – it says 'Pay . . .'. It does not say 'Provided you are satisfied with our goods, pay . . .'. Once you put your name on a bill of exchange you must honour it. To dishonour a bill usually means you will have to cease trading.

b *Addressed by one person to another* – it is the 'drawer' who is addressing the 'drawee'.

c *Signed by the person giving it* – the drawer signs the bill and at once becomes liable on it. This seems a strange idea, because the drawer does not owe the money, but if the drawee accepts the bill and becomes the 'acceptor' he/she will become the chief person liable on the bill.

d *On demand, or at a fixed or determinable future time* – the tenor of the bill (the time it has to run to maturity) must be clear. Some bills are payable on demand, or at sight, or on presentation. A bill payable 'three months after date' is easily understood; we can determine the due date from the date on the bill. A bill payable '30 days after sight' must be presented for acceptance, so that we know when it was 'sighted'.

e *A sum certain* – this is not the same as a certain sum. A sum certain means a fixed, definite, known amount. If the bill is going to be as good as money, we must know how much money it is worth.

f *To, or to the order of* – the drawer names the *payee*, the one to be paid, but that person may order the acceptor to pay someone else by endorsing the bill to this effect.

g *Or to bearer* – a bill which is payable to bearer does not need to be endorsed – the bill passes by delivery from hand to hand. It can present problems if stolen.

'Sight' bills and 'usance' bills

If a bill is payable at sight it is payable as soon as the drawee sees it, and there is no period of credit open to the drawee. Other bills payable at a later date are called 'usance' bills – the word implies 'by ancient usage or custom of the trade'. It harks back to olden days when merchants frequently had to wait until ships came in before they could pay their debts.

Cheques

A cheque is defined in the Bills of Exchange Act, 1882 as follows: 'A cheque is a bill of exchange drawn on a banker payable on demand'. The drawer of the cheque orders the banker to pay a sum certain to the person named on the cheque.

12.3 Drawing bills of exchange

A bill of exchange can be written on any piece of material – one irate fishmonger recently paid his rates with one written on a large fish – but it is usual to buy blank forms like the ones reproduced in Fig. 12.2 by courtesy of Formecon Ltd. Note the various parts of the bill, and how they fit the definition given in section 12.2 above.

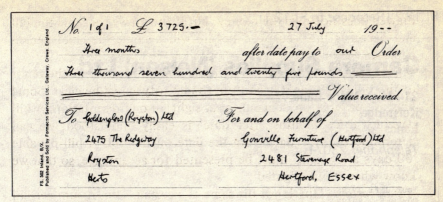

Fig. 12.2 An inland bill of exchange

12.4 Letters about inland bills of exchange

SL12.1

R V PHOTOGRAPHICS (Burnley) Ltd

2714 High Street, Burnley.   Tel. 358359

```
Camera Supplies (Nelson) Ltd                 Our Ref  JT/RS
214 High Moor Lane
Kelstedge
Lancs                                        17 September 19--

Dear Sirs

As is usual at this time we are stocking up for Christmas and write to
ask whether you will supply us against a bill of exchange drawn at
four months from the date you fulfil the order.  This should mean you
receive payment about the end of January.

I enclose the order, but my prices may be out of date and consequently
the total may not be correct for the value of the bill.  I will leave
you to draw on us for the correct figure.  I trust that you can accommo-
date us as you have done in former years.

Yours faithfully



J Thomas
Managing Director
```

Camera Supplies (Nelson) Ltd

214 High Moor Lane
Kelstedge
Lancs
Telephone: 23071

Your Ref: JT/RS
Our Ref: SD/SH

1 October 19--

R V Photographics (Burnley) Ltd
2714 High Street
Burnley

Dear Mr Thomas

In accordance with the request in your letter dated 17 September we
have today despatched to you goods valued at £3850. We present our
bill of exchange drawn on you for this sum at 4 months from date, for
acceptance and return.

We hope you will have a successful season, and look forward to accommodating you in the same way on future occasions.

We have a most interesting development in the spring of next year with
a first camera from the Singapore based 'Zoomview' Camera Co. I hope
we may draw this to your attention at our February 'Spring Show'.

Yours very sincerely

S Driver
Sales Manageress

G B Borrowdale (Contractors) Ltd

2846 Darwen Drive
Wethoughton
Lancs
Telephone: 846739

```
Your Ref   TS/DC
Our  Ref   JBB/CL
```

29 September 19--

```
Rawtenstall's Bricks (Bedford) Ltd
The Clay Hill
Langford
Beds
```

Dear Sirs

I write with regard to my letter of 3 September in which I warned you
that due to the recession in building we were unlikely to be able to
honour the full value of the bill of exchange due on 4 October (£8500).
The position has improved somewhat and my directors would like to
propose as follows:

(a) Payment of £5500 by cheque on 7 October
(b) A new bill for £3046 at one month after date from 7 October to be
accepted by us. This represents the balance of £3000 and interest at
14 per cent on £8500 for 3 days (4-7 October) and £3000 for 31 days
(7 October - 7 November).

We should be able to meet this further bill of exchange on the due
date.

I hope very much that you can accommodate us to this further extent;
we do seem to be finding buyers for our houses at last and there
should be no further problems.

Yours faithfully

```
T Stannard
Chief Accountant
```

12.5 Foreign bills of exchange

When bills of exchange are used to settle debts between firms of different nations the procedure outlined above has to be extended to provide a simple solution to the problem of the international transmission of money, which is also in different currencies. Many arrangements can be made, of which the following is a simple example:

Imagine John Smith of London who draws a bill of exchange on Macquarrie Bros of Wellington, New Zealand, requiring them to pay for goods supplied £10 000 sterling, three months after date. He discounts the bill with a London bank which charges 12 per cent interest, thus paying £9700.82 for the £10 000 bill. The bank is now the **holder in due course** of the bill, which means it holds the bill in good faith, for value (in other words it has paid for it). A holder in due course is entitled to collect the value of the bill on the due date.

The bank sends the bill to its Wellington branch, or to a 'correspondent bank' prepared to act on its behalf. The sum is converted to New Zealand dollars, and is then collected on the due date. It thus forms a fund, belonging to the London bank in its account in Wellington. There is little point in returning the money to the UK for in the course of business the bank is sure to be approached by a British importer wishing to pay a New Zealand firm for goods supplied. The bank will sell this importer a banker's draft in favour of the New Zealand supplier, and this will be settled in New Zealand from the New Zealand fund created when Macquarrie Bros honoured their debt to Smith.

Uniform rules for the collection of commercial paper

Many difficulties can arise in the collection of money by bills of exchange, and it is essential for the trader to give clear instructions about any eventuality that occurs. For example a bill may be dishonoured on presentation for acceptance (the drawee will not accept the bill). It may be dishonoured when presented for payment (the acceptor will not pay on the due date). In either of these cases an inland bill must be 'noted' (a note is made on the bill of its dishonour, by an official called a **notary public**). A foreign bill must be 'protested'. This is a formal legal process in which the notary public presents the bill again in his official capacity. If it is again refused he writes out a document (the protest) which formally declares that on presentation it was dishonoured. This can then become the basis for a legal case which may result in the bankruptcy of the debtor.

To reduce the difficulties as much as possible a set of rules has been drawn up in English and French by the International Chamber of Commerce, 38 Cours Albert 1er, 75008 Paris. These specify exactly what each party should do, and clarify many situations. It is always advisable to quote these rules in any letter about foreign bills of exchange. This is referred to again in Chapter 15.

12.6 Letters about the collection of commercial paper
SL12.4

Joseph Nakanda

**2174 Port Highway,
Lagos, Nigeria**

Our Ref: JN/ST

13 January 19--

T Grimshaw and Co Ltd
1702 Cannon Street
London
EC4 1ST
England

Dear Sirs

The sale of your goods proceeded satisfactorily last Friday, and we enclose our account sales which shows that the sum of £3724.68 is due to you. This payment is covered for exchange control by the Form M already in your possession. Will you please draw on us for this amount at 30 days and present it through your bankers at once, for collection subject to the Uniform Rules for Collections.

We hope we may act for you on a future occasion.

Yours faithfully

Joseph Nakanda
Commission Agent

Enc: Account Sales

Norton and Son (Merchant Bankers)

2748 Liver Bird View, Liverpool, England
Telephone: 051-246 8021

Our Ref: AZ/TD

10 June 19--

The Manager
The Royal Banking Company
986 Hudson Avenue
Toronto
Canada

Dear Sir

We are pleased to enclose the following bills, which we wish you to
collect subject to the Uniform Rules for Collections. They are clean
remittances unencumbered by any documents. Please present the usance
bills for acceptance and retain them until the due date, when they
should be presented for payment. All charged are for our account and
to be deducted from the proceeds, which should be credited to our
Toronto Account. Please protest at once any bill dishonoured by non-
acceptance or non-payment. The amounts are:

$ 9 000 - at sight on Mackenzie & Co
$ 4 500 - for 25 July on Austin Bay Co
$ 5 600 - for 24 August on Martin & Co

$19 100 - payable in Toronto

Yours faithfully

A Zimmerman
Norton and Son

Enclosures: 3 bills

RICHARD LEONE

Attorney at Law, Lepontoland,
2475 Chaka Way, Leponto City

Your Ref: Bill of Exchange 2175
Our Ref: RL/JS

14 July 19--

Messrs Sullivan and Son
98 Irlam Road
Liverpool 14
England

Dear Sirs

By a decision of the Ministry for External Affairs foreign exchange
regulations have been imposed over all payments for non-essential
items, and your bill of exchange has been passed to us by the Bank of
Lepontoland because you named us in the block 'In the case of need
refer to' on the 'Bank Instructions' form.

We have protested the bill, and retained a copy; the original protest
is enclosed. I am sure you will appreciate that the drawee is in no
way to blame for this decision, and has deposited the total sum due
with us, which we have placed on deposit, to bear interest at the best
rate obtainable. Whether this sum can ever be paid remains to be seen,
but in the meantime there is nothing we can do, and no doubt you will
approach the Export Credit Guarantees Department with whom I note you
are insured against this eventuality.

Yours faithfully

Richard Leone
Attorney at Law

12.7 Difficulties with bills of exchange

The law about bills of exchange is complex and cannot be studied fully in a book of this type. The chief feature of a bill of exchange is that it is a negotiable instrument. This means that when it passes from hand to hand it transfers to a person who takes it in good faith for value, a perfect title (right of ownership). Even if the person I take it from has no right to it I obtain a good title to it, provided I took it in good faith for value at that date. Such a holder in due course has rights against the acceptor, who has the first duty to pay the bill. If he/she dishonours it the holder turns to the first endorser, or any other endorser, but usually to a first class name on the bill (a major bank).

The letters below illustrate some of the difficulties that arise.

12.8 Letters about difficulties with bills of exchange

SL12.7

MALLET BROS

2174 High Tor Road
Matlock, Derbyshire
Tel: Matlock 54323

Our Reference: TD/BD

31 January 19--

Messrs Groves & Co
1192 Welbeck Road
Manchester M3 2PQ

Dear Sirs

We regret to find that your bankers have dishonoured your acceptance for £375 in favour of the Lancashire Metal Co, in spite of our notification that no extension could be arranged. This action has caused us considerable embarrassment and made it necessary for us to discharge the debt to Lancashire Metal Co ourselves.

Your attitude in the matter is most unsatisfactory, and compels us to insist on receiving the amount due within forty-eight hours. Failing this we shall place the matter in the hands of our solicitors.

Yours faithfully

T Donaldson
Mallet Bros

Servicit Merchant Bankers Ltd

214 St Mary Axe
London EC3 2LR

Telephone: 01-365 8000

Your Ref: Bill 1218
Our Ref: JT/CD

24 July 19--

G H Setchfield Industries (Weybridge) Ltd
2047 Downsway
Weybridge
Surrey

Dear Sirs

Your bill drawn on Stirling Timber Co (Chertsey) Ltd for £850 which
we discounted on 11 May last has been dishonoured for non-payment
today. As endorser of the bill we must ask you to put us in funds
forthwith. We also reserve the right to charge you with interest at
16 per cent per annum on a daily basis until your cheque is cleared.
On receipt of your cheque we shall return the bill to you for
appropriate action. We have not yet had the bill noted since no
doubt you will prefer to see a notary public yourself.

Yours faithfully

J Thompson
Short-term Funds Manager

Morton Bros (Construction) Ltd

3874 New Road, Newhaven, Sussex   Tel: 079 12 7565

Messrs Barton & Co   Our Ref: JM/TS
196 Michigan Boulevard
Ottawa
Canada   17 May 19--

Dear Sirs

We regret to advise you that the bill for £7250 in our favour on
Messrs Garfield & Co has been presented for acceptance today; this
was refused on the grounds that you have no authority to draw. Owing
to our long connection we are reluctant to take immediate action, and
propose to leave the matter until 17 November when the bill falls due.
If at that date payment is refused we shall be compelled to draw on
you for the amount of the bill plus charges incurred through protest.
In the meantime we have had the bill protested for non-acceptance to
safeguard our position at a later date.

Yours faithfully

J Morton
Managing Director

12.9   Exercises on bills of exchange

1 Draw up a number of inland bills of exchange, or obtain a supply
from Formecon Services Ltd. Then draw the following bills:

   a Security Equipment (Mansfield) Ltd, 528 Newark Road, Mansfield, Notts draw on A Locksmith, 2527 Hornsey Road, London,
   N4 for £850, payable three months after date. The bill is dated
   1 November 19--, and payable to Security Equipment Ltd.

   b Photosupplies (Nottingham) Ltd, 2386 Beeston Way, Nottingham draw on Studio 91 Ltd, 91 Old Grange Way, Long Eaton,
   Notts on 21 January 19-- for £1360 value received. The bill is
   to be payable to their order, 6 months after sight.

   c Survey Equipment (Spondon) Ltd, of 1381 Derby Road,
   Spondon draw on Aerial Surveys (Southend) Ltd, of 2486

Rochford Road, Southend-on-Sea, Essex for £855 value received. The bill is payable to 'our' order, and is payable three months after date which is 21 October 19--.

2 *a* Cyril Farley (Tottenham) Ltd, of 247 Wood Way, Tottenham, London, N15, write to Peter Gibbs & Co (Midhurst) Ltd asking for goods to the value of £1850. They are prepared to accept a bill of exchange drawn at three months from the date of delivery, the goods to be collected by their vehicle from 2087 Chichester Road, Midhurst, Sussex. Write the letter, using your own name, as the accountant of Cyril Farley Ltd. The date is 11 September 19--.

b Peter Gibbs & Co agree to the arrangement, and enclose the bill of exchange drawn on Cyril Farley (Tottenham) Ltd, but point out that due to an increase in prices they have had to draw the bill for £1985. They express their willingness to accommodate their customer in this way whenever necessary. The date of delivery was 18 September 19--, and the letter was written, and the bill drawn, on the same day.

3 *a* You are the chief cashier of Nathanael Gibbs and Partners, opticians, of 2184 Sunderland Street, Peterlee, Co Durham. You wrote to Brian Young Optical Manufacturers Ltd, of 3847 Nile Street, South Shields on 4 January 19-- to express your regret at not being able to honour a bill of exchange for £1780 due on 21 January. You ask them to accept payment of £1200 on the due date, the balance of £580 to be renewed by a further bill drawn on that date, at one month for £580 and interest at 12 per cent per annum.

b The manufacturers reply expressing concern at the failure to honour the bill in full, but agreeing to the new arrangement, except that they wish the interest rate to be 15 per cent. This is the price they are paying for the use of money at this time. They reserve the right to sue upon the bill on the due date if the £1200 is not actually paid as promised. Their letter is dated 9 January 19--.

4 You are the export manager of Peter Grimes Export (Grimsby) Ltd, of 4275 East Coast Road, Grimsby. Write to your bankers Silverstone Trust Co Ltd, 5876 Lombard Street, London EC2 5ST asking them to arrange collection of a usance bill drawn on Isaac Olaleye, 2842 Port Compound, Port Harcourt, Nigeria. Refer to the Uniform Rules for Collections as a basis for action. The bill is for £1850,

due three months after date, which is the date of your letter. Instruct them to protest the bill in the event of either dishonour for non-acceptance or dishonour for non-payment, and to retain the accepted bill for presentation on the due date. Funds to be remitted to you net of their charges as soon as possible after collection.

5 *a* As the result of a successful lawsuit in the courts in Hong Kong you have been awarded damages of 10 000 Hong Kong dollars and costs of 23 000 Hong Kong dollars, against the Hong Kong Mercantile Marine Co, (I T Sung) Ltd, whose vessel damaged your wharf. Write on 1 April 19-- as chief accountant of Tentergate Wharf and Haulage (Greenwich) Ltd, 2745 Pier Road, Greenwich, London, to your bankers Solvent & Carefree (London) Ltd, 249 St Mary Axe, London EC3 2LA. Enclose a sight bill of exchange drawn for the amount mentioned. Ask them to present the bill for collection, under the Uniform Rules, and to place the equivalent sterling amount, less charges, to the credit of your account.

b Write as the bankers named above on 21 May 19-- to notify Tentergate Ltd that £3124.56 has been credited to their account. The details are that the 33 000 Hong Kong dollars were exchanged at \$10.12 = £1, to yield £3250.87. Charges were £136.31.

12.10 Appendix on the English language: extending your vocabulary

Writers and speakers are constantly seeking better ways to express what they want to say to the world. You should always seek to use words, phrases or expressions which convey your idea with absolute precision, better than any other phrase could do it. The French phrase *mot juste* is used to describe such a phrase or expression — it means the word (*mot*) that is exactly right (*juste*).

In section 1.4, reference was made to a **thesaurus**, and a short extract was given from a traditional-style thesaurus. More modern styles are also available, as shown below. The extract shows the word 'animal', which is a noun (n). There are three chief uses of the word animal, which are labelled 1, 2, 3. The first of these is an animal as a *mobile organism* (as distinct from vegetables which are generally immobile). The second meaning of animal is a non-human creature, contrasting the animals with the higher species, man. The third use of the word is *a brutish human,* as where a man is described as an animal because he behaves in a way that lowers him to something less than human.

The complete extract, reproduced by courtesy of Collins Publishers, from *Collins New World Thesaurus* is as follows:

animal, n 1. (A mobile organism) — Syn. living thing, creature, human being, beast, being, fish, crustacean, amphibian, cetacean, vertebrate, invertebrate, reptile, insect, bird, wild animal, domestic animal, mammal, a representative of the fauna, animalcule; see also bird 1, fish, insect, man 1, reptile.

2. (A nonhuman creature) — Syn. beast (of burden), brute, lower animal, quadruped, beast of the field, creeping thing, varmint, pet, farm animal, dumb animal, wild thing, one of God's creatures, monster, critter. — Ant. man*, spirit, soul*.

3. (A brutish human) — Syn. brute, savage, monster; see Beast 2.

A thesaurus, either of the modern or traditional type, or a good dictionary is an invaluable aid to anyone who wishes to expand his knowledge of words and thus his effective use of language.

12.11 A practical exercise to extend your vocabulary

A simple, effective way of expanding one's vocabulary is to get into the habit of writing down any new words met, checking their meanings in a dictionary and learning both their spellings and their meanings.

Invest in a small notebook. Title each double-page with a letter of the alphabet. Draw a vertical line a third of the way across each page. When you see a new word in a newspaper, novel, textbook, business letter, etc., make a note of it on one side of your page; when you have time, check the word in your dictionary and write its meaning on the other two-thirds of your page. Then learn both spelling and meaning.

Within a short time you will find that you have developed the habit of noting new words and discovering their meanings. Periodically, once a week perhaps, check back through the pages and see how many words you can remember. If you do not have anyone to test you, you can test yourself by placing a sheet of paper over the column of words and try to remember (and spell) the words by looking at the meanings. When you have tried this method, reverse the process by looking at each word while its meaning is covered and attempt to give the correct definition of the word.

If you only discover two new words a day, within a short time your vocabulary will have expanded considerably and your powers of communication improved accordingly.

13 Import trade

13.1 Importing commodities

Importing commodities is of fundamental importance to the economy of any nation. No country in the world has every commodity it requires, and some countries (Singapore for example) need to import almost everything for their manufacturing industries. The chief commodities are metals (iron ore, tin, copper, zinc, manganese, silver, gold, lead, etc.), fibres (wool, cotton, jute, sisal and many more, including synthetic fibres), timber (both hardwoods and soft woods), beverages (tea, coffee, cocoa), grain, fishmeal, etc. Since many of these products are most easily moved in bulk, and are of fairly uniform quality, they can be bought and sold on special markets without any need to be seen and inspected in the market place (though some can be inspected at sampling warehouses and depots around the country). Correspondence about them tends to be much reduced these days, since telex messages and telephone calls are widely used to notify that cargoes are on the move, and to make arrangements for storage, warehousing, delivery, etc. Such correspondence as is required might be related to the inspection of consignments, the prices obtained, etc. A selection of typical letters is given in section 13.2 below.

13.2 Letters about bulk commodities

SL13.1 (See Glossary for **C and F**, laydays and **liquidated damages**)

Australian Iron Ore Co Ltd

Port Hedland, Western Australia

Our Reference Contract No 2178

1 October 19--

Special Steels Ltd
Hunterston
Ayrshire
Scotland

Dear Sirs

Your representatives Messrs McCardy and Dalry have signed the
contract for iron ore to be delivered to your Hunterston terminal
and we now confirm that shipment will start on 10 October next with
our class of 'Southern Cross' 120 000 ton bulk ore carriers sailing
at fortnightly intervals.

May we remind you that the contract price is based on CFR terms
and consequently all insurance on the cargoes is to be arranged by
you in London and is for your account. May I also remind you that the
laydays for unloading our vessels are limited to 7 days reckoned from
noon on the day following notice of availability for unloading at your
terminal. Any delay over this time limit, for whatever reason, will
invoke the 'liquidated damages' clause in the contract.

We look forward to a long and mutually beneficial business relationship.

Yours faithfully

R Stewart
Australian Iron Ore Co Ltd

SINGAPORE CHEMICALS CO LTD

BEDOK DEPOT
BEDOK
SINGAPORE

Your Ref: AS/TD
Our Ref: ML/BC

14 February 19--

Antipodes Extraction Ltd
2148 Beach Road
Newcastle
New South Wales

Dear Sirs

With reference to the consignment of ethanol (order No 1684), we have arranged for one of our clean-product carriers to bring this consignment in after making its major delivery at Sydney in the last week of this month.

Our Sydney agents Ayres and Co will be in touch with you as soon as they have firm news of her arrival there, since there is some congestion in the port. In any case it seems certain she will be cleared well before your final date for delivery, 10 April 19--.

Yours faithfully

Man Lee
Sales Manager

Orlando Alvarez

1024 Calle Alboraya
Valencia
Spain

Our Ref: B/L 217/RA/DC

13 October 19--

Messrs Smith & Sons
605 Royal India Building
Liverpool 21

Dear Sirs

We have despatched to you by SS Libertad a consignment of oranges
for which we enclose the bill of lading. As an advance payment of
the freight could not easily be arranged, it was necessary to leave
this payment to you on arrival, and we hope that you have no objection to meeting it. We ask you to make all other payments arising
from the clearing of the goods, and their sale.

The demand for oranges seems brisk at the moment, and we look forward
to receiving an 'account sales' showing that this consignment has
achieved satisfactory prices. We trust that you will be satisfied with
your usual commission based on the gross proceeds, and del credere
commission of $2\frac{1}{2}$ per cent, also on the gross proceeds.

Yours faithfully

Roberto Alvarez
Export Manager

Enc: B/L 217

POTOSI TIN MINING CO LTD

**POTOSI
BOLIVIA**

Your Ref: Order No 1714
Our Ref: LQ/RE

17 October 19--

Rio Pilcomayo Manufacturing Co Ltd
Avon Road South
Bristol
BS3 1TW

Dear Sirs

This is to notify you that your cargo of pellets (28 000 metric
tonnes) sailed today in the SS Valparaiso from Iquique. We enclose
the short-form Bill of Lading, which also confirms the tonnage
mentioned above. Upon arrival and unloading we shall appreciate the
transfer of the purchase price within fourteen days, as required by
our contract, to our account with the Bank of London and South
America.

Yours faithfully

Leo Quetzal
Export Manager

Enc: S/F Bill of Lading

Smith and Sons

605 Royal India Buildings, Liverpool 21

Telephone: 66734

Your Ref: BL 217/RA/DC
Our Ref: TS/DG

15 November 19--

Orlando Alvarez
1024 Calle Alboraya
Valencia
Spain

Dear Senor Alvarez

The consignment of oranges dispatched on 13 October duly arrived in perfect condition and was cleared from the docks at once. We were able to obtain good prices as shown by the following account sales:

Account Sales: 13 November 19--

		£
6000 boxes oranges, sold as follows:		
2000 boxes at £10.50		21 000
3500 boxes at £8.75		30 625
500 boxes at £6.20		3 100
		54 725

Less charges as follows:	£	
Normal commission at 5% on gross proceeds	2736.25	
Del credere commission at 2½%	1368.12	
Freight	4750.80	
Landing charges	685.00	
Port dues	425.00	
Road haulage	286.50	10 251.67
		£44 473.33

A banker's draft for this balance is enclosed. We should like to express our appreciation of your passing this transaction to us and hope we may handle consignments for you in the future.

Yours sincerely

Trevor Smith
Junior Partner

Enc: Banker's draft

Peters and Coleporter Ltd

Silversmiths,

Great Winchester Street, London EC2 7PQ
Telephone 01 - 550 7839

Your Ref: B/L 17685
Our Ref: TJD/RA

14 March 19--

Tupac Yupanqui Inc
Calle Porto 175
Tumbes
Peru

Dear Sirs

We have to notify you that we are in dispute over the quality of the
silver bars shipped to us on the bill of lading referred to above.
As we are entitled to do we selected two ingots at random and had
them assayed at the Assay Office here in London. Both ingots were
below specification (95 per cent pure), as the assay report shows.
There appear to be three options:
(a) We can have the whole consignment refined to the agreed level, at
your expense
(b) We can accept the bars in their present condition and adjust the
price accordingly. If so we suggest that the price be the value of
silver of a purity equal to the average purity of the two bars
assayed.
(c) If this is not acceptable we are prepared to have each bar
assayed separately and pay for each bar according to its assayed
purity, but we must charge you for the assay charge on the remaining
28 bars out of 30.

Would you please let us know at once how you wish this matter to be
resolved.

Yours faithfully

T J Dixon
Purchasing Officer

Enclosure: Assay Report

13.3 Importing manufactured goods

Whilst the import of bulk commodities is essential for most nations, the import of manufactured goods has only recently become a major feature of United Kingdom imports, and many developing nations are anxious to restrict imports of manufactures so that they can protect 'infant' home industries and develop an industrial work force.

A major preoccupation of international trade is to arrange affairs in such a way that both parties are sure of satisfaction. Thus the exporter would like to be paid for the goods supplied as soon as they leave the factory, while the importer half a world away would like to receive the goods before parting with the purchase money. How this is arranged applies equally well to both import and export trade, but is probably better left to the next chapter, Export Trade. A full discussion of documentation is also necessary, but is best left to that chapter too.

Here we will simply follow through a single import transaction for a sophisticated manufactured product, to be paid for on open-account terms. Open-account means that the parties concerned will treat one another as if they lived in the same country, and will settle accounts at regular intervals without any special protective documentation.

Leisure-Pleasure Mail Order Ltd

Camside Industrial Estates, Cambridge, CB4 1PQ   Tel: (0223) 79347

Our Reference RC/DBE

31 January 19--

Singapore Manufacturing Co Ltd
Entrepot Buildings
Collyer Quay
Singapore O1O4

Dear Sirs

We note from your recent advertisement in the 'Economist' that you
are seeking outlets for your Singa 235 automatic flash camera and
accessories in the United Kingdom. We are an expanding Mail Order
house in the leisure-pleasure field and would be interested in dis-
cussing with you the possibility of marketing your camera under our
subsidiary brand name of 'Picnic Products'. All 'Picnic Products'
carry the manufacturer's own name tag, manufacturing codes etc but in
addition carry a 'logo' plate with the words 'Picnic Product' and a
picture of a countryside scene, which establishes our brand image.

It would not be necessary to give us any sole agency for the marketing
of your camera in this way, since we have no major facilities for
servicing etc. All it does mean is that in return for the placing of
regular orders for your products, and featuring them in our catalogues,
you will arrange to incorporate an unobtrusive brand image label in
your design on the items sold to us.

We would also hope that the trade discount you would give us would
reflect the marketing effort we were making. Do you have a representative in the United Kingdom with whom we could discuss this? If
not, one of our buyers will be passing through Singapore in late
February, and could break his journey to visit you.

We are a highly reputable Mail Order house and can furnish bankers'
references etc as required.

Yours faithfully

Richard Cookson
Importer

Singapore Manufacturing Co Ltd

Entrepot Buildings, Collyer Quay, Singapore 0104

Your Reference   RC/DBE
Our Reference   TSL/JD

26 February 19--

Leisure-Pleasure Mail Order Ltd
Camside Industrial Estates
Cambridge
CB4 1PQ

Dear Sirs

After the visit of Mr Ferris today we are pleased to confirm the
following arrangements:

a   You will place an order for 1000 Singa 235 cameras per month, for
    three months, at the special price of £2.50 per camera.
b   You will also place an initial order for 100 each of the other five
    units in our accessories range, at a trade discount of 55 per cent
    of catalogue price.
c   You will make an immediate payment of £1000 sterling on account, the
    balance to be payable on open-account terms 15 days from delivery of
    statement, which will be made out on the last day of each month
    commencing with the last day of April.
d   Our design staff will adapt your logo to appear on a metal plate on
    the camera, as required.
e   Goods will be consigned by air freight, at our expense, you to pay
    all clearance charges and duty (if any) from Heathrow Airport, London.
f   Payment to be by bank transfer into our Singapore account, the
    details of which have been supplied confidentially to your repres-
    entative Mr Ferris.
g   Any complaints about equipment, or any repairs, are to be referred to
    our English agents, Technoproducts (Nottingham) Ltd, Beeston Road,
    Nottingham.
h   Any disputes between us are to be settled in the courts of the party
    making the complaint, using English Law, both parties agreeing to
    honour the judgments as if they had been made in their own countries.

We look forward to receiving your first order, the notification of the
transfer of the deposit of £1000 and a long and mutually beneficial
course of business.

Yours faithfully

T S Lee
Singapore Manufacturing Co Ltd

Brixton Trading Co Ltd Tel: 01 - 792 6699

2174 Coldharbour Lane, Brixton, London SW9 4ED, England

Benzinger (Locarno) AG   Our Ref HD/PT
CH 127884
Via San Gottardo
Locarno   31 July 19--
Switzerland

Dear Sirs

Order for Benzinger Chronometers

We are interested in acting as a marketing outlet for your gold
chronometers. We are an established wholesaler in this class of
goods serving retailers throughout the United Kingdom. We can make
arrangements to pay by letter of credit, and provided you are agreeable will place an order at once for 100 each of the ladies' and
gentlemen's models with day-date and automatic self-wind facilities.

Would you please advise whether you are prepared to supply us, and
likely delivery dates. Our order will then be placed at once and
notified to you by a letter of credit through our bankers Childe,
Fortescue and Co Ltd, of 1784 New Bond Street, London W1.

Yours faithfully

H Donaldson
General Manager

13.5   Exercises about imports

1 Write on 11 February, 19--, as the factory manager for Central
Heating Products Ltd, 2764 Corporation Street, Newcastle 4 to the
Emerald Mountain Copper Mining Co, Rockhampton, Queensland,
Australia to ask about the supply of copper ingots. Ask them to
quote for 20-ton loads on FOB terms, to be dispatched in an initial
consignment of 30 loads and then 10 loads per month for three
years. Emphasise that you have a quotation from Spain which is
very competitive, especially in view of the shorter freight distance.

2 Ismael Muhammadu, of 2174 Zagazig Road, Abu Kebir, Egypt, has sent 2000 tonnes of early potatoes on consignment terms to an importer R T Gatward Public Co Ltd, Nine Elms Depot, London, SW8. As general manager of Gatwards you are able to sell 1800 tonnes at £80 per tonne and 150 tonnes at £60 per tonne. The balance is sold for cattle food at £5 per tonne. You deduct 7½ per cent for commission of which 2½ per cent is del credere commission. You also charge £1800 handling and transport charges. Write a letter on 10 April 19--, and draw up an account sales. The balance due is sent by banker's draft, in Egyptian pounds which convert at E£1.5 = £1 sterling.

3 *a* The Oriental Trading Co, 2145 Ghaziabad Road, Delhi sends J Gately (Bloomsbury) Ltd of 1846 Bedford Row, London WC1 a consignment of brassware by SS *Arabia* due in London on 20 October 19--. As import manager you clear the goods from the docks (handling charges £85, transport £45), sell them for a total proceeds of £18 250 (auctioneer's commission £365) and include on the account sales charges for warehousing £62.50, insurance £76.50, delivery £65. Your own charges are 10 per cent of the *net* proceeds. Draw up the account sales, and write a covering letter explaining the outcome of the venture and hoping that similar consignments will be placed with you in the future. A banker's draft for the balance is enclosed. The date is 15 November 19--.

  b An inquiry from a customer in the jewellery trade concerns Burmese jade. Write to the Oriental Trading Co to ask them if they are dealers in Burmese jade and silverware. Would they kindly furnish you with full details, and would they be agreeable to sending any goods ordered by air mail to arrive in the United Kingdom before 20 February, against a letter of credit from a major bank.

4 *a* The Brazilian Trading Co, 3584 Calle Jose dos Campos, Sao Paulo, Brazil sends a consignment of coffee to their London import agents, Howard, Hollow and Partners, 2185 Mark Lane Buildings, London, EC3. Write a letter from Sao Paulo to the partners on 4 April 19--, enclosing the bill of lading and asking them to defray all expenses at Tilbury and elsewhere from the gross proceeds. After deducting their commission the balance

should be paid into the London branch of the Bank of South Sao Paulo, for transfer to Brazil.

   b On 24 April 19--, Howard, Hollow and Partners acknowledge the safe arrival of the shipment and agree to dispose of it at the best price possible.

   c The sale is arranged at the following prices: 275 tonnes at £980 per 5 tonnes and 45 tonnes at £972 per 5 tonnes. Charges in the United Kingdom totalled £5760, and commission on the gross proceeds was charged at 7½ per cent. Write a letter to Sao Paulo confirming that the net proceeds have been paid into the Bank of South Sao Paulo, and enclosing the account sales.

5 *a* Nautical Gear (Newcastle) Ltd, 2045 Tynemouth Way, Newcastle have ordered navigational instruments from Tor Ericsen, Port Compound, Bergen. The crates as listed are cleared from the docks, and the bill of lading surrendered, but on opening, one item included in the packing sheet (10 chronometers) is not included in the contents. Write to ask what can possibly have led to this omission, since the crates appeared intact on arrival, and no claim appears possible against the ship-owner.

   b Tor Ericsen reply that by an error in their packing department the goods were packed with another consignment sent to the Marine Dry Dock Company Ltd, The Dry Dock, Hebburn on Tyne. This company are holding the goods available for collection and Ericsen ask you to collect them and deduct the expense from your account before settlement. They apologise for the inconvenience.

13.6   Appendix on the English language: synonyms

In the previous chapter the importance of expanding your vocabulary was stressed, if precision of communication is to be improved. The English language has developed over many centuries, and its stockpile of words has grown to cover the multitude of objects, feelings, actions, appearances, etc. which make up the world. Inevitably more than one word may have emerged to cover the same idea, for example the words 'assist' and 'help' are so similar in meaning as to be virtually interchangeable. A word which is the same, or similar, in meaning to another word is called a **synonym**.

However, synonyms are not always exactly the same in meaning.

One word may carry a slightly different emphasis, and be more appropriate in a certain situation than another word. Take, for instance, the fine distinctions in meaning between these nouns covering relationships:

> A *friend* is someone who is personally close to us, while a *companion* may just be someone who keeps us company; someone whom we can merely recognise but with whom there is no intimacy is an *acquaintance,* while *comrade* suggests a fellow member of a group. A *colleague* is a person with whom one works.

The successful communicator will be able to choose from a range of possible synonyms the correct word to use in a particular context. It is important to know the precise meaning of synonyms if you are to choose the most appropriate word, and to avoid using a word in an unsuitable context.

13.7   Exercises on synonyms

1 Use each of these words in a sentence which shows that you understand its meaning:
   a1 mysterious
   a2 peculiar
   b1 slandered
   b2 libelled
   c1 antiquated
   c2 obsolete
   d1 mob
   d2 crowd
   e1 trespasser
   e2 intruder.

2 Using a *Roget's Thesaurus*, compile lists of synonyms for the business words given below, and distinguish between the words in each list. You could enter these in your vocabulary book in a section on synonyms:
   a money
   b debtor
   c security
   d commerce
   e production.

14 Export trade 1

14.1 The pattern of activities in export trade

Export trade calls for a special pattern of activities, because when the people of one country trade with the people of another country they are operating across national boundaries where different systems of law prevail. This leads to what are known as 'conflicts of law'. Conflicts of law may centre around the following areas:

a Are the things that the parties to a contract wish to do illegal in one or other of the countries?
b Which set of laws shall prevail, in the event of a dispute?
c Will the courts have jurisdiction (the right to make a judicial decision) in any matter, or will jurisdiction lie elsewhere?
d Once a judicial decision has been made, can it be enforced against the offending party, or not?

Clearly there are many problems that can arise, and to try to solve them a great many international conventions about the laws of carriage, trade, insurance, documentation, arrest, etc. have been held.
   The pattern of activities in export trade is as follows:

a Pre-contract negotiations take place with the buyers or their representatives. These representatives are often buying agents in the exporting country (sometimes called **export houses** or **confirming houses**). At other times the negotiations may be conducted in the foreign country by our sales representatives travelling abroad.
b Unless already known to us, the credit status of our customers is important and will be one of the subjects discussed.
c Quotations will be prepared for the supply of goods and services. Special clauses may need to be inserted at this point about inflationary charges, and about possible changes in foreign exchange rates. It will be essential to discuss the methods of payment. There are five methods: cash with order, letters of credit, documents against payment, documents against acceptance and open-account terms. Each of these is a story in itself, and will be explained in the correspondence later in this chapter, and the next chapter.

d Compliance with the regulations of both countries is essential and requires us to check on the export regulations in our own country and the import regulations in the foreign country. It may be necessary to obtain licences to export or import; sanitary certificates may be required to show goods are free of pests before being moved across borders; packing materials often have to be of a special type.

e If all these matters are covered an order must be placed, acknowledged, checked against the pre-contract negotiations and then formally accepted.

f The goods then have to be manufactured or obtained.

g The route for delivery of the goods has to be selected and shipping space reserved, or airline space reserved or chartered.

h Packing specifications have to be drawn up and instructions given to the packers.

i Insurance cover has to be arranged.

j Documentation must be prepared, including the documentation about carriage by road, rail, sea or air (or possibly some combination of these, known as multi-modal transport). Documentation about payment must be prepared, including invoices, bills of exchange, bank instruction forms, etc.

k Finally goods will be dispatched, documents presented, payment arranged and letters of appreciation soliciting further business will conclude the train of events.

While many of these activities will not call for business correspondence, telex messages and telephone calls conveying many of the messages required, at almost all stages in particular circumstances business letters will be called for, if only to ensure that written evidence is available at a later date should it be necessary.

14.2 Exporting on 'cash with order' terms

'Cash with order' is the most secure method of payment for exporters, since they already have the money before they dispatch the goods abroad. Naturally it is less popular with the foreign importer, who must make funds available before the exporter has done anything at all to deserve payment. It is most commonly used in small-scale exporting, such as the export of textbooks by post to individual customers.

A new system called 'Postabroad' provides a package of export documentation to simplify exporting by post. These 'postpacks' may be obtained from Formecon Services Ltd, Gateway, Crewe, CW1 1YN, in two-part, five-part or eight-part sets, according to the problems to be faced by the exporter in meeting the customs' requirements.

14.3　Exporting with a letter of credit

Often the exporter is worried that the foreign importer may not pay for the goods sent abroad. The importer, by contrast, fears to part with his money in case the exporter does not send the goods at all, or sends inferior, unsatisfactory goods. To solve these problems we can use the 'documentary credit' system. The full name for the system is 'the irrevocable documentary letter of credit system' and these may also be 'confirmed', or 'unconfirmed'. Under this system the importer states exactly what he requires, and provides a sum of money to pay for it, which he lodges with his bank. The exporter is then told by the bank in a 'letter of credit' what the importer requires, and if he provides it in exactly the correct way – correct quality, type, etc. and on time, with documentary proof that it has left the country – the bank will pay the exporter. The system requires the following arrangements:

a *The importer* arranges with his/her bank to make a sum of money available for payment to the exporter when the bank is satisfied that the goods concerned have left the exporter's country in good order and condition. This sum of money is 'irrevocable' i.e. it cannot be withdrawn without the exporter's consent.

b *The importer's bank* notifies a bank (the correspondent bank) in the exporter's country of the availability of the credit and the terms on which the credit will be released. It asks the correspondent bank to notify the exporter of these terms in a 'letter of credit', and it may ask them to 'confirm' the credit. This means that the correspondent bank in the exporter's country adds its good name to the order, promising to pay if the exporter does everything correctly.

c *The correspondent bank* sends the exporter a 'letter of credit', with full details of what is required.

d *The exporter* manufactures or obtains the goods, packs them, dispatches them and obtains documentary proof of the departure of the goods by sea, air, road or rail. He presents these documents to the banker, and the credit is released either at once (a **confirmed credit**) or after the documents have been sent to the foreign banker (an **unconfirmed credit**).

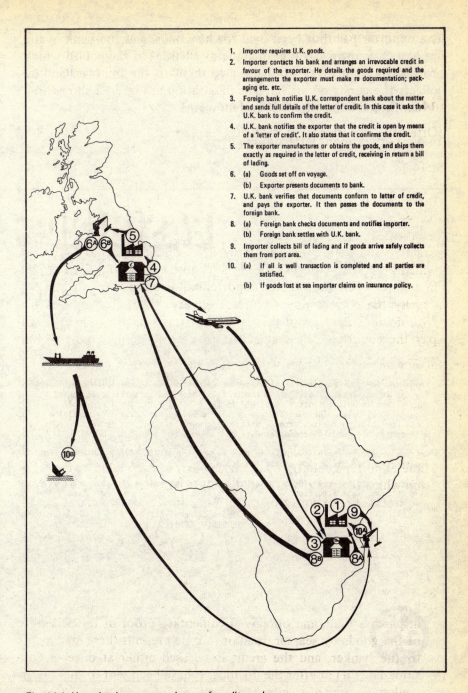

1. Importer requires U.K. goods.
2. Importer contacts his bank and arranges an irrevocable credit in favour of the exporter. He details the goods required and the arrangements the exporter must make re documentation; packaging etc. etc.
3. Foreign bank notifies U.K. correspondent bank about the matter and sends full details of the letter of credit. In this case it asks the U.K. bank to confirm the credit.
4. U.K. bank notifies the exporter that the credit is open by means of a 'letter of credit'. It also states that it confirms the credit.
5. The exporter manufactures or obtains the goods, and ships them exactly as required in the letter of credit, receiving in return a bill of lading.
6. (a) Goods set off on voyage.
   (b) Exporter presents documents to bank.
7. U.K. bank verifies that documents conform to letter of credit, and pays the exporter. It then passes the documents to the foreign bank.
8. (a) Foreign bank checks documents and notifies importer.
   (b) Foreign bank settles with U.K. bank.
9. Importer collects bill of lading and if goods arrive safely collects them from port area.
10. (a) If all is well transaction is completed and all parties are satisfied.
    (b) If goods lost at sea importer claims on insurance policy.

Fig. 14.1 How the documentary letter of credit works

205

The exporter has thus been paid for his goods, and the bank in the importer's country has the 'documents of title' to the goods, which prove ownership of them. They give these to the importer and he collects the goods on arrival. The illustration in Fig. 14.1 shows how the confirmed letter of credit system works.

14.4   Letters about letters of credit

SL14.1

Your Ref: FU/LIB/21
Our Ref: EZ

9 March 19--

I Urukehu Esq
2475 Port Compound
Suva
Fiji

Dear Mr Urukehu

Thank you for your enquiry for A4 binders. We specialise in supplying Easibinders for use in university, college and commercial libraries and shall be delighted to supply them in bulk against a confirmed letter of credit through a reputable international bank. The quantity you require would appear to be only part of a container load, but we can arrange with our forwarding agents to group the goods with compatible goods destined for Fiji.

We supply binders for A4 journals in four capacities of 43, 54, 63 and 83 mm, so you can see there is a wide choice available.

We look forward to receiving a letter of credit in due course and your order will have our immediate attention.

Yours sincerely
EASIBIND LIMITED

Kenneth Coad
General Manager

Easibind Limited
Eardley House
4 Uxbridge Street
Kensington
London W8 7SZ
Tel 01-727 0686/7/8
Telex 23894

Registration number : 307469
Registered Office :
Wilson Road, Huyton,
Liverpool, L36 6HQ.

Directors
G. Bussey

D. A. Morgan
R. F. Wood

Fig. 14.2 A reply to an overseas enquiry

A I Bank Public Co Ltd

107 Lombard Street, London EC2P 2BX   Tel: 01 - 724 3388

Our Ref: AB/CD/DC217/564

14 April 19--

Easibind Ltd
Eardley House
4 Uxbridge Street
Kensington
London W8 7SZ

Dear Sirs

ADVICE OF POPULAR BANK OF OCEANIA, SUVA, FIJI

We inform you that the above-named bank have opened with us their irrevocable credit in your favour on account of Isaac Urukehu, 2475 Port
Compound, Suva, Fiji to the extent of £32 500 (say Thirty two thousand
five hundred Pounds). The credit is valid at this office until 12 noon
on 23 May 19--, on or before which your drafts on us at sight may be
paid if accompanied by the under-mentioned documents evidencing current
shipment from Southampton to Suva of the goods described below. The
buyer's order number and reference is UK 1385. Part shipments prohib-
ited. All documents to be in English. We confirm that no import
licence is required for these goods on entering Fiji.

Two copies consolidator's House Bill of Lading issued in favour of Popular Bank of Oceania marked 'FREIGHT PAID' showing the amount of freight
paid, and 'INSURANCE PAID' showing the amount of insurance paid.

Two copies of a packing list covering the contents of the container of
which the goods are part, being an LCL (Less than Container Load).

Four copies of a commercial invoice bearing the declaration required by
the Dominion Government regulations, and bearing a clause 'warranted
packed free of grass, straw, chaff and hay'. The invoice covering
10 000 A4 binders 83 mm capacity at a quoted price of £32 500.

All drafts under this credit to bear the clause 'Drawn under Documentary Credit 217564'.

We are requested to advise you of the terms of the credit, which is
irrevocable on the part of our principals and also bears our confirmation. Subject to Uniform Customs and Practice for Documentary Credits
(1974 Revision) International Chamber of Commerce Publication No 290.

Yours faithfully

A Baldwin
Overseas Manager

Your Ref: FU/LIB/21/UK1385
Our Ref: PP/EZ

14 April 19--

I Urukehu Esq
2475 Port Compound
Suva
Fiji

Dear Mr Urukehu

LETTER OF CREDIT DC 217 564: POPULAR BANK OF OCEANIA

We have been advised of this documentary credit but would like to make one
representation about it. Your specification of Southampton as the port of
dispatch is unnecessarily restrictive, since in the event of a strike or other
difficulty at that port the goods could not leave from a trouble-free port, and
would be subject to delay - which might extend beyond the validity of the letter
of credit.

In these days of multi-modal transport the container company which is acting as
the combined transport operator has agreed to be liable for any loss incurred
wherever it happens, and therefore there is no need to limit his freedom to use
whichever port is most convenient. All ports are equally good. Will you please
instruct your bank to telex the A I Bank (their correspondents in the matter)
authorising them to modify their instructions to read 'from the United Kingdom
to Suva'. As soon as we receive this modification we will accept your offer to
buy, and proceed to pack and dispatch the goods.

Yours sincerely
EASIBIND LIMITED

Kenneth Coad
General Manager

Easibind Limited
Eardley House
4 Uxbridge Street
Kensington
London W8 7SZ
Tel 01-727 0686/7/8
Telex 23894

Registration number : 307469
Registered Office :
Wilson Road, Huyton,
Liverpool, L36 6HQ.

Directors
G. Bussey

D. A. Morgan
R. F. Wood

Fig. 14.3 A letter concerning a letter of credit

BARCLAYS International

168 Fenchurch Street, London, EC3P 3HP.

date 20th July 19..

DOCUMENTARY CREDITS DEPARTMENT

SPECIMEN

IRREVOCABLE CREDIT No:- FDC/2/6789
To be quoted on all drafts and correspondence.

Beneficiary(ies)	Advised through
Speirs and Wadley Limited, Adderley Road, Hackney, London, E.8.	

Accreditor	To be completed only if applicable
Woldal Incorporated, Broadway, New York, U.S.A.	Our cable of Advised through Refers

Dear Sir(s)

In accordance with instructions received from The Downtown Bank & Trust Co.
we hereby issue in your favour a Documentary Credit for £4108
(say) Four thousand, one hundred and eight pounds sterling   available by your drafts
drawn on us

at sight
for the 100% c.i.f.   invoice value, accompanied by the following documents:-

1. Invoice in triplicate, signed and marked Licence No. LHDL 22 19..
2. Certificate of Origin issued by a Chamber of Commerce.
3. Full set of clean on board Shipping Company's Bills of Lading made out to order and blank endorsed, marked "Freight Paid" and "Notify Woldal Inc., Broadway, New York."
4. Insurance Policy or Certificate in duplicate, covering Marine and War Risks up to buyer's warehouse, for invoice value of the goods plus 10%.

Covering the following goods:-

400 Electric Power Drills

To be shipped from	London	to	New York c.i.f.

not later than   10th August 19..

Partshipment not permitted	Transhipment not permitted

The credit is available for   presentation to us   until   31st August 19..

Documents to be presented within 21 days of shipment but within credit validity.

Drafts drawn hereunder must be marked "Drawn under Barclays Bank International Limited 168 Fenchurch Street London   branch, Credit number   FDC/2/6789   "
We undertake that drafts and documents drawn under and in strict conformity with the terms of this credit will be honoured upon presentation.

Yours faithfully,   *R. E. Dawnty*

Co-signed (Signature No. 9847   )   Signed (Signature No. 1024   )

Subject to Uniform Customs and Practice for Documentary Credits (1974 Revision.) I.C.C. Publication No. 290

Fig. 14.4 A specimen irrevocable letter of credit

Popular Bank of Africairia

2074 Liberation Square, Zanzibasa, Africairia

Our Ref: WSG/TA

27 October 19--

London Bank of Commerce and Industry
2714 Lombard Street
London
EC2 4FC

Dear Sirs

Letter of Credit in favour of Timbercutters (Leeds) Ltd

We have had established in an account in this bank an irrevocable
credit on behalf of Timbercutters (Leeds) Ltd, 2475 Pennine Way,
Leeds, England, in the sum of six thousand pounds (£6000) sterling.
The credit will be released by this bank when we receive the following:

(a) Short-form bill of lading (set of one original and one copy)
evidencing the shipment to this bank of the goods named at (c) below.
(b) Clean Certificate of Inspection from Machinery Inspections
(Tilbury) Ltd, 3275 Dock Way, Tilbury, proving that the goods listed
at (c) below have been fully tested and run in operational conditions
on suitable test benches at the premises of Timbercutters (Leeds) Ltd.
(c) Commercial invoices (1 original and 8 copies) referring to 3 power
saws, driven by 230 volt AC electric motors, Timbercutters trade mark,
at the agreed price of £1800 per machine, on CIF terms. Insurance to
be effected with Lloyd's underwriters including War Risks. Shipping
ex Tilbury on Palmate Line (Africairia) vessel only. Shipment on deck
not permitted.
(d) This credit is valid until 12 noon on 4 December 19--.

We do not wish you to confirm this letter of credit, but will release
the credit to you for onward transmission to the exporter as soon as
we receive a satisfactory set of documents. Will you please let the
exporter know the terms of this credit, Number 27310, which is subject
to the Uniform Customs and Practice of Documentary Credits (1974
Revision).

Yours faithfully

Thomas Kisumu
Import Control Manager

SL14.6 (Telex message related to SL14.5)

```
45254   POPBANK QZ
207989 SUPSN G

30.10.19--

POPULAR BANK AFRICAIRIA
ZANZIBASA


NOTIFIED YOUR CREDIT NUMBER 27310.  REGRET PRICE
QUOTED TIME EXPIRED (SEE OUR LETTER TO IMPORTER
27 MARCH 19--).

PRICE SUBJECT TO TEN PER CENT INCREASE 1980 POUNDS
STERLING PER MACHINE.

PLEASE CONFIRM AGREEMENT AND NOTIFY VIA CORRESPONDENT
BANK.  CANNOT PROCEED UNTIL CORRECT PRICE AGREED.


TIMBERCUTTERS LEEDS LTD


207989 SUPSN G
45254   POPBANK QZ
```

Fig. 14.5 A telex message concerning a letter of credit

14.5 Exercises on 'cash with order' and letters of credit

1 Write a letter to Pitman Books Ltd, 128 Long Acre, London, WC2E 9AN, from your own address in a foreign country asking them to send you copies of their literature on Pitman 2000, and in particular specimen tapes from their Voice-Link home tutoring courses. Enclose a banker's draft drawn on London for £10 sterling and express your willingness to be invoiced for any further sum necessary.

2 Write a letter to Formecon Services Ltd, Douglas House, Gateway, Crewe, CW1 1YN asking them for details of their Postabroad packages of export documentation which you wish to use in your export trade to 'cash with order' customers. You are employed at 'Books for Foreigners', 1248 Birchangar Lane, Bishops Stortford, Essex, England.

3 The Calle de Caracas Supervende, Maracay, Venezuela wishes to purchase goods from the clothing manufacturers Personal Contact Ltd, 93 Mortimer Street, London W1. On 4 April 19-- they instruct the Commercial Bank of Venezuela (Caracas) Ltd to arrange an irrevocable letter of credit to the value of £15 000, valid until 15 May 19-- in favour of Personal Contact Ltd, on the following terms:

   i The credit will be released when a set of documents is presented to a major London bank proving that the goods have been shipped from the UK aboard a Venezuelan vessel (three bills of lading, all original copies).

  ii Seven copies of a commercial invoice, in English, and seven Spanish translations, referring to the following goods:
4000 garments in all, made up of 200 each of styles 1-20, each in sizes 10-16 represented by 40 each of sizes 10-12 and 20 each of sizes 14-16.

 iii The prices to be £3.50 per garment FOB, freight and insurance to be effected by Personal Contact Ltd and added to the FOB price, shown separately, two copies of the insurance policy to be supplied.

Write the letter from Calle de Caracas Supervende to the Commercial Bank of Venezuela, 2174 Calle Garibaldi, Caracas, Venezuela instructing them to arrange the credit.

4 Write the letter dated 7 April 19-- from the Commercial Bank of Venezuela to their correspondent bank in London, the Bank of London and Venezuela, 18957 Great Portland Street, London, asking them to convey the terms of the letter of credit in Question 3 above to Personal Contact Ltd, and to confirm the credit. Ask them to refer in their letter to the Uniform Customs and Practice of Documentary Credits (1974 Revision).

5 Write the letter dated 12 April 19-- from the Bank of London and Venezuela to Personal Contact Ltd, notifying them of the establishment of a confirmed irrevocable letter of credit in their favour, and stating the terms on which the credit will be released (see Question 3 above).

6 Send a telex from Personal Contact Ltd to Calle de Caracas Supervende pointing out that the prices mentioned in their letter of

credit have risen to £4 sterling per garment and the credit is therefore not large enough. Suggest they raise it to £18 000 and ask them to instruct their bank to telex the necessary approval to their London Correspondent Bank.

7 Write a letter on 12 May 19-- from Personal Contact Ltd expressing your appreciation of the order which has been completed by the dispatch of the goods on board the vessel *President of Venezuela*. Thank them for the arrangement of the credit, which has now been released, and express your willingness to deal in future on similar terms at any time.

14.6 Appendix on the English language: confusion of words

In business communication it is easy to use a wrong word and to convey either an incorrect meaning, or no meaning at all. This is because the English language contains many words which sound the same as, or similar to, other words. For example the words 'accept' and 'except' are similar in sound, but very different in meaning. Consider the following sentences:

I found all the offers interesting, but I accept your offer.
I found all the offers interesting, but I except your offer.

The first seems a sensible sentence; a contract has been made, because the writer has accepted an offer. The second one is not at all clear; has the writer said that our offer was the only one that was not interesting, or was the intention to say 'accept' not 'except'? The student must be careful not to use a word which has a similar sound to the one he really requires, but which has a very different meaning.

If you wish to become an audio-typist, that is a typist who transcribes letters from a dictation machine, it is particularly important that you can spell well, and that your typing makes sense. A particular difficulty with audio-typing, or the taking of oral notes, is the confusion which arises from **homophones**.

Homophones are words which have the same sound, but different meanings and different spellings. For example, 'principal' and 'principle' are homophones. An audio-typist hearing this word will have to rely on the context of the sentence to know which spelling should be typed. For example:

The principal of the local college visited the office to persuade young clerks to attend night school.

The principle on which the firm has always operated is 'Be prompt and be competitive'.

In the first sentence the principal is the chief figure in an institution, such as a college, and the rest of the sentence makes it quite clear which word is required. Similarly, the second sentence is about a belief which governs the actions of a firm, and the spelling must be correct if the sentence is to make sense.

Students whose knowledge of English is weak often confuse homophones, or words which sound similar. If you are to avoid such mistakes, always use a good dictionary to check your spelling.

14.7 Exercises on avoiding confusion of words

1 In each of the following sentences choose the correct word from the two in brackets.
  a The welfare officer gave the girl some (adverse, advice).
  b (Oral, Aural) evidence will be given to the investigating committee by the witnesses to the (incidence, incidents).
  c The lawyer sought to (elicit, illicit) information from the witness.
  d The local (route, rout) for the procession ran through the business district.
  e A car engine which uses lead-free petrol would be as (economic, economical) as an ordinary engine.
  f The factory is situated in the heart of the newly developed (industrious, industrial) area.

2 Use each of the following *homophones* in a sentence, showing that you understand the meaning of each word:
  a1 stationary   d1 ascent
  a2 stationery   d2 assent
  b1 compliment   e1 board
  b2 complement   e2 bored
  c1 lightning
  c2 lightening

3 Start to make a list of homophones in your vocabulary book. Add new homophones to your list as you come across them.

15 Export trade 2

15.1 Exporting on 'documents against payment' terms

In export trade, documents frequently represent the goods to which they refer, which are moving across the high seas or through the stratosphere. When documents change hands the goods change ownership, and the benefit of insurance policies transfers to the new owners. We have seen that from the exporter's point of view 'cash with order' terms and 'letter of credit' terms ensure payment is received at an early date. A third way of ensuring payment is to export goods on 'document against payment' terms. This means that the documents which represent ownership of the goods will only be surrendered to the importer on payment of the cash. This system is therefore also called 'cash against documents'.

'Documents against payment' is also of benefit to the importer, who is not obliged to part with the purchase money until the documents representing ownership actually arrive, and even then it is possible to pledge the documents against a loan from the bank until the goods actually arrive and are available to the importer at the port or airport.

Eastern Electronics (Harlow) Ltd
Motorway Approaches, Harlow, Essex.   Tel: Harlow 33792

Our Ref: JFK/TR

27 July 19--

The Merchant Bank Ltd
72 St Mary Axe
London EC3 5PG

Dear Sirs

Documents against Payment

We present herewith the documents relating to a shipment to The Excelsior Trading Co Ltd, 66 Malabar Causeway, Singapore. The documents are as follows:

Set of two original copies of Bills of Lading, signed by the master of
   the SS Cathay for the shipment on board of the goods listed on the
   invoice;
Two sets of commercial invoices (three copies for Customs in each set);
Set of two insurance certificates under our open cover policy;
Set of two bills of exchange for the value of the invoices enclosed.

Would you please arrange for these documents to be sent out in two equal sets, by air mail posted on successive days, to your correspondent bank in Singapore. The bills of lading may be released on payment in full of the draft - all charges being for our account and not the account of the Excelsior Trading Co Ltd. When one set of documents has been honoured the other will be rendered void.

Please remit the net proceeds by telegraphic transfer and credit our account with the balance left after deducting your UK charges.

In the event of dishonour please protest the bill and deliver the documents to Kim Lee (Auctioneers) Ltd, 2074 Port Way, Buona Vista, Singapore, who will dispose of the goods at the best price possible and pay your foreign charges. Please debit our account in this situation with your UK charges.

Yours faithfully

J F Kemp
Export Manager

Enclosures: 2 sets of documents

Eastern Electronics (Harlow) Ltd

Motorway Approaches, Harlow, Essex.   Tel: Harlow 33792

Your Ref: Order No 1274
Our Ref: JFK/TR

27 July 19--

The General Manager
The Excelsior Trading Co Ltd
66 Malabar Causeway
Singapore

Dear Sir

We thank you for your order No 1274, and have dispatched the goods
required by SS 'Cathay', due at Singapore on 18 August 19--.

We have felt it necessary on this occasion to make this a 'documents
against payment' transaction, since we have not had time to secure
credit references on your organisation. I am sure you appreciate that
we must safeguard ourselves in this way. A copy invoice shows the sum
involved.

Our bankers are the Merchant Bank Ltd of London, and their correspondent bank in Singapore will approach you in a few days for payment of
our sight draft. They will then hand to you the full documents to
enable you to claim the goods from the docks on arrival.

We hope that in due course we will be able to establish regular
trading with you. In such circumstances we would be agreeable to
giving you a three month bill for future transactions once credit
references are secured. We hope that this will be only the first of
many orders you will place with us.

Yours faithfully

J F Kemp
Export Manager

Enc Copy Invoice

Steelcraft (Harlow) Ltd

2175 London Way, Harlow, Essex.

Telephone: (0279) 458201

Your Ref: AAM/24 October 19--
Our Ref: TSD/AK

30 October 19--

Ahmed Abdul Muhammadu
2174 Port Approaches
Manama
Bahrain Island

Dear Sir

Thank you for your enquiry about our 'steelcraft' range. As requested
we have sent you D/P (Documents Against Payment) an FCL containing
specimens of each of our products in the full catalogue. To complete
the container load - to secure packing advantages - we have also sent
a small selection of our brassware fittings, which can be gold-plated
if required. We are naturally pleased with this initial order, and
hope you will find the items appropriate to the housing project you
have in mind.

Our bankers are Bank of London and the Near East, of Gracechurch
Street, London, and their correspondents in Bahrain will approach you
with the documents in due course.

Your offer to pay for the secondment of a representative to Bahrain
should this sample order lead to a massive adoption of the fittings
in the new town is most welcome. We would be happy to pay the representative's salary during his secondment if you are prepared to pay
the incidental expenses of accommodation, fares etc.

Yours faithfully

T S Doncaster
Export Manager

ANTIPODES TRADING CO LTD

2024 CORNHILL, LONDON EC3 2JD   *Telephone* 01 - 324 8467

Our Ref: CP/DG

13 June 19--

The Overseas Manager
Antipodean Bank Ltd
856 St Mary Axe
London EC3 3JA

Dear Sir

As arranged by telephone earlier today, we enclose a bill to our order
for £7560 drawn on Messrs Anzai and Co, Sydney, New South Wales. You
will find attached to the bill:

(a) a short-form bill of lading referring to a container shipped on
    board the SS 'Southern Star'
(b) an invoice detailing the goods shipped
(c) a letter of specific hypothecation, permitting you to sell the
    goods through any auctioneer of your choice should the consignee
    fail to take delivery.

Our consignees have been told by telex today that your Head Office will
present the bill for payment before the documents can be surrendered.
This is the first transaction we have had with Messrs Anzai and Co and
on this occasion we feel we should insist on a documents against payment transaction. All charges are for our account. Please credit our
account with the net proceeds, by telegraphic transfer.

Yours faithfully

C Paterson
Export Manager

Encs

15.3 Exporting on 'documents against acceptance' terms

Frequently an importer is only prepared to place orders with an overseas supplier if attractive credit terms can be arranged. Even a three
or six months period of credit (given by a 3 month or 6 month bill of

exchange) gives the importer an opportunity to sell goods before payment falls due. The importer is then in a similar position to the home trader who accepts a bill of exchange to be honoured at a later date, and becomes liable upon it (see section 12.1). From the exporter's point of view this system is less reliable as regards payment than the letter of credit system, or the 'documents against payment' system, but it is possible to insure the risk of non-payment with the Export Credits Guarantee Department at very reasonable rates of insurance.

Should such a bill be dishonoured, either by non-acceptance or non-payment, the remedy is to 'protest' the bill. A protest is a formal document drawn up by a notary public after official presentation of the bill to the drawee. It records the exact nature of the bill, the fact that it was officially presented and that the drawee refused to accept it, or refused to pay it, whichever the case may be. Such a 'protest' will be recognised in the Courts as documentary evidence of dishonour, and may be the subject of an action for damages.

15.4   Instructions to the bank

As mentioned earlier in Chapter 12, since foreign bills of exchange are used all over the world, where different legal systems apply, it is easy for disputes to arise about them. This problem has been resolved to a considerable extent by a body of rules called 'The Uniform Rules for Collections, ICC Brochure No 322, the latest published by the International Chamber of Commerce. It is also necessary to instruct banks fully and carefully about the procedures you wish them to follow. This can most easily be done by the use of an aligned document, such as the form designed by SITPRO reproduced by courtesy of the SITPRO Board as Fig. 15.1. Note the detailed nature of the instructions about the release of documents, the charges payable, the protest of the bill on dishonour, etc. Notice also the passage at the bottom right-hand corner referring to the Uniform Rules incorporating them into the instructions, so that they form part of the instructions to the banker. This is an excellent example of the sort of document devised by SITPRO (The Simplification of International Trade Procedures Board, whose address is Almack House, 26-28 King Street, London, SW1Y 6QW).

FOREIGN BILL AND/OR DOCUMENTS FOR COLLECTION

Drawer/Exporter	Drawer's/Exporter's Reference(s) (to be quoted by Bank in all correspondence)

Consignee	Drawee (If not Consignee)

To (Bank)	For Bank use only

FORWARD DOCUMENTS ENUMERATED BELOW BY AIRMAIL. FOLLOW SPECIAL INSTRUCTIONS AND THOSE MARKED X

Bill of Exchange	Comm'l. Invoice	Cert'd./Cons. Inv.	Cert. of Origin	Ins'ce Pol./Cert.	Bill of Lading	Parcel Post Rec'pt.	Air Waybill

Combined Transport Doc.	Other Documents and whereabouts of any missing Original Bill of Lading

RELEASE DOCUMENTS ON	ACCEPTANCE	PAYMENT		Protest	Do Not Protest
If documents are not taken up on arrival of goods	Warehouse Goods	Do Not Warehouse	If unaccepted ⟶ and advise reason by	Cable	Airmail
	Insure Against Fire	Do Not Insure	If unpaid ⟶	Protest	Do Not Protest
Collect ALL Charges			and advise reason by	Cable	Airmail
Collect Correspondent's Charges ONLY			Advise acceptance and due date by	Cable	Airmail
Return Accepted Bill by Airmail			Remit Proceeds by	Cable	Airmail
In case of need refer to				For Guidance	Accept their Instructions

SPECIAL INSTRUCTIONS: 1.   Represent on arrival of goods if not honoured on first presentation.

Date of Bill of Exchange	Bill of Exchange Value/Amount of Collection
Tenor of Bill of Exchange	
Bill of Exchange Claused:—	
	Please collect the above mentioned Bill and/or Documents subject to the Uniform Rules for Collections (1978 Revision), International Chamber of Commerce, Publication No. 322. I/We agree that you shall not be liable for any loss, damage, or delay however caused which is not directly due to the negligence of your own officers or servants.
	Date and Signature

Fig. 15.1 Instructions to a banker re foreign bills for collection

FRIESIAN FARMS LTD

**MILTON ROAD
WISBECH
CAMBRIDGESHIRE
ENGLAND**

Your Ref: AK/TD/Order No 2847
Our Ref: SJ/BJ

20 May 19--

The General Manager
Royal Estates
Safa
Emirate of Rasa Kun

Dear Sir

The five friesian pedigree cattle selected on your recent visit have
been granted veterinary certificates and are free to move as arranged
through Gulf Air Transport. Our representative Mark Tyler will
accompany the animals on their journey, carrying with him the necessary documents and a bill of exchange for the full amount. He will
take these documents to our bankers Rasa Kun Merchant Bank Ltd, who
will present the bill to you for acceptance, payable six months after
sight. On accepting the bill the documents will be released to you
and the cattle may be collected from the airport.

Please note that the insurance policy only covers the cattle to the
point where they leave the airport building, and consequently you
should arrange cover in Rasa Kun in advance of delivery, effective
from that time on.

Thank you for your custom on this occasion. We hope His Royal High-
ness is pleased with the animals, and that they form the nucleus of a
prosperous herd in the future.

Yours faithfully

S Johnston
Herd Manager

Denver Heavy Plant (Hertford) Ltd

Warrenwood Avenue, Hertford, England. Tel. Hertford 864021

```
Your Reference: Order 1218
Our Reference:  JD/TG

1 October 19--

Jugolinia Belgrada
Koper
Yugoslavia

Dear Sirs

Thank you for your order for electrical power units.  We have started
manufacture and hope to ship the units by Jugolinija North Europe Line,
Rijeka, Yugoslavia on the container vessel 'Ledenice', leaving South-
ampton on 24 October.

We shall route the documents to you by our bankers, East Mediterranean
Bank Ltd, who will make them available in due course on acceptance of
the bill of exchange presented to you at that time.  Thank you for
clearing all import difficulties in Yugoslavia, and we look forward to
shipping the goods on time, and receiving payment six months after
sight of the bill in Yugoslavia.

Yours faithfully



J Desoutter
Export Manager
```

15.6   Exercises on export trade using bills of exchange

1 As general manager of Messrs Hilton & Son, 2384 Trumpington Road, Felixstowe, Suffolk, England you write a covering letter to your bankers, Middle East Merchant Bankers Ltd, 2075 Gracechurch Street, London EC3 2AD to accompany the documents you are lodging with them. The documents include a form giving instructions to the banker. Refer to this document and remind them that it requires them to act on your behalf according to the Uniform Rules on the Collection of Commercial Paper.

2 Middle East Merchant Bankers Ltd write to Messrs Hilton & Son (see Question 1) to notify them that they have been advised by their branch in the Gulf that the drawee at Bab-el-Wad refused to pay the bill of exchange on the grounds that they had never ordered the goods. Accordingly they have protested the bill, but they have also notified the 'notify party' named in the Instructions to Bankers. He has taken delivery of the goods, which he considers marketable at a fair price, and will accordingly sell by auction at the best price obtainable. He will contact Hilton & Son direct, but in the meantime Middle East Bankers Ltd have debited the account of Hilton & Son with their charges, including the cost of protesting the bill.

3 Muhammed al Kalifah, of 27 Avenue of the Prophet, Bab-el-Wad, writes to Hilton & Son enclosing an 'account sales' which shows that the gross proceeds of the sale of the goods (see Questions 1 and 2) were £7384. Deductions are made for insurance and transport charges £35.50, warehousing £84.00, commission (5 per cent of gross proceeds) and del credere commission (2½ per cent of gross proceeds). A banker's draft for the balance is enclosed. Write this letter, showing your calculations for the sum due to Hilton & Son. Express your hopes that you may act as 'notify party' in the future if similar difficulties arise.

4 Write to a customer abroad to whom you have just dispatched goods, stating that owing to your lack of knowledge as to their standing you have been compelled to put the transaction on a 'documents against payment' basis.

5 Write to your bankers instructing them to hand the documents in connection with the above transaction (see Question 4) to your customer when he has honoured the bill of exchange. Instruct them that in the event of dishonour by non-payment they are to protest the bill and warehouse the goods pending your further instructions. Ask them to advise you of such dishonour by telex. Instruct them that if the bill is honoured they should remit the proceeds, after deduction of charges, by telegraphic transfer to the credit of your account in your home town.

6 Write to the Tandy Tea Estates, Dravidian Peninsula, Sri Lanka notifying them that the fermentation plant they require has been shipped on a Far East Traders vessel after certification by the

Bureau of Inspection. As agreed the documents have been sent to the Bank of Southern Sri Lanka and will be released against acceptance of three bills of exchange dated four months, eight months and twelve months after sight. Thank them for their order and express the hope that when further expansion is undertaken you may quote them for further plant and equipment. You are the export manager of Agricultural Machines (Dedham) Ltd, Willy Lots Way, Dedham, Suffolk, England.

7 Write to the Bank of Southern Sri Lanka referring to the documents for Tandy Tea Estates (see Question 6), and requesting them to act on your behalf as instructed in the 'Foreign Bills for Collection' document supplied. Ask them to present the bills for acceptance, and on the due dates for payment, remitting you the sums received net of their charges, and notifying you by telex of any dishonour.

15.7   Appendix on the English language: ambiguity and obscurity

If errors are not to be made in business transactions it is important to avoid ambiguity and obscurity in written and oral communication.

Ambiguity is a 'double meaning' in a sentence, which leaves the reader or listener unsure about what is actually meant. It may arise for a variety of reasons. Sometimes a word has a double meaning. Many a teacher has given an ambiguous comment on a pupil by saying he was 'trying'. Sometimes ambiguity arises from the confusion of a pronoun, which appears to refer to one noun but is meant to refer to another. Thus in the sentence 'When the patient reached the doctor he was anaesthetised' we are not quite sure who lost consciousness.

Adverbs act to modify verbs, and they are frequently misplaced so that they appear to modify the wrong word. Consider the sentence:

'Those who work rapidly get ill in these conditions.'

Does 'rapidly' refer to the speed of the work, or the speed of getting ill? The sentence needs revising, to read:

'Those who work in these conditions rapidly get ill.'

It is also possible to misplace modifying clauses, such as the clause in italics in the following sentence:

'The container going through the documentation process *made of steel and aluminium* belongs to our best customer, Transpolar Suppliers Ltd.'

To correct this we should put the modifying clause immediately after the noun to which it refers, though a complete rearrangement of the sentence might be preferable. Thus:

'The steel and aluminium container going through the documentation process belongs to our best customer, Transpolar Suppliers Ltd.'

Obscurity occurs when a sentence is so badly organised or expressed that its meaning is not clear. Even more serious than an obscure sentence is a longer piece of writing which is so confused that it is not possible to understand what the passage as a whole is trying to tell us.

In order to detect such obscurity or ambiguity in your writing you must put yourself in the place of the reader, and ask yourself whether you would understand what the writer was trying to communicate if you had no prior knowledge of the subject. If the communication is at all unclear, then rewriting is necessary. You should always read through any letter or report after you have written it to check for clarity and precision of expression.

15.8 Exercise on ambiguity and obscurity

Revise the following sentences to remove any confusion of meaning:
a Braking frequently ruins the tyres.
b People who repair machines rarely get rich.
c The exporter promised as soon as possible to use the air freight service.
d In Wales there is a harbour used by bulk ore carriers called Port Talbot.
e He promised to visit us as we said 'Goodbye!'
f When the container shifted on the lorry it was damaged.
g He located the trouble with his tachograph in the workshop.

16 Agency

16.1 The nature of agency

An agency arises when one person (the principal) authorises another person (the agent) to make contracts on his/her behalf with third parties. It follows that there will usually be an actual **appointment** of an agent to confer the necessary authority on the agent. Sometimes the law will recognise an **agent of necessity**, as where a passer-by acts without authority — for example in extinguishing a fire, or preventing an accident.

An agent should always act within the authority given by the principal — for example a limit may be placed upon the amount to be bid by an agent at an auction. If the agent acts outside the authority, and the principal refuses to ratify the act, the agent may be sued for **breach of warranty of authority**. Thus if an agent bids at an auction at a price higher than the limit, he/she will be liable for the bid personally, and if unable to honour it an action for breach of warranty of authority could follow.

The chief types of agency are special agency, general agency and universal agency. A special agent acts for a short time while a particular act is being carried out. Thus an estate agent may be appointed to sell a house, and once the sale is completed the agency is ended. A general agent acts on a continuing basis, for example 'main dealers' in the motor car trades are authorised to represent major motor manufacturers in their areas. They keep supplies of spares, carry out repairs, etc. and generally develop and maintain the manufacturer's brand image in the area.

Universal agents have the same powers as a principal, even to the point of signing legal documents. This is called a 'power of attorney' and in the United Kingdom has to be formally conferred upon the agent, under seal, by the Powers of Attorney Act, 1971.

16.2 Letters about the appointment of an agent

SL16.1

```
                                        2045 Searle Street
                                        Hughes
                                        Canberra
                                        Australia
                                        ACT 2605




Gray, Cook and Partners
27 Saint Andrews Street
Cambridge
CB2 3BS                                 16 November 19--


Dear Sirs


My wife and I wish to appoint you as our agents in the sale of a
property we own jointly in Cambridge: 2164 Wandlebury Avenue,
Chesterton, Cambridge.  We are hoping that we can get at least £25 000
for the property and hereby authorise you to inspect the property and
draw up sale particulars at your earliest convenience.


Our solicitors are Wildeblood and Partners, 2754 Grantchester Road,
Cambridge, and we are arranging for my father, Hugo Weisskopf of
116 Camside, Chesterton, Cambridge to have power of attorney to sign
on our behalf.


Would you please liaise with these parties as necessary.


Yours faithfully




P G Weisskopf (Dr)                J Weisskopf
```

SL16.2 (Response to SL16.1)

Gray, Cook & Partners

CHARTERED SURVEYORS-ESTATE AGENTS

ALEX R. COOK, FRICS
CHRISTOPHER J. DODSON, FRICS
DAVID T. WARD, FRICS
PERRY C. SENNITT, FRICS
D. ROGER DRIVER, ARICS
P. C. GRAY, MA, FRICS

Gordon E. Long FSVA consultant

27 St. Andrews Street	1 King Street	8 The Pavement	6 Queen Street
CAMBRIDGE CB2 3BS	SAFFRON WALDEN CM10 1HE	ST. IVES PE17 4AD	HAVERHILL CB9 8AH
Tel: 0223 - 68811	Tel: 0799 - 23563	Tel: 0480 65065	Tel: 0440 3171

Please Reply to: **Cambridge office**

Our ref: ARC/CW   25 November 19--

Dr P G Weisskopf
2045 Searle Street
Hughes
Canberra
Australia
ACT 2605

Dear Dr Weisskopf

Re: 2164 Wandlebury Avenue, Cambridge

We thank you for your instructions to place your property on the market for sale.

We enclose our folder with several copies of our particulars together with a pamphlet giving a few points of information which may be of assistance to you.

Our normal scale of fees is at the rate of 2% on the selling price plus VAT. However, as long as we remain your SINGLE AGENTS our charges will be on the concessionary single agency scale of 1.75% on the first £20 000 and 1.5% on the residue of the selling price, plus VAT.

You can be assured that we will do all we can to effect an early and satisfactory sale and all offers, as and when received, will be submitted to you for your decision, together with our advice thereon.

If you have not already been in touch with your solicitor, we would advise that, at this stage, you inform him of your intention to sell. He can then arrange to obtain or hold your Title Deeds, if necessary getting them from the Building Society, so that he is in a position to submit a draft Contract immediately a firm and satisfactory sale has been negotiated.

Yours sincerely

GRAY, COOK & PARTNERS

Fig. 16.1 A letter accepting instructions to act as an agent

H J Guyer and Co

Schillerstrasse 1227
Hamburg
West Germany

Our Ref HJG/RA

1 December 19--

Messrs Horace Watkins & Son
900 Old Street
London EC1

Dear Sirs

You will remember that last month you offered your services as
London agent for our china and glass. As we pointed out at the
time, it did not seem fair that we should terminate our existing
agency. Conditions have changed in the meantime and made our
present arrangement unworkable. You have, we understand, a wide
connection among United Kingdom buyers, and, as we are convinced that
our product is appropriate to the British market, we think there is
every chance of our developing a mutually profitable arrangement.

Should you be willing to consider taking over the sole agency for us
we should be glad to hear as early as possible the terms and conditions on which you are prepared to assume the agency. If your
position has changed in such a way as to render such an agency
inconvenient we should be glad to know the name and address of some
other reliable firm who might be persuaded to represent us.

Yours faithfully

H J Guyer
Managing Director

Horace Watkins and Son

900 Old Street, London EC1 4SX

Telephone: 01 443 7489

Your Ref   HJG/RA
Our Ref   HW/CB

5 December 19--

Messrs H J Guyer & Co
Schillerstrasse 1227
Hamburg
West Germany

Dear Sirs

Thank you for your letter of 1 December offering us the sole agency
for your products in the United Kingdom. Your proposal interests us,
and we think that our 15 years' experience with similar goods should
prove invaluable. Most of our orders would come directly from the
firms whose buyers use our showrooms and warehouse facilities for
viewing a large variety of merchandise. We not only display goods
passively but feature each brand of merchandise periodically in
special 'weeks'. Thus in February next we have a special China and
Glassware Week where we shall display samples of your wares. All
buyers who do not attend this particular week will be mailed with
your literature, at our expense.

Since this is a sole agency arrangement, and orders will come direct
to you, we hope you will agree that all orders from the United Kingdom
shall count as an order from us, and earn a commission of 5 per cent.
We are also prepared to guarantee all accounts, in return for a
further 'del credere' commission of 2% per cent on all sales. Any
account which is more than six weeks in arrears will be paid to you
by us, and we shall pursue the debtor in the United Kingdom.

We look forward to receiving your response to this offer, and to
making firm arrangements for the sole agency.

Yours faithfully

H Watkins
Senior Partner

SWITCH-A-CALL LTD

2071 Moora Way, Perth, Western Australia

R Chalmers Esq
I K Brunel Ltd
3284 Portway Road
Portsmouth
England

Your Reference: RC/KT
Our Reference: Agency/21/BB

Date: 27 April 19--

Dear Ron

We are pleased to inform you that after our visit to your workshops in
Portsmouth and our evaluation of the UK market for Switch-a-Call, we
have decided to appoint you as our UK servicing and marketing agent.
The terms of this agency are confirmed as follows:

1. The agency will commence on 1 July 19--, and will run for an initial
   period of three years, with an option open to you to continue for a
   further three year period if you wish, on the same terms. Further
   periods will then call for revised terms.
2. The commencement of the agency is conditional upon adequate servicing
   staff being available. Four of your UK employees will report to our
   Perth works on 15 May for a four week servicing and maintenance
   course. You will pay their air fares and wages while in Australia.
   We will pay all hotel and other expenses while they are here.
3. Supplies of Switch-a-Call and components will be invoiced to you at
   50 per cent of recommended sale price. If you allow agents to develop the sale of these devices around the UK their margin of profit
   must come out of the 50 per cent trade discount given to you. We
   will not supply any other UK outlet than yourselves.
4. Every effort will be made to ensure that you receive supplies as soon
   as possible after an order is placed by telex or post. It will faci-
   litate delivery if goods can be ordered in FCL (full container loads)
   of 1000 devices. This still leaves room for a reasonable order of
   spare parts. We acknowledge receipt of your deposit of £5000 sterling for the first FCL.
5. Payment will be made on open-account terms, by the payment of a deposit of £5000 per FCL and the balance payable in full, two months
   after the date of our statement.
6. If either party feels obliged to discontinue the arrangement over
   the first three year period, or any subsequent agreed contractual
   period, the agreed liquidated damages are £10 000 for each year
   remaining to run, or pro rata for part-years.

I think you will find that these are the terms which we discussed whilst
in the UK. We hope to receive your acceptance of these terms and look
forward to a long and successful cooperation in marketing Switch-a-Call.

Yours sincerely,
Switch-a-Call Ltd

Blake Brignull

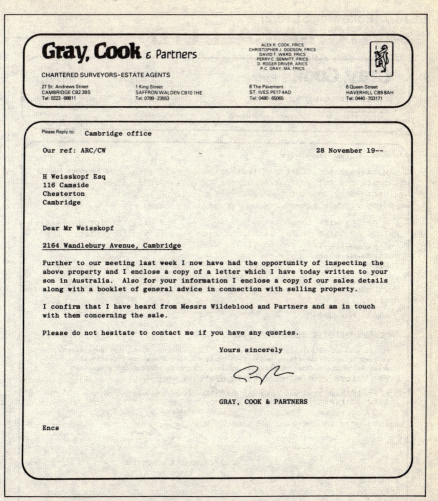

Gray, Cook & Partners

ALEX R. COOK, FRICS
CHRISTOPHER J. DODSON, FRICS
DAVID T. WARD, FRICS
PERRY C. SENNITT, FRICS
D. ROGER DRIVER, ARICS
P.C. GRAY, MA, FRICS

CHARTERED SURVEYORS-ESTATE AGENTS

27 St. Andrews Street	1 King Street	8 The Pavement	6 Queen Street
CAMBRIDGE CB2 3BS	SAFFRON WALDEN CB10 1HE	ST. IVES PE17 4AD	HAVERHILL CB9 8AH
Tel: 0223 - 68811	Tel: 0799 - 23553	Tel: 0480 - 65065	Tel: 0440 - 703171

Please Reply to: **Cambridge office**

Our ref: ARC/CW   28 November 19--

H Weisskopf Esq
116 Camside
Chesterton
Cambridge

Dear Mr Weisskopf

2164 Wandlebury Avenue, Cambridge

Further to our meeting last week I now have had the opportunity of inspecting the
above property and I enclose a copy of a letter which I have today written to your
son in Australia. Also for your information I enclose a copy of our sales details
along with a booklet of general advice in connection with selling property.

I confirm that I have heard from Messrs Wildeblood and Partners and am in touch
with them concerning the sale.

Please do not hesitate to contact me if you have any queries.

                              Yours sincerely

                              GRAY, COOK & PARTNERS

Encs

Fig. 16.2 A letter from the acting agents

16.3 Subsequent ratification of an unauthorised act

Where an agent acts outside the authority of the principal it is perfectly possible for the principal to ratify the unauthorised act subsequently, and thus honour the bargain made on his/her behalf. This
may happen in certain fields, such as fine art, antiques etc., or in dealings on the commodity market where prices fluctuate fairly widely.
Some illustrations of this are given in the specimen letters below.

SL16.7 (Following SL16.2)

Gray, Cook & Partners

ALEX R. COOK. FRICS
CHRISTOPHER J. DODSON. FRICS
DAVID T. WARD. FRICS
PERRY C. SENNITT. FRICS
D. ROGER DRIVER. ARICS
P. C. GRAY. MA. FRICS

Gordon E. Long FSVA · consultant

CHARTERED SURVEYORS–ESTATE AGENTS

| 27 St. Andrews Street
CAMBRIDGE CB2 3BS
Tel: 0223 · 68811 | 1 King Street
SAFFRON WALDEN CM10 1HE
Tel: 0799 · 23553 | 8 The Pavement
ST. IVES PE17 4AD
Tel: 0480 · 65065 | 6 Queen Street
HAVERHILL CB9 8AH
Tel: 0440 · 3171 |

Please Reply to: **Cambridge office**

Our ref: ARC/CW   22 December 19--

Dr P G Weisskopf
2045 Searle Street
Hughes
Canberra
Australia
ACT 2605

Dear Dr Weisskopf

<u>Re: 2164 Wandlebury Avenue, Cambridge</u>

We are pleased to be able to confirm that, in accordance with your instructions,
we have accepted the offer, subject to contract, for the above property as
detailed on the enclosed Memorandum of Sale. We have advised the respective
solicitors and look forward to matters proceeding smoothly.

In the meantime if we can be of any further assistance please let us know.

                                       Yours sincerely

                                       GRAY, COOK & PARTNERS

Enc

Fig. 16.3 A letter confirming the actions of an agent

GALLERIE GRECQUE

17956 KING'S ROAD
CHELSEA
LONDON
SW3 8UP

Telephone: 01 399 7642

Your Ref: NV/RS
Our Ref: TR/VR

21 May 19--

N Vassilis
2075 Ag. Sofias St
Corfu
Greece

Dear Mr Vassilis

Important find in Shipwreck: Aphrodite of Cnidus

A recent underwater expedition has recovered from the sea off Cornwall
a torso of Aphrodite of Cnidus. It is almost certainly a Roman copy
of the original by Praxiteles, and from the same school as the one in
the Louvre. It appears that it was part of the cargo of the vessel
'Mediterranean Trader' which sank in a storm in 1777. The statue is
somewhat encrusted, and is at present being cleaned, but it should
come up for auction in 2-3 months time. The likely price would, we
estimate, be in the region of £10 000. Knowing your interest in the
period, and acting on the general authority given to us some years
ago we propose to attend the auction on your behalf.

We do not envisage any difficulty about an export licence, since this
is not a unique piece, but just a very attractive sculpture.

Would you please advise us what limit we should place on our bids.
Mr Prendergast has seen the statue, and says it is in good condition,
and ideal for your villa at Gouvia.

Yours sincerely

T Reinhardt
Dealer

GALLERIE GRECQUE

17956 KING'S ROAD
CHELSEA
LONDON
SW3 8UP

Telephone: 01 399 7642

Your Ref: NV/RS
Our Ref: TR/VR

23 July 19--

N Vassilis
2075 Ag. Sofias St
Corfu
Greece

Dear Mr Vassilis

<u>Aphrodite of Cnidus: £13 250 Sterling</u>

Your letter authorising us to bid for you up to a figure of £12 500
sterling was received and we attended the auction on your behalf.
However you will see from the price mentioned above that we have in
fact exceeded our authority. It so happened that the statue, when
fully cleaned, proved to be an improvement on the one in the Louvre,
having the neck and part of the hair of the original statue, and both
upper arms. This naturally increased the interest in the statue and
raised the price.

In the circumstances, since we were only bidding against one other
dealer, Mr Prendergast held on, and secured the statue for £13 250.
We hope very much that you will ratify the purchase, and on receipt
of your instructions to this effect we will pack the statue for air
freighting to you. Mr Prendergast will accompany the statue in the
usual way, and supervise its erection at Gouvia. A telex message
ratifying the purchase would help us greatly.

Yours sincerely

T Reinhardt
Dealer

16.5 Duties of agents and principals

Each party in a contract between an agent and a principal has certain duties to perform. The duties of the agent may be listed as follows:

a To comply with the instructions of the principal, showing due care and diligence.
b To disclose all relevant material information, and in particular not to make any secret profit.
c Not to disclose to another party any secret information which has been given by the principal (such as a reserve price below which the principal will not sell an article).
d To render full and honest accounts as required.
e Not to let his/her own interests conflict with those of the principal.

The duties of the principal are:

a To pay the agreed remuneration or commission.
b To indemnify the agent against all expenses legitimately incurred in the performance of his/her duties.
c Not to interfere with the agent in such a way as to prevent the earning of the commission.

An agency may be revoked by giving notice to the agent, or if the agent has been found to have made secret profits the agency may be terminated without notice.

FRIESIAN BREEDERS LTD

Maori Homestead, Hastings, North Island, New Zealand

```
Your Ref: A/c No 1287
Our Ref:  TR/BC


31 May 19--


Thomas Heffer and Sons Ltd
Twenty-pence Lane
Brockenhurst Road
Brockley
Hampshire
England


Dear Sirs

You recently acted as our agents in the purchase of the prize bull,
Lord John of Friesland, which your account says was purchased for
£10 000 at the premises of Friesland Cattle Breeders Ltd.  Today we
read in the Cattleman's Journal that their annual report includes a
mention of the highest price ever paid for a prime bull '£8500 for
Lord John of Friesland'.

We must confess to feeling not a little annoyed at this, since it
seems to indicate that you have made a secret profit out of the trans-
action, in breach of your duty as agent.  I am sure you know that in
the case of a secret profit being made we are entitled not only to
the return of the secret profit, but also of our commission of 10 per
cent.  This means that we are entitled to a refund of £2500.  However,
not to be too hard on you, we will accept an immediate refund of £1750,
being the excess price charged by you plus £250 compensation for loss
of use of this money.  I might add that we shall need a lot of per-
suading to place our business with you in future.  Your banker's draft
for £1750 will help matters.

Yours truly




Tom Richardson
Buyer
```

Thomas Heffer and Sons Ltd

Twenty-pence Lane, Brockenhurst Road
Brockley, Hampshire, England
Telephone: 845733

Your Reference TR/BC
Our Reference TH/AJ

11 June 19--

T Richardson Esq
Friesian Breeders Ltd
Maori Homestead
Hastings
North Island
New Zealand

Dear Mr Richardson

I am absolutely shocked by your letter of 31 May; injuring as it does
our long business relationship with you. I have been on the telephone
to Holland all morning about it, and the matter is now in the hands of
the Dutch police.

It appears highly probable that a conspiracy between our Dutch agent
and one of their employees led to false documentation being prepared.
They certainly only received £8500 sterling for the bull, yet we have
an invoice for £10 000.

We are asking our bankers to make a credit transfer through the Bank
of New Zealand to your account for £1750, the figure which you state
you are willing to regard as a full settlement. This should only take
a few days.

We shall keep you informed as a matter of mutual interest about the
enquiries being made in Holland, but we do hope this will not cause
you to withdraw your business from us. There is no question that we
have both been defrauded, and we regret the incident very much indeed.

Yours sincerely

Thomas Heffer
Managing Director

TUAS EXPORTERS LTD

2174 Straits View Road
Tuas, Singapore

Your Ref.
Our Ref   UK 176/BC

Date   3 October 19--

Messrs Skinner Bros
9 Wyburn Street
London SW2 4DP

Dear Sirs

We are concerned that your statement of expenses for the past month
is unusually high. It is possible that special items of expenditure
have had to be met, but we think you will agree that we are entitled
to some explanation of the whole position. We must point out that
the goods in question do not warrant the heavy charges you have made.

You may be interested to know that exactly similar agencies in West
Germany, France, Holland and Eire have expenses per unit of less than
half the charges you are making - in the case of West Germany the
charges are 30 per cent of your charges.

It is essential that closer control of expenses is achieved in the
United Kingdom, otherwise we shall have to consider revoking your
agency when it comes for renewal next June. Please let us have a
detailed break-down of these expenses, including photocopies of any
hotel bills, travelling expenses, vouchers etc which are the basis
of the claims made.

Yours faithfully

Thomas Wak
Chairman of the Cooperative
Tuas Exporters Ltd

Permafrost Ltd

24 Orchard Estateway
Hargrove
Norfolk
England
Telephone: 55478

Our Ref: PH/TS

27 July 19--

Umo Eyo
2748 Zaria Road
Kaduna
Nigeria

Dear Umo

Your returns for the month of June have not yet reached us although
they normally do so by the 15th of the month. We appreciate that
you have been very busy because of the sales drive in the Kano area,
but they may have gone astray. Will you send us either the actual
returns, or a duplicate set by air mail at once.

We should also like to have a report on the trouble at the refrigera-
tion depot at Jos. Were you able to help Isaac, and is the customer
perfectly happy now?

Our respects to Mrs Eyo, and the children.

Very sincerely

Peter Hall
Manager - West Africa

UMO EYO

2748 Zaria Road, Kaduna, Nigeria

Your Ref: PH/TS 27 July 19--
Our Ref: UE/SD

4 August 19--

Peter Hall Esq
Permafrost Ltd
24 Orchard Estateway
Hargrave
Norfolk
England

Dear Peter

I really cannot understand why the returns have not arrived, since
they were sent off on the usual date in the normal way. I enclose
herewith a duplicate set with full details of both the June sales and
the progress at Kano up to 4 July. We are very pleased with these
results so far.

The trouble at Jos was a temperamental compressor, which seems to have
an internal fault on it of an intermittent nature. Fortunately the
back-up machine prevented any losses but Isaac got worried about it
because once the back-up machine is in use there is no real safeguard
if a further break-down occurs. We replaced the whole compressor and
sent it down to Lagos for investigation. All is now well, therefore,
at Jos.

Thank you for your good wishes, which are reciprocated.

Yours very sincerely

Umo Eyo
Kaduna Agency

Enclosures: 1 Duplicate Returns
            2 Report on Kano drive

Compagna El Dorado

2598 Calle del Prado, Madrid, Espagne

Our Ref: EST/DA

24 May 19--

Gold of Ophir (Bond St) Ltd
2895 Bond Street
London W1

Dear Mr Mathews

REVOCATION OF AGENCY

We regret to inform you that we must give you notice of the termina-
tion of your agency. Under the terms of our contract this means that
the agency will terminate on 31 December next. We very much regret
the necessity to do so but it is connected with the recent absorption
of Compagna El Dorado by Compagna Almagro, of Mexico City. They
prefer to market our products through their own agents in London.

We understand that these agents will be in touch with you direct
about the transfer of stock balances, and with a proposal for compensation for the outstanding period so that they can in fact assume
the sale of our products sooner than 31 December.

On a personal note may I say how sorry I am to lose a valued business
relationship in this way. I hope that you will continue to keep in
touch; you will always be welcome if you visit Spain in the future,
and I hope I may still call on you on my periodic visits to the
United Kingdom.

Yours sincerely

Juan Cortes
Export Manager

Marine Pleasurecraft (Lymington) Ltd
The Hard, Lymington, Hants. England.   Tel: 44832

---

27 September 19--   Our Ref: TM/ag

'Plaisir Maritime'
La Plage
Barfleur
France

Dear Sirs

REVOCATION OF AGENCY FORTHWITH

I am sure you will appreciate that the recent conviction of your
employee, Pierre Malheureux, for smuggling, leaves us no alternative
but to revoke your agency for the sale of 'Pleasure Craft' in
Northern France.

Our chairman and managing director were detained for three days on
suspicion of being accomplices and our books and records were
impounded for over a month, completely disrupting our activities.
We appreciate that your organisation has been exonerated from
criminal acts itself, but you must accept responsibility for employ-
ing this person in the first place, and your liability therefore
for the disruption, and for the suspicion we have been placed under.

Yours faithfully

T Mortonstern
Export Manager

16.7   Exercises on agency

1 Imagine you have a house to sell and decide to appoint a firm of
local estate agents to act on your behalf in the sale of the property.
Write a letter asking for details of the commission required and
other likely charges should you decide to offer the property for
sale through them. Give them a full description of the property
and your asking prices.

2 Reply, as a partner in the firm of estate agents mentioned in Question 1, offering to act in the sale of the property, to prepare a 'sale details' sheet to be sent to potential purchasers, and stating your terms for commission, fees, etc.

3 Reply to the firm mentioned in Question 2, formally asking them to act on your behalf as agents in the sale of the property.

4 The firm mentioned in Question 1 notify you that they have accepted on your behalf, subject to contract, an offer to purchase the property which is rather higher than your asking figure, from a purchaser who is in a great hurry to obtain premises and can pay in cash. They have been in touch with both sets of solicitors and are pressing them to conclude the arrangements as soon as possible.

5 Chesapeake Sunray Electric Corporation Inc, of 1844 Main Street, Mesa, Arizona, USA, 85201 appoints Gerard Montier SA, 1784 Rue de Paris, Arois sur L'Aube, Aube 10700 to market their products as sole agents throughout the European Economic Community. The terms are that the sole agents shall pay the Chesapeake Sunray Corporation the usual trade price, except for a deduction of 5 per cent which will be allowed in view of their assuming del credere responsibilities for all debts. The retail prices charged to customers shall be entirely at the discretion of the agents who assume all responsibilities in the European market. Write the letter of appointment.

6 Gerard Montier (see Question 5) write to Chesapeake Sunray Electric Corporation to protest that they have seen advertisements in the German press for products manufactured by the Chesapeake Sunray Corporation. These have been placed by a Finnish subsidiary of the Corporation, Finsun NV, of Helsinki. This exploitation of the German market is in breach of their contract to be sole agents for the products in the European Economic Community. In your letter suggest that Finsun be forced to give a written undertaking to your firm that they will not continue selling in Germany.

7 Finsun NV of Nobelstraade 2175, Helsinki write to state that their own agency agreement permits them to market in the Comecon countries and this includes the German Democratic Republic. By mistake two magazines, having the same name, one published

in West Berlin and one published in East Berlin, were muddled by the advertising agency and advertisements inserted in the wrong magazine. A list of 29 applicants is enclosed with their letter. These are West German customers who have already been notified that their orders have been passed to Gerard Montier SA for fulfilment. They apologise for the error and hope this clarifies the situation.

8 A firm of dye and paint manufacturers, Franken Posthema, NV, 1724 Spoorlaan, Gouda, Holland write to Herbert Donaldson (Barrow) Ltd, Barrow on Soar, Loughborough, England to notify them that due to the decline in sales below the lowest limit (25 000 guilders per month), they propose to terminate their agency for the sale of dyes and paints in the United Kingdom with effect from the last day of the present year. At this date all stocks will be purchased back by the principals at the invoiced price plus 10 per cent as compensation. They regret the unsatisfactory results of the arrangement, but must seek a more successful agent to act for them.

16.8 Appendix on the English language: faulty agreement of subject and verb

Grammatical errors often occur in correspondence because the writer does not understand basic rules of agreement between subject and verb. Common examples are as follows:

a When the subject is separated from the verb by several words, phrases or clauses it is easy to lose sight of the subject of the sentence, or clause. Thus:

> 'I ordered the accused to turn out his pockets and a collection of money, keys and small pilfered articles, including several pieces of costume jewellery, were listed by the desk sergeant.'

The subject of the second clause is the word 'collection', a singular noun, so the verb should be the singular 'was', not the plural 'were'.

b Compound subjects need a plural verb, but the word 'with' can lead to difficulties. Thus:

> The sales manager and the representatives are dining at the Grand Hotel.
> The sales manager with the representatives is dining at the Grand Hotel.

In the first sentence the use of 'and' makes it clear that the subject is compound and needs a plural verb. In the second sentence the word 'with' is a preposition leading to an extension of the subject 'sales manager'. This is a single subject and takes a single verb.

c The words *this, that, each, every, either* and *neither* are singular and take a singular verb. *These* and *those* are plural and take a plural verb. Hence:

> Every shareholder is expected to use his/her vote at the Annual General Meeting.
>
> Those letters are for first-class mail but this can be sent second-class.

Where secretaries have to correct the English errors of executives whose work they type it is always difficult. The best thing is to correct it anyway. If the executive does not notice it will make no difference. If the executive complains it will be necessary to justify the changes and demonstrate that you can always be trusted to do the correct thing. Once again, standard reference books, such as Fowler's *Modern English Usage,* published by Oxford University Press, are essential.

16.9 Exercises on the correction of sentences

1 Choose the correct word from those in brackets to ensure agreement in the following sentences:

a An assortment of fruit, apples, oranges, grapes and plums (was, were) displayed on the wholesaler's forecourt.

b A list of arguments and counter-arguments (has, have) been prepared.

c Migrations of the cabbage white butterfly (occur, occurs) in April.

d The consignment of food, clothing, toys and other relief materials (is, are) available for shipment immediately.

e The officer and his crew (is, are) celebrating at the Harbour Inn.

2 Which of the italicised words is correct in the following sentences?

a One of the dogs (*bite, bites*) strangers.

b The cause of hurricanes (*is, are*) well known.

c Two vessels from the company's fleet (*is, are*) missing.

d The pilot with the flight engineer (*is, are*) arriving by taxi shortly.

e The nation expects every man this day will do (*their, his*) duty.

17 Carriage by land, sea and air

17.1 The nature of carriage

Carriage is the transport of goods or passengers. Transport is one of the most important branches of commerce. Its function is to bring goods to the point where they are required, either the point of production (for raw materials) or the point of consumption (for finished goods). As far as services are concerned transport moves people to the point where they can benefit from the services available, whether it be the dentist, the hospital, the college or the holiday hotel. Carriage takes place by land, inland waterway, sea and air. Land transport may be by road or rail.

A division in transport is between inland transport (which is within a particular nation-state) and international transport. All transport is subject to peculiar difficulties, for even in inland transport the carrier goes great distances with our property, so that there have to be safeguards against improper behaviour. In international transport not only are the journeys longer but the codes of laws change too, so that we may find it difficult to exert our legal rights if property is lost, stolen, damaged or delayed. For this reason a new type of carrier has appeared, called the **combined transport operator** who operates in the international field, using **multi-modal transport**. Thus he may operate on a road-sea-road operation, or a road-sea-rail journey, and assume legal responsibility for all damage occurring on the different parts of the journey.

17.2 The legal consequences of carriage

Carriage is one of the most ancient activities, and the laws which govern it grew up centuries ago before legislatures of any sort existed. In England and many other countries with legal systems derived from English law the law of carriage is governed by the ancient custom of the realm. This holds that the carrier is a common carrier, and liable for every loss that occurs, except for a few special cases called the 'common-law exceptions'. One of these exceptions is an 'Act of God'. Thus a carrier who loses goods is held to be liable for their loss, but if he can prove that the goods concerned were – for example – struck by lightning and burned up he can escape liability. Later the severity of this harsh law was somewhat reduced, by the introduction of the concept of a **private carrier**. A carrier who makes it quite clear in his **Conditions of Carriage** that he is not a common carrier, but only a private carrier, is allowed to escape the full severity of the law. He does not carry by the ancient custom of the realm, but by virtue of a contract he has made with those who want him to carry their goods, or their persons, to the destination agreed. This is the usual arrangement today as far as most carriers are concerned, and they are careful to mention their 'Conditions of Carriage' in any correspondence, to send copies of them to regular customers and to display them in their offices where goods are received for carriage.

There are three parties involved in most movements of goods, the consignor – who sends the goods; the carrier – who carries them, and the consignee – who receives them at their destination. Because of legal difficulties which have arisen in the past the carrier is in some difficulty to know with whom he has made a contract. Was it the consignor, who delivered the goods to his depot for carriage, or was it the consignee (who probably owns the goods)? As he has never seen the consignee (until the moment of delivery of the goods at the end of the journey) one would think that the carrier must make the contract with the consignor. Unfortunately the law often holds otherwise, and the carriers therefore usually say in their 'Conditions of Carriage' that if the consignor is not the owner of the goods he is deemed to be acting as the agent for the owner of the goods, and in this way he makes a contract on behalf of the owner of the goods.

Clearly, the law of carriage is very involved. Those who are interested might like to read *The Law of Carriage of Goods by Land, Sea and Air,* by Jaspar Ridley (Shaw and Sons Ltd). Here we need only note that in any correspondence about the carriage of goods (or passengers) it is very important to refer to the carrier's Conditions of Carriage. These form the basis of the contract between the parties. The carrier undertakes to carry with due care. If the goods fail to arrive at all (lost goods) or arrive late (delayed goods) or arrive damaged then the consignee, or perhaps the consignor, will be able to claim compensation for the loss, delay or damage. Whether the claim will be met depends upon the facts of the particular case, but since most carriers are honourable, and expect to be held liable for their own faults, they will meet any claim which is justified. They may be able to reject the claim for perfectly good reasons, like an Act of God, an Act of the Queen's enemies, bad packing of the goods, and **inherent vice**. Inherent vice is the bad nature of some goods — for example an expensive bull once worked itself into such a temper in the vehicle that it injured itself and had to be destroyed. The carrier was held not liable; it is in the nature of bulls to be violent — an inherent vice.

17.3 Correspondence about contracts of carriage

SL17.1

```
                                                24 Flowery Avenue
                                                Highcliff on Sea
                                                Essex   2SS 1JD

Grants Removals Ltd
20 Crown Way
Rochford
Essex                                           14 May 19--


Dear Sirs

Removal to Hertfordshire: Quotation

Would you please give me a written quotation for the removal of my
personal effects from the above address to

                        27 The Rodings
                        Bishops Stortford
                        Hertfordshire

The move must take place in the week commencing 30 May 19--, vacant
possession of the new property being available from Monday 30 May.
This would also be the most convenient day for me if you have a
vehicle free.

I appreciate that you will need to send a representative to see how
much property we have to move.  We are available every evening from
5 pm, or on Saturdays from 9 am onwards.

                        Yours faithfully



                        G T Merryweather
```

GRANTS REMOVALS LTD

20 Crown Way, Rochford, Essex 5SS 1DT. Tel: 53942

Our Reference: JT/DC
Your Reference: Letter of 14 May 19--

16 May 19--

G T Merryweather Esq
24 Flowery Avenue
Highcliff on Sea
Essex 2SS 1JD

Dear Sir

Quotation for Removal

Thank you for your letter. After the visit of our representative,
Peter Marker, yesterday we are able to quote you as follows for
removal at 8 am, Monday 30 May 19--.

To removal of all goods from the house, garage and outbuildings, packing, transport, unloading and installation of same in the property at Bishops Stortford	£185.00

(This cost includes the packing of all china, glassware, etc,
and the relaying of carpets on arrival at the new premises.)

Would you please note that we only carry goods under the Conditions
of Carriage published by our Trade Association, a copy of which is
enclosed. Please read these carefully, since they limit our liability
in certain circumstances.

I understand that the removal expenses are to be charged to your new
employers, Eden Products (Bishops Stortford) Ltd. Please ensure that
if you accept the quotation you send us a written authority from them
confirming their willingness to pay all charges.

We look forward to your acceptance of this quotation, and to assisting
you on 30 May.

Yours faithfully

John Thompson
Manager

Raymond Foster (Cambridge) Ltd

207 Camside, Cambridge, Essex
Telephone: 33421

Your Ref:
Our Ref: RF/ST

Date: 27 July 19--

Tony Young Esq
Park Air Services Ltd
Room 112G
Building 521
Heathrow Airport
London

Dear Mr Young

We note from your advertisement in the Journal of Commerce that you
offer a worldwide airfreight service. We are manufacturers of electrical switchgear selling small orders (average 50 kg) to firms in
many parts of the world, but chiefly the Middle East, Far East and
Australia. Our average daily dispatch is about 20 cases, which have
been handled by sea, but we feel airfreight would be more appropriate.

Would it be possible please for you to send someone to see us to
advise how this might be arranged, and perhaps advise on packaging
charges, documentation etc, as well as to discuss collections (or
deliveries by us to your depot at Heathrow). We feel we could put a
useful amount of business your way, and reap the benefit ourselves of
faster deliveries and more economic operations when seen from a
'total cost' point of view.

Yours faithfully

Richard Farnham
Export Manager

Park Air Services Ltd.

AIR FREIGHT AND INSURANCE AGENTS
AUTHORISED I.A.T.A. CARGO AGENTS
ROOM 112G · BUILDING 521 · STANSTED ROAD
HEATHROW AIRPORT LONDON
HOUNSLOW · MIDDLESEX · TW6 3LX
Telephone: 01-759 0028 (3 lines)   Telex: 263739

Our Ref: RB/TJ
Your Ref: RF/ST   28 July 19--

Raymond Foster (Cambridge) Limited
207 Camside
Cambridge ·
Essex

Attn: <u>Mr Richard Farnham - Export Manager</u>

Dear Mr Farnham

We are in receipt of your enquiry dated 27 July 19-- and would thank you for the
interest shown in the services we offer.

We have over twenty years experience handling exports by air worldwide as well
as arranging customs clearance for importations of all types into the United
Kingdom. Being licenced by IATA we have access to all services operated by
member airlines in addition to the many carriers who are non-participating.

We have a small but efficient staff and being moderately sized can offer a fast,
economical and personal service. The latter we consider to be of great importance.
To be able to contact the person dealing with your consignment direct, rather than
through various Customer Liaison Clerks etc, as employed by larger agencies, saves
time and a great deal of aggravation. We deal with your shipments as though we
are <u>your</u> Shipping Department.

Our Export Department is fully conversant with all available airfreight rates and
will always arrange the most economical transportation, given the time factor
involved. All customs documentation is completed as is consular work, certificates
of origin etc, if required. A fast packing service is offered for those shipments
requiring same and insurance cover can be arranged upon receipt of written
instructions.

Collections of export airfreight shipments are available throughout the UK and
provided we are notified by 10.00 am will be carried out the same day.

The shipments mentioned in your enquiry are ideally suited for airfreight and the
undersigned would be delighted to come and discuss arrangements for shipping same.
Please advise when this would be convenient.

We attach hereto our tariff for your perusal and would once again sincerely thank
you for your interest and the opportunity to provide for your airfreight requirements.

I very much look forward to meeting you.

Yours faithfully

A Young
Export Manager

Registered in England No. 664661 Registered Office Dominion Works, Thames Road, London, W4 3RF

Fig. 17.1 A response to an inquiry about carriage by air

17.4 International conventions on carriage — exclusionary clauses

One of the difficulties about contracts is that the parties to the contract can agree to all sorts of clauses. The law takes the view that both parties to the contract are equally knowledgeable, and equally well-advised legally. This is of course quite ridiculous, and perhaps the early railway companies proved the point more clearly than anyone else. They wrote all sorts of clauses into their contracts and would not carry goods for anyone who did not agree to them. The clauses were called 'exclusionary clauses' because they excluded liability for all sorts of things that might happen.

Imagine an old lady who calls at the railway station to send a parcel. Can we say she is as well advised legally as the railway, with the finest lawyers on its payroll? If she does not like a clause can she strike it out and say 'Not agreed'? Of course not. These exclusionary clauses became very troublesome in the Law of Carriage, and especially with shipping lines, railways and road hauliers. Eventually international conventions had to be held on the carriage of goods by road, rail, sea and air. These conventions have resulted in reasonably fair arrangements. The general conclusion is that if the carrier is at fault he is held liable. If he is not at fault, because of an Act of God or some other reason, he will be excluded from liability. Any exclusionary clause that is inserted which tries to protect the carrier when loss, damage or delay is the carrier's fault will be null and void, and the law will disregard it. The rules are known by the following names:

Carriage by Air:	The Warsaw Rules
Carriage by Sea:	The Hague-Visby Rules
	(*Note:* New 'Hamburg Rules' are awaiting ratification)
Carriage by Rail:	The CIM rules
Carriage by Road:	The CMR rules

17.5 Documentation of freight movements

One feature of the freight-forwarding industry today is that much of the business formerly conducted by correspondence is now dealt with by telephone and telex. More important than the correspondence involved is the documentation, which is really a standardised form of communication. In the case of all major types of international carriage this takes the form of a consignment note or waybill which conforms with an international convention, and the requirements of an Act of Parliament or other ruling body of the nation-state concerned. These notes are named as follows:

a Road transport in the European Economic Community – the T form, which is part of the CT (Community Transit) procedure.
b Other international road haulage – the CMR consignment note (CMR is from the French for Convention on Merchandise by Roadhauliers).
c The TIR carnet for international road haulage where several frontiers have to be crossed (but in the EEC the T form procedure applies instead).
d Rail transport – the CIM consignment note (CIM is from the French for Convention on International Merchandise. This convention was held in 1914 before international carriage of goods by road started, so the word 'rail' does not appear in the title – in those days everything went by rail as far as inland transport was concerned).
e Sea transport – the bill of lading, the common short-form bill of lading or the liner waybill.
f Air transport – the air waybill.

In each case the wording of the convention is important and covers many vital elements in the 'conditions of carriage' which form the basis of the contract between the parties. Some items of the 'conditions of carriage' could be rendered null and void by the convention, and the consignor and consignee could also be affected by the rules about notification of claims, time limits on claims and on legal action and the jurisdiction of the courts in any dispute. If you enter this field of business, and it is a vital and interesting field of modern commerce, it is essential to make a detailed study of these documents and to know the importance of each box on the form.

Bateman Brothers

317 Philpot Lane
London EC3 1DT
Telephone 01 339 2054

Your Ref:
Our Ref: AB/CO

Date   17 February 19--

The Goods Manager
British Rail, Western Region
Marlington Station
London
W2 5SE

Dear Sir

We regret to advise you that 10 boxes of apple concentrate forming
part of the consignment for Messrs Queen & Son of Bristol, and
covered by your Receipt No A1234, were found on arrival to be unfit
for use. The consignees inform us that a note to this effect was
made when they took delivery, and as the consignment was sent at your
risk we should be glad to have your credit note for £75, representing
the value of the boxes damaged, as shown by the invoice enclosed.

Yours faithfully

A Bateman
Manager

BRITISH RAIL

WESTERN REGION

Marlington Station, London W2 5SE

Tel: 01 488 6555

Your Ref: AB/CO
Our Ref: JK/AP

20 February 19--

Messrs Bateman Bros
317 Philpot Lane
London
EC3 1DT

Dear Sirs

Consignment No A1234 Damaged in Transit

We regret to state that no claim for compensation on this consignment
can be considered, because the damage has in our opinion resulted
from an Act of God. Investigations have shown that the deterioration
was due to the presence of rain water which penetrated the tarpaulin
covers during the storm which occurred on 7 February. As these tar-
paulins are known to afford adequate protection against ordinary
adverse weather conditions, and as the storm was exceptionally
violent, we trust that you will agree that our obligations were dis-
charged when all ordinary precautions were taken. The Bristol meteoro-
logical office described the storm as 'the worst tornado to hit the
West country, since records began'.

Yours faithfully

J Kelly
Claims Manager
Marlington Station

UMO EYO LTD

2174 Kano Road, Kaduna, Nigeria

Our Reference UE/AK

21 October 19--

Euro-Nigeria Multi-Modal Ltd
Building 5187
Kano Airport
Northern Nigeria

Dear Sir

Damages for delay: Consignment No 2164 to London Airport

On 7 October you undertook to carry to the United Kingdom a consignment of semi-manufactured parts which were declared to be of vital
importance to our customer in the United Kingdom. You undertook to
deliver them within 36 hours, but in fact they have only been
received today, despite repeated requests for you to trace them and
expedite delivery.

Our contract with the UK customer required us to pay liquidated damages
of £50 per day if the goods did not arrive by 12 October. We have thus
been made liable for damages of £450 sterling. As the carriage was
carried out under the Uniform Rules for a Combined Transport Document,
and as you were the Combined Transport Operator you are liable for this
delay, and I shall be glad to receive your cheque in settlement.

Yours faithfully

Umo Eyo
Managing Director

Euro-Nigeria Multi-Modal Ltd

Building 5187
Kano Airport
Northern Nigeria

```
Your Reference   UE/AK
Our Reference    NM/AT
```

24 October 19--

```
Umo Eyo Ltd
2174 Kano Road
Kaduna
Nigeria
```

Dear Mr Eyo

We are most apologetic about this unfortunate delay to your goods, which were placed in error aboard a plane bound for Lomé in Togo, instead of London. An employee in the airport, who has since been dismissed, was found to be almost illiterate and quite unable to distinguish the two names.

Even so this would have presented little difficulty had the aircraft not been damaged in a tropical storm in Lomé. We eventually had to rescue the consignment by road. It has been a most expensive exercise, but that is no fault of yours. Our cheque for the compensation will reach you shortly; in the meantime we must make a claim against our sub-contractors at the airport.

I hope this unfortunate experience will not prejudice you against us in the future. We feel it is most unlikely to occur again.

Yours sincerely

E Odina
Freight Manager

THE PRECOCIOUS OIL CO LTD

2487 WEST ROAD
LONDON W5 2AJ

Telephone: 01 657 4873

Your Ref:
Our Ref: GW/JG

1 October 19--

Linford, Linton and Lightbody
176 St Mary Axe
London
EC3 1DT

Dear Sirs

We have an expanding activity in Algeria in connection with oil and
natural gas development under official contracts with the Algerian
Department of Energy. We therefore need a regular facility (three
times weekly) for flying spares, crews etc into and out of Algiers.
To some extent these arrangements could be flexible to meet the needs
of carriers with 'empty leg' journeys to fill who would be prepared
to charge an economical rate. Can you please negotiate the charter of
aircraft on the Baltic Exchange to meet our needs from carriers serving the Southern Mediterranean area?

If you wish to discuss the exact details of our requirements perhaps
you would contact me by telephone, or in my absence my deputy, Peter
Driver.

Yours faithfully

G Waterford
Managing Director

Madison Engineering (Fabrication) Ltd
Western Industrial Estate
Harlow, Essex
Telephone: Harlow 565483

Our Ref: JJ/BD

31 March 19--

Fillbox Faster and Co Ltd
Milton Depot
Milton
Cambridgeshire

Dear Sirs

Regular Consignments to Bombay, Madras and Calcutta

We are specialists in the fabrication of small plants for biomass
energy supply, and ship regularly to official agents in India,
Pakistan and Bangladesh. We rarely have a full container load, our
plants being packaged to fit in a standard container, but occupying
only five feet of length, but full container width and height. The
new express service from Felixstowe, for which you are one of the
consolidators,interests us very much.

We are considering appointing you as agents for regular LCL consignments, but would first like to see the extent of your operations,
handling facilities, etc. Would you please suggest a time and date
which would be convenient for members of our Board to visit you at
Milton and discuss such arrangements.

Yours faithfully

Jack Johnstone
Manager: Physical Distribution

The Freight Forwarders of Africairia

2174 Chaka Street,
Washonaland, Africairia

Our Ref: NM/RS

27 July 19--

W Zeilbeck Esq
Director General
International Federation of
Freight Forwarders Association
29 Brauerstrasse
POB 177
CH 8026
Zurich, Switzerland

Dear Mr Zeilbeck

Membership of FIATA

Our membership is anxious to extend its links outside Africairia, to forge bonds of friendship with freight forwarders all over the world.

Would you be kind enough to explain the aims of FIATA, and how we may become members of your association. Perhaps you could supply, or invoice me for, brochures and literature for discussion by our management committee.

Africairia is a developing African country with a huge hinterland, without any railway system, so that road haulage is the very lifeblood of the nation.

Thanking you in advance for your courtesy,

Ndaisa Muhammadu
General Secretary

FEDERATION INTERNATIONALE DES ASSOCIATIONS DE TRANSITAIRES ET ASSIMILES
INTERNATIONALE FÖDERATION DER SPEDITEURORGANISATIONEN

INTERNATIONAL FEDERATION OF FREIGHT FORWARDERS ASSOCIATIONS

29, BRAUERSTRASSE · POB 177 · CH-8026 ZURICH · SWITZERLAND · ☎ 241 90 45 · 🖂 CH 57278 · 🖂 FIATA

THE FREIGHT FORWARDERS OF AFRICAIRIA
Att: Mr. Ndaisa MUHAMMADU
General Secretary
2174 Chaka Street

<u>WASHONALAND</u>, Africairia

Zurich, April 6th 19--
WZ/cs

<u>Ordinary membership with FIATA</u>

Dear Mr. Muhammadu,

Thank you very much for your friendly lines of July 27th and your interest
shown in the world-wide Community of Forwarders assembled in FIATA.

It is with pleasure that we send you by separate mail the following:

- Brochure "All about FIATA"
- Brochure "The Forwarder, the Architect of Transport"
- Brochure "The Documents of FIATA"
- Brochure "The Services of FIATA"
- Brochure "The Forwarder Past and Present"
- List of FIATA members world-wide
- Application form for Ordinary Membership

We would suggest you study this material and after receiving your formal
application we would engage the registration procedure as usual.

We would like to draw your attention to the fact that the statutory requirements as shown on the application form should be complied with and reach us
in good time so that the matter can be dealt with by the next meeting of our
Executive Committee due to take place in September 19-- in Dublin.

We thank you in advance for your kind consideration and look forward with great
interest to hearing from you.

Yours sincerely
F I A T A

W. Zeilbeck
Director General

<u>Encl</u>:

Fig. 17.2 An international organisation for freight forwarders

17.7 Exercises on the carriage of goods

1 Write to Deakins Removals Ltd, 1745 Talbot Street, Nottingham asking them to give you a quotation for removing your office equipment from 2174 Young Street, Nottingham to 3258 Bath Road, Bristol. The removal must be carried out in the week commencing 3 May 19--, preferably on Monday 4 May.

2 Reply to the inquiry in Question 1, quoting £184.50 plus VAT for the work. Refer in your letter to the visit you made to inspect the amount of goods to be moved, and also to your Conditions of Carriage, a copy of which you enclose. Point out that the quotation is subject to owner's risk, but you are prepared to carry the goods at your risk for an insurance premium of £18.50, payable on acceptance of the quotation.

3 Write a letter on 15 January 19-- to All-Destinations Freight (Hamble) Ltd, 1384 High Road, Southampton asking them whether they would be prepared to handle regular consignments to Atlantic Coast destinations in France — particularly Quimper, Lorient, Nantes, St Nazaire, La Rochelle and Bordeaux. Explain that the packages would be cubes 2 feet square, designed to be consolidated into containers of standard size, and approximately 40 packages per week-day would need to be moved between 1 February and 31 May, to meet seasonal needs in connection with the leisure-pleasure industry along that coast. Offer to settle the account monthly in arrears, and for goods to be carried at carrier's risk. You are the export manager of Beachwear (Winchester) Ltd, 2174 Southampton Road, Winchester, Hants.

4 Reply on 17 January 19-- to the letter mentioned in Question 3 above, stating that you would be pleased to undertake the forwarding of the goods concerned provided it can be fitted in with your present arrangements to serve the area concerned. You send a container-load twice weekly on Wednesdays and Saturdays. Can the goods be held at your depot for a day or two to fit in with this arrangement, or are they perishable? If this arrangement is possible, and a daily collection is only required to clear production lines, then you will arrange to collect daily and dispatch twice weekly. Goods would be perfectly secure and under guard at all times. If this is acceptable a costing exercise will be put in

hand and a quotation submitted. A set of your Conditions of Carriage is enclosed.

5 On 16 May 19-- write to All-Destination Freight (Hamble) Ltd notifying them that because of the arrest of one of their drivers in France for smuggling, your goods have been delayed at Quimper and a customer at La Rochelle has cancelled the order as a result. You demand the return of the goods to the United Kingdom as soon as they are freed from control, and damages of £120 for loss of profit on the order. Failing this you propose to ask your solicitor to commence a legal action on your behalf.

6 All-Destinations Freight (Hamble) Ltd (see Question 5) reply expressing their regret for the delay, and the loss of business that has resulted. While expressing their own total innocence in the matter, they accept liability for delay and promise the return of the goods free of charge. With regard to the claim for damages they accept that damages are payable, but consider £120 rather high. They offer £85, in settlement of the claim, and hope to hear that this is acceptable.

7 Airship Services (Zimbabwe) Ltd are proposing to operate an airship lifting service to all parts of Central Africa. Airship lifts are particularly useful for areas where roads are bad, or goods are of awkward size or weight. Write to them asking if they would be able to airlift generators weighing 20 tonnes each to a range of destinations in Zambia, Malawi, Tanzania and Zimbabwe. You are importing via Beira, and airlifts from Beira Airport, or ideally direct from a special quay which is under construction at the port, would reduce handling costs in Beira itself. The generators are required for hospital surgical units where electricity is not available, or liable to interruption.

8 Down-under Ltd operate an air freight service to New Zealand and Australia which delivers goods within 56 hours door to door to all destinations. Reply on their behalf to an inquiry from Roll-over Doors (Huntingdon) Ltd requesting the possibility of dispatching garage parts in this way. The dimensions of their doors are 8 foot by 7 foot. Reply that it would be possible to carry these in one of your aircraft and offering to visit them and discuss the matter.

17.8 Appendix on the English language: avoiding unnecessary words and phrases

Tautology is the repetition of the same statement or idea, but using different words. As brevity is an important quality of good communication, you should try to avoid the unnecessary use of words or phrases which merely repeat what you have already said. Take, for example, the following sentence:

'The consignment should arrive by 7 am in the morning.'

As the abbreviation am stands for *ante meridiem,* the Latin phrase meaning 'before noon', there is clearly no need to include the phrase 'in the morning' in the sentence, as it merely repeats what has already been said.

Just as it is important to avoid using unnecessary words and phrases within a sentence, so you should avoid unnecessary repetition of information or ideas in a longer passage, such as a report. Although it may be appropriate to repeat an important aspect of a report, either in order to emphasise it, or as part of a final paragraph summarising what has already been said, any superfluous repetition will only help to confuse your communication.

While brevity and precision of expression will hold a reader's interest, rambling 'waffle' will not. The advice given in earlier chapters applies here too. Only careful re-reading of your writing from the recipient's point of view will reveal whether it contains the unnecessary use of words and phrases.

17.9 Exercise on the avoidance of unnecessary words and phrases

Rewrite these sentences omitting any unnecessary words and phrases:
a It was exactly seven o'clock precisely when the final conclusion to the meeting came.
b The twins were perfectly identical.
c We shall advertise the washing powder and give a free gift with every packet purchased.
d The different sections of the firm worked together with mutual cooperation.
e The electrically-powered car will be a new innovation to the car market.
f I myself saw the secretary personally.
g The problems associated with inflation are continually recurrent.

18 Insurance

18.1 The nature of insurance

Insurance is a process by which losses fall lightly upon many people instead of heavily upon a few. Thus most people insure their homes against storm damage by paying a few pounds into a 'pool' of insurance money. In any storm that occurs it is rare for the lightning to strike more than one house. The unfortunate victim whose house is damaged draws compensation from the pool to repair the damage. Thus the loss falls easily upon all who pay premiums, and the one who actually suffers damage does not suffer more than the rest.

There are several important principles when arranging insurance, of which the two most important are 'insurable interest' and 'utmost good faith'. **Insurable interest** holds that we may not insure anything unless we shall actually suffer a loss if it is harmed or damaged. I may insure my own house, car, business premises, etc. because I shall suffer a loss if they are damaged. I may not insure my neighbour's house, car or other property because if they are damaged I shall not suffer loss (and I might just be tempted to help the unfortunate event happen, to gain the 'compensation' from the insurance company). It is against public policy to allow people to insure property when they have no insurable interest. This means that it would encourage crime, which is never a good policy for the public.

Utmost good faith is a principle which holds that a contract of insurance is one which requires the parties to tell the absolute truth at all times. In any contract we must show 'good faith', but in insurance contracts we must show the 'utmost good faith'. This is because the insurance company is going to cover a risk which it can only assess on the basis of the answers we give to certain questions on a **proposal form**. For example, A decided to insure the life of his partner, B. The proposal form asks 'Has Mr B enjoyed good health over the last ten years?' He has, but yesterday he had a heart attack and is dying. If A replies 'Yes' he is telling the truth to some extent, but not the absolute truth. The insurance company is likely to be defrauded if clients do not show the utmost good faith.

18.2 Arranging insurance cover

The stages of arranging insurance cover are as follows:

a The person seeking cover completes a proposal form, with utmost good faith.
b The insurance company assesses the risk and fixes a **premium** to be paid.
c The premium is paid into the insurance pool, and cover commences.
d The insurance company invests the pool to earn interest and thus increase the pool.
e In the event of a loss being suffered the insured makes a **claim** for compensation.
f The claim is investigated, and if found to be valid the compensation is paid from the pool — if necessary some of the investments are sold to obtain the money required.

This chain of procedure is used in the vast majority of insurance contracts, where almost all citizens are insuring their homes, motor vehicles, valuables, etc. Since all these arrangements are similar, standard procedures can be followed and forms can be prepared which will fit almost all situations.

Rather more specialised is the insurance of goods and passengers moving around the world by sea and air. The wide variety of goods on the move, the different classes of ships and aircraft, etc., make the insurance of such movements rather different from the standard transactions in other fields. This type of business is frequently carried out through Lloyd's of London, an organisation with several thousand **underwriters** prepared to cover risks of every sort, each risk being considered on its merits. The procedure is described in most commerce textbooks, but the basic idea is that a Lloyd's broker, acting for a client seeking insurance, draws up a 'slip' which describes the risk to be covered. He then takes this slip to a leading underwriter in the field, and discusses a fair premium. The leading underwriter will then give him 'a lead' by writing on the slip his willingness to carry a share of the risk (say £20 000 at £12 premium per £1000). With this lead the broker will soon find others willing to participate, and when the full cover has been obtained a policy can be prepared.

R. G. Reis & Co. Ltd.

Members of:

British Insurance
Brokers Association

National Association
of Pension Funds

The Society of
Pension Consultants

Incorporated Life &
Mortgage Brokers

---

10 Jesus Lane Cambridge CB5 8BA   Telephone: (0223) 311471

A J Roe Esq
12 Abbots Way
Horningsea
Cambridge

Your Ref: AJR/31 May
Our Ref: DG/PMH

1 June 19--

Dear Mr Roe

Private Car Insurance - Newly Qualified Driver

We are pleased to hear that your son has now passed his driving test and is
considering purchasing his own car. Your own insurers have been notified
accordingly.

We shall be pleased to arrange insurance for him when he has chosen a vehicle,
and even if he starts College in September in another area a telephone call
at any time will enable us to assist him should a claim arise or change of
vehicle require the cover to be renegotiated.

It is important that he looks for a vehicle in either Group 1 or 2 and I
enclose a list which shows him the choice available. The reason is that until
he has established a few years 'no claims' bonus insurance will be quite
expensive as he is young and inexperienced. Cars in other Groups would really
be prohibitive.

We look forward to hearing from him.

Yours sincerely

D Gibbs
Director

Directors: R.E.W. Westgate A.C.I.I., F.C.I.B. J.R. Westgate D.G. Gibbs A.C.I.I., A.C.I.B.
A.J. Roe P.G. Neighbour A.C.M.B.
Consultant: D. Lincoln F.C.C.A.

Branch Office: 15 Angel Hill, Bury St. Edmunds, Suffolk IP33 1XG

City Office: 73 Cheapside, London EC2V 6FS
Registered Office: 10 Jesus Lane, Cambridge
Registered in England No. 515264

Fig. 18.1 Advice about insurance for a young driver

The Accident, Fire and Life Assurance Co (Singapore) Ltd

2816 Woodlands Causeway, Singapore

Your Ref: 1B/JK
Our Ref: Policy No 207146

14 July 19--

Pest Control (Tuas) Ltd
2456 Marine Road
Tuas
Singapore

Dear Sir

I set out below details of the premium payable to bring into effect our insurance of your buildings. To make payment of the Total Annual Premium please complete the direct debit form enclosed and return it to me. We will then present it at once, and also each year on the renewal date.

I do hope you appreciate why it is necessary to use a direct debit form, instead of the traditional banker's order. You have asked that this policy be index-linked, so that any rise in the value of your premises as inflation occurs will be fully covered in the future. In order to do this the value covered will be raised according to the inflation index, and this means that the premium must also rise in accordance with the index. A direct debit enables us to ask for the correct sum each year. You need not fear that such a sum will ever be excessive, for we have taken out a guarantee with our bank that any overcharge will be automatically refunded from a sum placed at the bank's disposal for this purpose.

Yours faithfully

Man Lee
Manager

Property Insured: 2456 Marine Road
Value of property covered S$80 000 - index linked
Policy commences 14 July 19--
Renewal date annually 13 July
Premium Rate per S$1000: S$1.25
Total Annual Premium S$100

The Commercial Insurance Co (Wilmington) Inc

3092 Main Street, North Carolina, USA

```
                                    Your Ref:  (by telephone)
Mrs Patricia Webster                Our Ref:   RTY/AB
35 Roseville Road
Westport
Connecticut 06880                   1 November 19--
```

Dear Mrs Webster

Thank you for your telephone call today. We are happy to consider
giving you cover on your motor vehicle, and enclose a proposal form.
Please complete this as soon as possible and we will notify you of
the premium payable. In the meantime we are holding you covered,
fully comprehensive, except for the first fifty (50) dollars of any
claim, in anticipation of your completion of the form.

The above cover will be invalidated should any insurance company have
refused to insure you for any reason. If this is the case please
telephone us to notify us of the circumstances.

Yours faithfully

Richard T Younger
Manager (Motor Vehicles Department)

Many insurance situations can be dealt with by standard-form letters. Fig. 18.2 on page 272 shows such a letter from a major motor insurance company. It refers to the changed situation resulting from a change of motor vehicle. The motorist who changes cars is 'held covered' in the new car until the necessary paperwork has been concluded. If the new car is a more valuable car, or represents a higher risk, the motorist will be asked for an increased premium. If the new car is less expensive, or less powerful, a refund of some of the premium previously paid may be in order. Study this standard-form letter carefully.

AA

Automobile Association Insurance Services Limited

Monmouth Road Cheadle Hulme Cheadle Cheshire SK8 7BT

Telephone 061-485 6191

Directors Andrew H S Lewis MBE (Chairman) J Atkinson D A Griffiths O F Lambert R A Lovick D J Reynolds

Registered Office: Fanum House Basingstoke Hampshire M F Saunders D R Thomas R D Vaughan D Welton Professor E Wright

Registered Number 912191 England

Reference: GAD/.................................

Dear Member,

Thank you for your communication. We have altered your policy as indicated below.

The amendments are effective from:— ....

☐ Change of vehicle – from (Reg. No.) .... to

☐ Replacement/Additional Vehicle

Make and Model of Car	Cubic Capacity	Registration Number

☐ Change of address

☐ Cover amended to: ....

☐ Additional Drivers

Full Name(s): ....

....

☐ Use/Occupation amended to: ....

☐ Policy Options amended to: ....

☐ Other Information

The alteration results in:—

☐ A refund of premium for which we enclose our cheque. £ .

☐ An additional premium being payable. **Please return this letter, below perforation, with your remittance.** £ .

☐ No change in the premium payable.

☐ Where necessary revised documents are enclosed/will be sent to you.

☐

Policy No..

Renewal Date ....

Yours faithfully,

B L O C K   C A P I T A L S

Name and address of policyholder.

Date...

Automobile Association
Insurance Services Ltd.

Ins 429 (4/79)

Fig. 18.2 A standard-form letter about a change of vehicle

Electrical-Motors (Wisbech) Ltd

2074 South Quay
Wisbech, Cambridgeshire

Telephone: 0945 6825

Our Ref JRK/TD/2714

27 May 19--

Merriman, Walters and Co
2174 Market Approaches
King's Lynn
Norfolk

Dear Sirs

Open Cover: £100 000

For some time now you have been arranging insurance for us through
Lloyd's of London on a shipment by shipment basis. Our business has
been growing, and our expertise has attracted the attention of
several small firms who have asked us whether our Export Department
could act for them in dealing with export cargoes of various sorts.
We have expressed interest in these approaches, since it would enable
us to share our Export Department costs with these firms.

We would therefore like to change our present arrangements and arrange
an open cover against which all cargoes could be notified. Would you
please arrange an appointment so that we can discuss the implications
of such a change, and the procedures we must follow.

Yours faithfully

J R Kennedy
Export Manager

Thermodynamics (Gwelo) Ltd

2074 Umvuma Road, Gwelo, Zimbabwe

Our Reference   RL/TD

27 July 19--

African Continental Insurance Co Ltd
3965 Hartley Road
Salisbury
Zimbabwe

Dear Sirs

<u>Open cover for UK Airfreight</u>

We are about to start exporting our first consignment of electrical
components to the United Kingdom for onward transmission to customers
in all parts of the European Economic Community. It is essential that
we cover these for all risks by air, and since consignments will leave
daily an open cover under the Institute Air Cargo Clause (All Risks)
has been recommended to us. Would you please arrange such a cover to
the value of Z$250 000, effective immediately, at the most economical
rate you can obtain.

It so happens that our export manager, Joshua Lumumba, will be in
Salisbury next week and would like to visit you to discuss insurance
procedures. Would you please arrange an appointment for him on either
Tuesday or Wednesday (4 or 5 August) by telephone to this office.

Yours faithfully

Richard Luanda
General Manager

18.4 Claims

The cover provided by an insurance policy entitles the insured to make a claim for compensation out of the pool of funds available if the insured peril actually occurs. Where a loss is undoubtedly attributable to an insured peril the claim will be settled without delay. In a recent air crash where two aircraft were destroyed, to a value of over £40 million, the claim was paid within four days. Where a loss is clearly not attributable to an insured peril the Claims Department will explain the matter to the assured and show that the loss is outside the terms of the policy. Where a dispute arises it is commonly settled by an 'ex gratia' payment — as 'an act of grace'. This safeguards the insurer's goodwill, since it is undesirable to acquire a reputation as a bad settler of claims, but the sum is usually only a part of the sum claimed. Another type of settlement is a 'settlement without prejudice'. This means that the insurer disputes the claim, but will pay it on this occasion, without any admission that it is a precedent for future occasions.

Claims procedure may follow a pattern similar to the one shown below:

a The loss is discovered and immediate action is taken by the assured, to minimise the loss and to notify that a loss has occurred.
b Submission of the claim to the broker with the documentary evidence.
c The claim is recorded and the preparatory work is done by the broker.
d The claim is submitted to the underwriter.
e The claim is paid by the underwriter.
f The underwriter then passes the documents to a **recovery agent**, whose function is to recover what he can for the underwriter to restore some money to the pool. Clearly, if the loss suffered was an Act of God nothing can be recovered, but if the loss was due to the negligence of a carrier, for example, it may be possible to recover damages from the carrier.

The Megapolis Insurance Co Ltd

2174 Market Hill
Oxford
Telephone: 0865 44278

Your Ref: AB 17 October 19--
Our Ref: JT/TDC/17845

29 October 19--

R Larkin Esq
2975 Woodham Ferrers Road
Wickford
Essex

Dear Sir

Claim No 1294: Damaged Hand-Basin

I regret to say that your claim for compensation for a fractured
china hand-basin has been rejected on the grounds that the basin in
question has been installed in the house since it was built, some
twenty-eight years ago. It is our experience that such basins do
crack due to the changes of temperature from hot to cold water, and
their usual life is about ten years. This one has lasted longer
than most and the fracture is therefore due to 'fair wear and tear'
and not due to 'accidental damage' as referred to in your policy for
household contents. We cannot therefore offer compensation, because
our duty to other insured persons requires us to reject claims which
are not directly caused by the risk named in the policy.

Yours faithfully

J Tompkinson
Claims Manager

The Megapolis Insurance Co Ltd

2174 Market Hill
Oxford
Telephone: 0865 44278

Your Ref: Claim No 1279
Our Ref: JT/TDC/17986

22 May 19--

T Rose Esq
4175 Orbital Road
Watford
Herts

Dear Sir

Claim No 1279: Motor Vehicle Accident

Your claim has been considered and it has been agreed that the full
value of the car (less £25 excess) will be paid forthwith. We believe
this value to be £2850, rather than the £3500 you claim. We think
your estimate fails to take sufficient account of the fact that the
car was over two years old at the accident date, and had had three
previous owners. As you only paid £3600 for the car ten months before
the accident you are allowing £100 for ten months depreciation,
whereas a 25 per cent per annum deduction is normal for cars of this
type. We are therefore offering you £2825 in full settlement of your
claim. Will you please advise us whether this figure is acceptable,
and if so our cheque will follow about seven days later.

Yours faithfully

J Tompkinson
Claims Manager

Gayford and Partners (Leadenhall) Ltd

1001 Leadenhall Street, London EC3 1DT

Telephone: 01 - 328 4509

Our Reference JG/AC

12 October 19--

The Secretary,
Denham Bros. Ltd.,
321 Leadenhall Square,
London EC3.

Dear Sir,

<u>Sugar Claim - Policy 317533 (Declaration 19)</u>

We must refuse immediate liability for the damage to the shipment described in your letter of 10 October. Your claim, however, will receive consideration when you have supplied details of the damage.

For the purposes of adjudication please give us a full account of the accident and, if possible, a copy of the ship's log for that date.

Your method of calculating the damage is vague to a great degree, and we ask you to submit a survey report. If no surveyor has been appointed we should be ready to nominate one. Alternatively, should you prefer this course, we should be prepared to allow Lloyd's agent to act for our mutual benefit.

It is essential for office records that the policy be forwarded for endorsement and we should be glad to receive it as soon as possible.

Yours faithfully,
For Mercantile Insurance Co. Ltd.

Jabez Gayford
Adjuster of Marine Claims

Gayford and Partners (Leadenhall) Ltd

1001 Leadenhall Street, London EC3 1DT
Telephone: 01 - 328 4509

```
The Thoroughbred Training        Your Ref: Claim No.1
Stables (Cambridge) Ltd.,        Our Ref:  Claim No.2784
Stourbridge Common Road,
Cambridge.                       26 July 19--
```

Dear Sirs,

                    'Merry Man's Masterpiece'

     At last I am able to settle this claim after the latest round of
negotiations between yourselves and my principals, the Mercantile
Insurance Co. Ltd. I am sure you now appreciate that in giving
instructions to the veterinary surgeon at the racetrack to put down
the animal you were in breach of your duty to minimise our losses.
It was purely fortuitous that our representative at the track was
able to prevent this, and the animal is now fully recovered and is
about to be sold to a breeding consortium for a considerable sum.

     Accordingly the reservation made by my principals about the sum
payable has been withdrawn and you will be paid the full value of
£38 000 less the veterinary expenses and support costs of £3250.

     If you will notify me that you are prepared to accept the sum of
£34 750 in full settlement I will pass the claim for payment at an
early date.

                   Yours faithfully,
            For Mercantile Insurance Co. Ltd.

                        Aristotle Gayford
              Adjuster of General Accident Claims

18.6 Exercises on insurance correspondence

1 The Blewbury Festival Committee is about to hold a village fete
which it is hoped will raise £500 for a 'Village Theatre' project.
It is decided to insure the fete under two headings:
a Against damage to the public, or local residents, during the fete.
b Against bad weather, in the sum of £500.
Write to the Rural Insurance Co Ltd, of 2073 Leadenhall Street,
London, EC3 asking for a proposal form. Use your own name and
address, as treasurer of the Festival Committee.

2 Reply to the Committee (see Question 1) enclosing two proposal forms and referring to the scale of charges included in the sections on 'Instructions for Completion'. Ask that the premium be sent with the completed proposal form, so that if the proposal is accepted the event can be 'held covered' forthwith.

3 You wish your broker, T Smallwood and Co (Leadenhall) Ltd, of 3074 Lime Street, London, EC3 2PQ to arrange insurance for you for the following:

> 5000 sheets corrugated iron from Liverpool to Beira via Suez Canal, to be shipped on SS *Coral Coast* on 15 May 19--. Cover to include war risks and specifically mention possibility of Suez Canal closure. Estimated invoice value including freight and 10 per cent profit margin £27 500.

Write the letter on behalf of your employers Huyton Iron Merchants (Widnes) Ltd, 2074 Dock Way, Widnes, Lancs.

4 *a* Messrs Millington & Co (Southwark) Ltd of 2465 The Cut, Southwark, London SE1 2DT ask the Regal Insurance Company to survey their premises with a view to covering against fire the premises themselves and their stock of woollen goods. Write this letter, to their Head Office at 2045 The Dean's Way, Westminster, London, SW1 1PD.

 b Having inspected the premises, the Regal Insurance Company point out that owing to such internal hazards as wooden staircases with lift wells and such external hazards as proximity to a timber yard, they cannot grant cover on the premises at less than £1.50 per £100. They would reduce this figure to £1 per cent when a sprinkler device which they have drawn to the attention of the firm's safety officer is installed and operational. They also refer to their willingness to cover the stock, but would require a daily tally system to be set up to ensure that a knowledge of stock levels was available at all times.

5 Instruct your agent in Singapore to scrutinise very carefully claims submitted by a local importer, who is suspected of claiming for losses which occur in premises other than the insured premises.

6 Notify your insurers of a small fire at your premises. Ask them to send you a claim form and to arrange for an early inspection as you are anxious to restore order as soon as possible.

7 Goods arriving by sea in a container carried by a Combined Transport Operator are seriously damaged by sea water. Notify the carrier, Longhaul Container Co (Southampton) Ltd, that you are holding them responsible and asking them to appoint a surveyor. This letter should be addressed to the Agent, Mark Lane and Co, Harbour Way, Sydney, New South Wales. Your own address is Pilchards Quay, Crows Nest, Sydney, New South Wales.

Now write to your insurance brokers asking them to claim for you for the damage suffered, to the full invoice value of the goods, pending the results of the survey which you feel can only confirm your view that the goods are a total loss. They are Brigham, Young & Co, of Main Street, Crows Nest, Sydney.

8 You have received a claim from a merchant, Peter de Hooch, for damage by heavy seas to a shipment of sugar which was being taken ashore in small boats from a steamer some distance from shore. Point out that you have official evidence that on the day in question the sea was dead calm, with little or no wind. State that until he can reconcile these two conflicting statements no payment can be considered. His address is 2174 Harbour Street, Walvis Bay and your firm is Ison & Co, 259 St Mary Axe, London, EC3 2AB.

18.7 Appendix on the English language: the avoidance of slang and colloquialism

Slang words and phrases are never desirable in business correspondence. They are words and expressions which are in common use, but considered for some reason as outside the general body of standard English. They frequently start in a particular group — perhaps an ethnic group such as the Cockneys of London or a class or profession, such as the theatrical profession. Today the mass media may give a very wide currency to certain popular catchwords, while in wartime the vast numbers of people called into service may develop a specialist vocabulary of slang which passes into a wider use. Every pilot knows what a 'wizard prang' is, but it may turn into a 'prang' and eventually apply not only to an aircraft but to a motor car, or even a tray of teacups. The reader who cannot understand the last sentence will see why slang should be avoided — for not everyone knows what it means. This particular piece of slang is in the *Oxford English Dictionary,* which should be consulted by any perplexed reader.

A colloquialism is a word or expression which is on the verge of becoming slang. Thus a grand-daughter may be 'the apple of the old man's eye' to her grandfather, meaning that she is particularly dear to him. We speak of a character who is popular but not very well-mannered or cultivated as 'a rough diamond' and of a stupid person as 'thick in the head'. All these expressions are unsuitable for business use. Thus we do not write to a finance company saying:

'I am trying to *raise the wind* but my bank manager *smells a rat.*'

The very use of these phrases will lead the finance company to wonder whether a loan is desirable to a person who uses such informal expressions in formal correspondence. ('To raise the wind' is to borrow money, and to 'smell a rat' is to be suspicious of the real purpose of something.)

18.8 Exercises on the avoidance of slang

1 Re-phrase the following sentences to eliminate the phrases in italics:
  a The family interest is being maintained by Mr Mark Catesbey, who is *'a chip off the old block'.*
  b We are *under a cloud* as far as the Ministry is concerned at present, but we *begin to see a silver lining*.
  c Mr Hughes and I are *at loggerheads* at present and I should not wish *to rub him the wrong way* any more than I can help.
  d Shall we *put our foot in it* if we act before planning permission is confirmed?
  e I will have Mr Clarkson in the office and *haul him over the coals* for *letting the cat out of the bag,* but *it's no use crying over spilt milk.*

2 Replace the slang terms used in the following sentences by re-phrasing in standard English:
  a The price for this vehicle is two thousand five hundred *nicker*.
  b These American hotels charge fifty *smackers* for an overnight stay, but it does include a good dinner and an American breakfast.
  c Take care you are not *diddled* by these freight agents.
  d Thank you for arranging the lease for these new offices; we are certainly *on velvet* here.
  e I feel someone should sue him if only to *take the starch out of him.*

19 Personnel

19.1 Functions of the personnel department

The function of the personnel department is to find and recruit staff of the right type for every post within an organisation. Employees must have the right qualifications for the work they are to undertake. This may mean professional or educational qualifications, but it may also mean the correct physique, manual dexterity, mental qualities, toughness of character, etc. Asked what was the chief qualification for an engineering apprentice in a firm making bank safes the personnel officer replied 'Honesty'. Not quite what the young recruit was expecting, but obvious enough when you think about it.

The costs of finding suitable staff, inducting them into the firm, training them where necessary and re-training them to fit new developments in the industry or profession can be enormous. Labour turnover is a constant source of worry to managements, because the personnel costs are so high. Consequently personnel officers have an important part to play in retaining staff by encouraging staff loyalty in a variety of ways. Firms may offer staff 'perks' of various sorts: luncheon vouchers, staff shops where goods are available at discount prices, sports and clubhouse facilities, staff cars, etc. Personnel officers often supervise pension schemes, wages and incentive schemes, welfare services, etc. All these activities are important for the proper running of the firm, but their main purpose is to reduce labour turnover and ensure an adequate supply of the right quality of staff at all levels.

19.2 Personnel records: employee data folders

Adequate records are essential for any personnel department, and should be retained for many years, since inquiries from past employees are frequently made years later. One of the best sets of records available at present is that published by Formecon Services Ltd, Gateway, Crewe, CW1 1YN. It includes a data folder which becomes the employee's personal record with the company; two types of application

INDUCTION CHECKLIST

NEW EMPLOYEE FULL NAME	
DEPARTMENT & JOB	DATE STARTED

The object of good induction training is to obtain the best performance from the new employee and to relieve anxiety. Try to complete this form on the first day. Put a tick in each box when each point is understood by the new employee.

On completion hand second copy to new employee and return top copy to...

GENERAL INFORMATION		RULES, HEALTH AND SAFETY	
1. COMPLETE EMPLOYEE DATA FOLDER		31. COMPANY RULES (HAND COPY TO EMPLOYEE)	
2. OBTAIN P45 FORM (IF AVAILABLE)		32. DISCIPLINARY PROCEDURE AND APPEALS	
3. PROVIDE WRITTEN OR VERBAL JOB DESCRIPTION		33. INFORM WHERE FACTORIES/OFFICES ACT DISPLAYED	
4. EXPLAIN RATES OF PAY (a) BASIC		34. TIME KEEPING AND RECORDING	
5. (b) OVERTIME		35. LATENESS — EFFECT ON PAY	
6. (c) BONUS/COMM.		36. ILLNESS — SICK NOTE REQUIREMENTS	
7. (d) HOLIDAY PAY		37. ILLNESS — EFFECT ON PAY	
8. HOW, WHEN & WHERE PAID		38. ACCEPTABLE REASONS FOR TIME OFF OR ABSENCE	
9. HOURS OF WORK (OR SHIFTS IF ANY)		39. ABSENCE — EFFECT ON PAY AND COMPANY	
10. BREAKS		40. AFTER ABSENCE REPORT TO....................................	
11. OVERTIME AVAILABILITY AND ARRANGEMENTS		41. PROCEDURE FOR ARRANGING TIME OFF	
12. DEDUCTIONS (a) SAVINGS		42. SMOKING REGULATIONS	
13. (b) CHARITABLE		43. FIRE DRILL (a) WHAT TO DO	
14. (c) TRADE UNION (VIA COMPANY)		44. (b) EMERGENCY EXITS	
15. (d) OTHER (e.g. social club)		45. (c) WHERE TO ASSEMBLE	
16. EXPLAIN PAY SLIP FORMAT		46. (d) WHO TO REPORT TO	
17. CONFIRM COMPANY HOLIDAY ARRANGEMENTS		47. (e) LOCATION OF FIRE FIGHTING EQUIP.	
18. EXPLAIN HOLIDAY QUALIFICATIONS		48. SPECIAL SAFETY PRECAUTIONS/HEALTH HAZARDS	
19. CHECK CONFLICTING HOLIDAY COMMITMENTS		49. SAFETY REGS. AND POLICY STATEMENT (Show copy)	
20. PENSION SCHEMES AND/OR STATE SCHEME		50. YOUR SAFETY OFFICER/REP. IS..........................	
21. CANTEEN FACILITIES		51. SAFETY CLOTHING/SHOES/GLOVES/ETC.	
22. SOCIAL AND RECREATIONAL FACILITIES		52. EAR/EYE PROTECTORS/HELMETS/BARRIER CREAMS ETC	
23. TRANSPORT AND PARKING		53. SAFETY CLOTHING/PROTECTORS Obtain from..............	
24. PERSONAL PROBLEMS CONSULT......................		54. LIFTING AND HANDLING INSTRUCTIONS	
25. TRADE UNION MEMBERSHIP AND THE COMPANY		55. ENCOURAGE TIDINESS TO REDUCE ACCIDENTS	
26. COMPANY/GROUP PRODUCTS OR SERVICES		56. ACCIDENTS/Dangerous Occurences report to..............	
27. COMPANY HISTORY		57. ACCIDENT BOOK/Gen. Register held by......................	
28. COMPANY ORGANISATION AND COMMITTEES		58. FIRST AID BOX/ROOM IS SITED AT............................	
29. EDUCATION TRAINING PROMOTION AND TRANSFER		59. FIRST AID OFFICER IS..	
30. SUGGESTION SCHEME (give booklet if available)		60. EMPLOYEE COMPLAINTS are dealt with by..................	
61. TOUR OF PREMISES:— *Introduce to other members of department and ensure that they will help the newcomer to settle down. Explain each persons job. Point out location of toilets, washroom, lockers, cloakroom, fire exits and equipment, first aid box/room, canteen, special hazards and prohibited areas etc.*		I have received the above induction training:- New employee signature	
		Induction Supervised by:— Signature on behalf of employer	
62. OTHER INFORMATION:		Notes	

Fig. 19.1 A useful form for the induction of personnel

form to be completed by applicants for employment; an interview record to be completed by members of the selection panel at an interview; an induction check-list; an attendance record card, etc. Such a range of forms will save personnel staff hours of work, and provide a framework of records to meet almost all eventualities. The thorough coverage given to each area is best illustrated by an example. Figure 19.1 shows the induction check-list to ensure that every new employee is thoroughly briefed on the company, its history, activities, organisation and procedures. The reader is recommended to consider Fig. 19.1 in detail.

19.3   Routine correspondence from the personnel department

SL19.1

Giwa Mining Developments Ltd

2071 Mkusi Road, Kabwe, Zambia

13 August 19--   Your Ref: Letter of 4 August 19--
                                   Our Ref: KK/ab

Thomas Cook Esq
2174 Leyden Lane
Loughborough
Leicestershire
England

Dear Mr Cook

Thank you for your application for the post of mining engineer's assistant, forwarded to me from our London office. We hope to appoint some new staff in October, and your degree appears to be relevant. Will you please complete the enclosed application form and send it to me here by air mail, together with two references one of which should be from your University tutor. I will then let you know whether we can call you for interview.

Yours faithfully

Keis Khamis
Personnel Manager

THE OFFSHORE BANK LTD

2074 Chapman's Quay
Cayman Islands

Your Ref: Application No 21
Our Ref: JD/TD

1 July 19--

Miss Mary Cordoba
2147 Portobello Road
London W11 2DT

Dear Miss Cordoba

I am pleased to advise you that your application to join the bank
has been successful, and we are able to offer you an appointment in
the Investment Department starting on 1 September 19--. Your ability
to speak both Spanish and French was one factor which influenced your
selection and we hope that after suitable training in investment
banking you will join a team of negotiators handling our Latin-American
and European business.

Would you please let me know at once if you are prepared to accept the
post, and I will then send you full details of the joining procedure,
medical arrangements, work permit regulations, etc.

May I congratulate you on your success, and express the hope that you
will find working in the Cayman Islands both interesting and rewarding.

Yours sincerely

Jonathan Davidson
Personnel Officer

Personnel Officer, Gary and Clements Ltd

To   Peter Dawson, Base Metal Shop   27 October 19--

Dear Mr Dawson

Disciplinary Panel - Decision

I am writing to you formally to let you know the decision of the
Disciplinary Panel as a result of the incident last week, when you
struck your foreman, Mr W Whitelaw, and used abusive language to him.
The ruling of the panel, which was unanimous, was as follows:

1. You are formally reprimanded for your behaviour, which was dis-
graceful, and could easily have led to a court action for assault.
Mr Whitelaw appealed to the Panel on your behalf, stating that your
work was of a good quality, and your apprenticeship so nearly completed that dismissal would have an impact on your future career out
of all proportion to the offence - bad though it was.

2. You will lose any merit reward which would normally have been
accorded to you on 31 December, and will be fined the sum of £10
which will be deducted from your wages and contributed instead to
the Welfare Fund.

3. If there is any repetition of this type of behaviour you will be
dismissed without notice. The Panel believe that the incident would
not have occurred had you not been slightly affected by drinking
alcohol during the lunch break and they strongly recommend you avoid
this practice in future.

4. Finally the Panel hope that you will apologise to Mr Whitelaw in
a quiet moment and restore the good relationship which formerly
existed. While such a blot on your record cannot be easily wiped out,
we do feel that you have a solid future at Gary and Clements Ltd, and
need not fear that this incident will be held against you in the future
if you re-establish yourself as a dependable and respected employee.

P Donnelly
Secretary to the Disciplinary Panel
Personnel Officer

```
Memo to: Tomasina Bell

From:     Personnel Officer                    Date: 27 July 19--
_____

Thank you for agreeing to take part in the interviewing panel on
Friday, at 10.00 am.  We are selecting two out of nine candidates
in the general field of fashion design, but especially for ladies'
blouses and children's wear.  Herewith photocopies of the nine appli-
cation forms, and nine 'Employment Interview' forms from Formecon.
Please go through the applications and prepare questions to all candi-
dates - especially in your own field.  Leave the general questions to
Mr Marshall and myself.

Please note that the last three are students.  Mr Marshall feels that
even though we only have two jobs really, we could easily take on one
(or even two) of these if they show a bit of talent.  It would give
them a start and even if they leave us later we would have their help
for routine work in the busy period leading up to the September show.
I've asked them to bring in a bit of work - final college creations
etc.  Perhaps you'd have a look at it during the interview.  Once
again - thanks for your help.  We'll use No 1 Interview Room, in the
Tower Building.
_____

Answer required:  No                         Signed: Richard Denova
```

19.4 Employment agencies and the personnel department

It is frequently more economical and more satisfactory to employ a specialist employment agency to recruit staff of a particular type. Thus there are specialist employment agencies for clerical and secretarial staff, accountancy staff, nurses, chefs and other catering workers, etc. The whole field is very competitive, so that charges to firms are reasonable, and the expertise of dealing with particular classes of staff is available to relieve the pressure on personnel officers. Such specialists will draw up job-descriptions; secure advertising space; write advertising copy; consider applications and send 'letters of regret' to those who are manifestly unsuited to the post; draw up a short list of candidates and join a panel of interviewers to assist in the actual selection process. For some important posts, where only a few candidates are available in the world, interviews are conducted over the international telephone to enable an applicant to be questioned by a panel of selectors.

19.5　Correspondence and employment agencies

SL19.5

Executemps Limited

Atlantic House, 351 Oxford Street, London W1R 1FA. Tel 01 409 2766
Offices in Australia, Birmingham, Glasgow, Leeds, London, Manchester
Newcastle, Nottingham, Preston and Sheffield

A division of Hoggett Bowers & Partners Ltd　　　　　　　　　　*Recruitment Consultants*

Your Ref:　AL/CD
　　　　　　　24th September

Our Ref:　　VMC/var

Mr N Little
Finance Manager
Uniroyal Ltd
62-64 Horseferry Road
London
SW1 2AH　　　　　　　　　　　　27th September 19·

Dear Mr Little

For many years Executemps has specialised in the supply of
temporary accounting staff at all levels within commerce
and industry throughout the UK, Europe and Middle East.

As part of the Hoggett Bowers Group we work to a strict
professional standard, maintaining and developing our
business by personal visits to existing and prospective
clients.

I would appreciate the opportunity of meeting you to discuss
more fully our operation and principles, and to determine
any possible application our services could have within your
organisation, either immediately or over the longer term.

With this in mind I shall look forward to contacting you in
due course.　In the meantime, please contact me if I can be
of assistance in any way.

Yours sincerely

V M Crawford (Mrs)
Director

Registration No 1185578 Registered in England at 41A New Crown Street, Halifax

Employment Agencies Act 1973　Licence No SE(A) 1229

Fig. 19.2　A letter from a specialist recruitment consultancy

Executemps Limited

Atlantic House, 351 Oxford Street, London W1R 1FA. Tel: 01 409 2766
Offices in Australia, Birmingham, Glasgow, Leeds, London, Manchester
Newcastle, Nottingham, Preston and Sheffield

A division of Hoggett Bowers & Partners Ltd   *Recruitment Consultants*

Your Ref: Letter dated
                21st October 19--
Our Ref: VMC/TD

B Smith Esq
43 Lexington Road
London
NW3 4BS   22nd October 19--

Dear Mr Smith

Thank you for your letter giving us an outline of your career
details to date, and enquiring about the possibility of
temporary work.

As you know Executemps specialises in the provision of
accountancy staff and I see that you have in fact completed
up to Professional Part I of your Cost and Management qualification. It is possible that we could offer you some temporary
work but prior to an assignment it is necessary to interview
you, and with this in mind perhaps you could contact me as soon
as possible to arrange a convenient date.

In the meantime I am enclosing an application form for
completion and I look forward to hearing from you shortly.

Yours sincerely

V M Crawford (Mrs)
Director

Enc.

Registration No 1185578 Registered in England at 41A New Crown Street, Halifax
Employment Agencies Act 1973 Licence No SE(A) 1229

Fig. 19.3 A response to an application, offering an interview

Tyzack & Partners Ltd.

P. T. Prentice

R. T. Addis	A. Longland
A. Barker	C. A. Riley
D. A. O. Davies	J. L. Rogers
J. E. B. Drake	K. R. C. Slater
G. W. Elms	J. B. Tonkinson
N. C. Humphreys	Dr. R. F. Tuckett
P. A. R. Lindsay	Sir Peter Youens

Scotland

P. Craigie	B. N. Innes-Will
J. A. Sturrock	

RTA:jb:56

10 Hallam Street,
London, W1N 6DJ

Tel. 01-580 2924/7

Cables TYZACKLON LONDON

and at

21 Ainslie Place
Edinburgh, EH3 6AJ

Tel. 031-226 6112/3

11 November 19--

**Personal and
Confidential**

Mrs A Cook
53 Queens Street
Rochester
Kent

Dear Mrs Cook

Thank you for coming to see me.

After careful thought in the light of our discussion, I have come to the
conclusion that the background and experience of other applicants are
more closely in line with the appointment than your own. I would not
feel justified, therefore, in putting your name forward for consideration
by the company.

As I explained to you when we met I would like to retain your papers, in
strict confidence, as it is always possible we may be asked to help on
other appointments which may interest you.

I am glad to have met you and hope that this decision will not be too
disappointing.

Yours sincerely

R T Addis
Partner

Directors: Sir Harold Atcherley (Chairman), P. T. Prentice MBE (Managing Partner)
Secretary. Miss B. G. Betts ACIS
Licensed by the Department of Employment (Licence No. SE (A) 1528)
Registered Office: 15/17 Eldon Street, London EC2M 7LJ. Registration: London—628523
Associates in Hong Kong, New York, Brussels and throughout Australasia

Fig. 19.4 A letter of rejection

Tyzack & Partners Ltd.

P. T. Prentice

R. T. Addis	A. Longland
A. Barker	C. A. Riley
D. A. O. Davies	J. L. Rogers
J. E. B. Drake	K. R. C. Slater
G. W. Elms	J. B. Tonkinson
N. C. Humphreys	Dr. R. F. Tuckett
P. A. R. Lindsay	Sir Peter Youens

Scotland

P. Craigie	B. N. Innes-Will
	J. A. Sturrock

10 Hallam Street,
London, W1N 6DJ
Tel. 01-580 2924/7
Cables TYZACKLON LONDON

and at

21 Ainslie Place
Edinburgh, EH3 6AJ
Tel. 031-226 6112/3

Our ref: RTA:jb

11 November 19--

Personal and
Confidential

T Thomas Esq
5 The Drive
Birmingham B2

Dear Mr Thomas

I was delighted to learn from Brian Hill that you have accepted their offer of appointment and will be joining A & K Ltd as Financial Controller at the end of December.

Please accept my congratulations and best wishes for your future success in this new appointment.

Yours sincerely

R T Addis
Partner

Directors: Sir Harold Atcherley (Chairman), P. T. Prentice MBE (Managing Partner)
Secretary: Miss B. G. Betts ACIS
Licensed by the Department of Employment (Licence No. SE (A) 1528)
Registered Office: 15/17 Eldon Street, London EC2M 7LJ. Registration: London—628523
Associates in Hong Kong, New York, Brussels and throughout Australasia

Fig. 19.5 A letter of congratulation

Atlantic House, 351 Oxford Street, London W1R 1FA. Tel: 01 409 2766
Offices in Australia, Birmingham, Glasgow, Leeds, London, Manchester
Newcastle, Nottingham, Preston and Sheffield

A division of Hoggett Bowers & Partners Ltd   *Recruitment Consultants*

His Excellency Shaik Abdullah   Your Ref: SA/DC
Metal Products Corporation   Our Ref: VMC/var
Refinery Road
Awali
Bahrain Island   18th May 19

Your Excellency

<u>Accounting Staff for Bahrain</u>

Thank you for your enquiry about expatriate accounting staff
prepared to work in Bahrain. We shall certainly be willing
to act on your behalf in this matter, and we have a panel
of qualified professional staff who could assist in interviewing applicants.

The best way to proceed is to send full details to me about
the posts you wish to fill, giving accurate job descriptions
and some indication of your preferences as to the qualifications
you feel are appropriate to each post. I will pass these to
our executives and they will take action accordingly. If you
let us know as soon as the itinerary is agreed for your visit
to the United Kingdom we shall arrange the interviews of short-
listed candidates to fit into your main programme.

We shall need to prepare advertisements on your behalf for
these posts. I am enclosing copy for two recent advertisements
so that you can see the style, and also typical details which
we shall need to know for each post concerned.

We look forward to hearing from you in due course.

Yours sincerely

V M Crawford (Mrs)
Director

Registration No. 1185578 Registered in England at 41A New Crown Street, Halifax

Employment Agencies Act 1973 Licence No. SE(A) 1229

Fig. 19.6 **Recruiting expatriate staff**

SL19.10 (Advertising copy for SL19.9)

```
                    COMMERCIAL  DIRECTOR

    *    THIS is a major opportunity to join a very large City-based com-
    pany.  A world leader in the provision of financial services, the
    company has a network of regional offices throughout the UK.

    *    THE ROLE is to devise and direct the commercial opportunities of
    the company in a wide range of fields.  The appointment includes
    significant line management responsibility, and the ability to com-
    municate with major clients at the highest level is essential.

    *    PREREQUISITES are professional or business school qualification
    or an Honours Degree with experience in line management on the com-
    mercial side of a substantial company.  The ability to contribute
    fully within a demanding environment is a major requirement.

    *    TERMS are for discussion.  £25 000 is the salary indicator, with
    a comparable benefits package.  Age under 45.

    *    INTERESTED applicants wishing to join this progressive company
    should write enclosing a detailed curriculum vitae.

    Executemps Ltd, 351 Oxford Street, London, W1R 1FA.
```

19.6 Exercises on personnel correspondence

1 The personnel officer of Melvyn Park Group Ltd replies to Arthur Reeves, a toolmaker, to thank him for his inquiry about employment in the firm's Australian subsidiary. He encloses an application form and promises to interview Mr Reeves as soon as possible, but also inquires whether he appreciates that it will be essential for his family to move with him to Melbourne, Australia. In his reply will he please assure them that his wife is in agreement with this idea.

2 Duracove Well-Plugging Ltd have a worldwide market for their technical services on oil and gas fields. They place an advertisement in the *Young Engineer* offering posts for graduates in mechanical engineering under 30 years of age, prepared to travel to trouble spots around the world after specialised training in their works training department. Salary will be in the range of £8000-£15 000 depending upon age and experience. Opportunities for promotion are excellent and facilities are available for short-stay visits by wives and dependants while on foreign attachments. Applicants should apply to the personnel department, Duracove Well-Plugging Ltd, Galveston, Texas, USA. Write the copy for this advertisement.

3 Write a letter as personnel officer of Thameshaven Television Ltd, inviting Mary Brown, of 22 York Way, Thameshaven, Kent, to come for interview at 10 am on Monday, 1 September to the studios at Riverview Road, Thameshaven.

4 Write a letter to Olaf Olaleye of 22 Refinery Way, Port Harcourt, Nigeria, referring to his poor attendance at work recently. Ask if he has any explanation for this unsatisfactory state of affairs, i.e. family difficulties or poor health? Warn him that if no satisfactory explanation is provided consideration will be given to dismissing him with effect from the last day of the month. Sign your own name as personnel officer of the Independence Refinery, Port Harcourt.

5 Write a circular to be sent to the 54 recruits on a technical training course at the local technical college associated with a major employer in the area. As personnel officer welcome them to the course, congratulate them on their passing the entrance examination and express the hope that they will take every advantage of the opportunity being offered to them. Assure them that success on the course leads to a good post in an established industry with a great future.

6 Write the text of an advertisement for an employment opportunity in any local firm with which you are familiar. Give a description of the work involved, the salary available, the qualifications required and the deadline for applications. Invite applicants to write to you, as personnel officer of the firm concerned.

7 Write a letter to an imaginary firm in a field of employment which interests you, and in which you would have some prospect of gaining employment. Give full details of yourself, your qualifications and your work experience to date.

8 Two advertisements in an evening paper read as follows:
   a Receptionist secretary/man-girl Friday required for small textile company. Must be reliable and have energy and initiative. Write for application form to the personnel officer, Khartoum Fabrics Co, Avenue de Toussaint, Paris, France.
   b Accountancy junior required, book-keeping to trial balance essential, suit second-job applicant or well-qualified college leaver. Apply to personnel officer, Multiple Plastics Ltd, 2045 Crown Way, Chelmsford, Essex.
   Apply for one of these posts giving a full account of yourself.

19.7   Appendix on the English language: avoidance of clichés

A cliché is a word or phrase which has been so over-used that it has lost its original meaning. Often we read in the newspapers or hear on the radio and television about the latest sporting or entertainment 'super-star'; the phrase 'super-star' is used so frequently that it has lost its original force as a description of a highly talented and popular person, and is instead applied to almost anyone in the public eye for a short time.

Although newspapers are generally most guilty of the use of clichés, we should all avoid the use of outworn phrases in our communications. In the past businesses have developed forms of commercial English which have been so over-used that they have become clichés, verbose and even meaningless. For example the following phrases using commercial clichés could be rewritten in more direct English.

i   'We beg to acknowledge receipt of your letter' could become 'Thank you for your letter'.
ii   'It will be our earnest endeavour . . .' may be written 'We will try . . .'
iii 'We have initiated the necessary inquiries . . .' simply means 'We have started to inquire . . .'

You should remember that good communication depends on a clear, precise use of language, and that the use of commercial jargon or clichés in business letters should be avoided.

19.8   Exercises on the avoidance of clichés

1 Explain clearly the following clichés:
   a to make both ends meet   e a dead cert
   b strike while the iron is hot   f a fly in the ointment
   c to throw in the sponge   g not worth the candle
   d to keep a thing dark   h the thin end of the wedge

2 Rewrite these sentences in more direct English, paying particular attention to the words in italics:
   a *It is our opinion* that the manager was correct.
   b *It is incumbent upon us* to inform you of the details.
   c *I beg to offer my services* as a typist for your firm.

d *We wish to acknowledge the receipt* of your letter dated 16 October 19--.

e *Pending the arrival of the goods detailed* in our catalogue, *we beg to inform you* that we are *withholding all payment due.*

20 Conferences and functions

20.1 The importance of conferences and functions to large firms

Today firms tend to be large and impersonal, with top management located at a head office which may be thousands of miles from individual plants, workshops, depots and sales outlets where the ordinary activities of manufacture, distribution and selling take place. As a result problems of internal communication arise, while the firm's impact on local communities may also call for conferences, seminars and public relations functions. The arrangements for conferences and functions can be extremely complex, and generate a great deal of business correspondence. Usually an executive will be appointed to undertake the supervision of the arrangements but the main body of the work will fall upon the executive's personal assistant, or personal secretary. The executive is concerned with the purpose of the conference, its place in achieving the objectives of management, and its success judged by the results obtained. The personal assistant is concerned with the whole range of detailed arrangements necessary for this success.

20.2 The organisation of conferences and functions

Whenever a conference or function is to be held the organisation starts with the opening of a file. At first this will outline the event; its purpose; the stages necessary to achieve the objective, etc. Later certain detailed activities may be separated into special files so that particular individuals may be made responsible for particular aspects. Thus the dispatch of invitations, and the handling of the responses may be a full-time responsibility of one clerk. The hiring, installation and maintenance of visual aids, display material, electrical and electronic equipment may be an essential element supervised by a technician with appropriate experience. If costing is important an accounts clerk may assume responsibility for budgeting, and monitoring costs as they occur, to ensure that the budget is not exceeded.

Check-lists of activities will be drawn up to ensure that every eventuality is envisaged and arrangements are made to meet it. It is impossible to list every requirement here, but some of the usual steps are described below:

a Preparation of a detailed programme with the conference organiser, to ensure that the objectives of management will be achieved.

b Contact guest speakers, celebrities or members of staff taking part to ensure that they are available and willing to appear. It may be necessary to agree terms with agents and draw up contracts with them.

c Arrange the venue, the detailed accommodation and sign contracts for its use. If it is 'in house' accommodation book it with the appropriate executive and get written acknowledgment of the booking, so that double-booking cannot occur. It is essential to inspect the accommodation to ensure it is adequate for the purpose. You may require meeting halls, a conference office, restaurant facilities, car parking space, toilet facilities, security surveillance, etc.

d Advertising the function may be important. This may require space to be booked in trade magazines or the daily press. It may require brochures to be written, leaflets to be distributed, in-house literature to be prepared, or even radio and television publicity to be devised. Call in the experts early for all these activities!

e Prepare invitations, programme notes, etc. Check all such material carefully so that details such as dates, times, venues, etc., are not omitted. Postage costs are high, and the labour involved in sending letters correcting or amplifying an invitation is enormous. If applications are invited a tear-off application form should be incorporated.

f Many conventions and seminars require the organisers to prepare a folder for distribution to each visitor. This requires a considerable amount of preparation, with the necessary lecture notes, diagrams and charts arranged in correct order; agenda prepared; plans of the buildings made available in case they are needed, etc. A well-staffed distribution centre may be necessary on the morning the conference starts, to ensure that the folders for each visitor can be found and given out. Frequently the same distribution centre is used at departure to make a small presentation to all visitors or delegates as they leave (see SL20.2 below).

g Transport often presents problems at such functions. It may be necessary to collect VIPs from stations or overnight accommodation; coaches may be needed for business or social visits; car parking and official or police supervision may have to be arranged.

Clearly there is much to do, but the basic requirement is for the organisers to 'think through' every proposal to its logical conclusion, so that every aspect is anticipated and adequate preparation made.

20.3   Letters about arrangements

SL20.1

City of London

Barbican Centre
for Arts and Conferences

Administrator
Henry Wrong

11 Cromwell Tower
Barbican
London EC2Y 8DD

Telephone
National 01-638 4141
International + 44 1 638 4141

Telegrams
Barbicen London EC2

PDC/8001-BI/ch   14 July 19--

Congress Organiser
4 International Congress on Viral Infections
International Society of Biorheology
c/o Division of Neurology
University of Great Falls
Health Science Centre
Great Falls
Oregon   97201
USA

Dear Sir or Madam

4 International Congress on Viral Biology

We note that the above congress will take place in Tokyo,
Japan, between 27 July and 1 August 19--, and in simple
terms we should like to encourage your organisation to
consider London, and our Centre in particular, as a possible
future venue.

The Barbican Centre is a new and exciting complex, situated
in the heart of the City of London and scheduled for completion
late this year; we are currently accepting bookings from
1 October 19-- onwards. Our main auditorium will accommodate
2000 delegates in plenary session, and additional theatres are
under construction for 1150, 280, 255 and 153 delegates,
together with a wide range of seminar and committee rooms.
We shall also have 86,000 square feet gross exhibition space
in two adjoining halls.

I am enclosing a copy of our conference brochure, and I
should welcome your guidance as to how the venue decision is
made, and whether there are any steps we might take to invite
your congress to our Centre.

Yours faithfully

Susan Robinson
Conference Sales Director

Enc

Fig. 20.1 A letter about conference facilities

Registered No. 162757. E gland   Established 1871

Advertising, Promotional & Goodwill Gifts — Cigars — Wines

REGD OFFICES & SHOWROOMS
WEST GATE . LONG EATON
NOTTINGHAM NG10 1EG
TELEPHONE LONG EATON (060-76) 4457

Your ref: TC/AB
Our ref: RA/JG

31 October 19--

Miss Penelope Masters
Word Processing (Ongar) Ltd
2094 Burnham Road
Ongar
Essex

Dear Miss Masters

<u>WORD PROCESSING EXHIBITION, COMMERCIAL HOTEL, ONGAR</u>

Thank you for your kind enquiry for Advertising and Promotional Gifts for use
at the above Exhibition. As requested, please find enclosed our general
catalogue and price list. We recommend the following as most relevant:

1) Mail shot enclosures to encourage visitors to your stand – see pages 3-5
2) Lapel Badges, Ties, for Stand Personnel – see pages 5-6
3) Folders etc, for presentation of Company literature – see pages 7-10
4) Give-away marketing aids for product promotion – for both Buyers and
    end-users – see pages 12-17
5) Bearing in mind that visitors to the Exhibition may be home later than
    usual, a small gift for the visitor to take home would create considerable
    goodwill – see pages 20-22.

Keeping within your budget is most important and we would recommend that our
District Representative makes an appointment to call and discuss your requirements in more detail. Alternatively, we will be pleased to forward samples.

We look forward to hearing from you and of being of service to you,

Yours sincerely
JOSIAH BROWN LTD

Roger D. Alton

R D Alton
Director

YOUR GOODWILL IS OUR BUSINESS

Fig. 20.2 A letter about business gifts

City of London

Administrator
Henry Wrong

**Barbican
Centre**
for Arts and Conferences

11 Cromwell Tower
Barbican
London EC2Y 8DD

Telephone
National 01-638 4141
International +44 1 638 4141

Telegrams
Barbicen London EC2

PDC/mmb-vk/7015

26 February 19--

Mrs P Smith
Conference Organizers Limited
3 New Street
London
EC2Y 8DD

Dear Mrs Smith

International Microbiology Convention Conference 19--

Referring to our telephone conversation yesterday, I enclose
a cost indication based on the outline programme suggested
by you at January 19-- rates.

Regarding dates, the following would be available:-
Monday 7 May to Friday 11 May inclusive
Monday 14 May to Friday 18 May inclusive
Monday 21 May to Friday 25 May inclusive

The week commencing Monday 28 May is reserved for a client.
It would be possible to note on the schedule a request for
first refusal on that week. I shall not reserve any of
these dates for FIADAI until I hear from you.

Please let me know if there is anything further we can do.
If you think it would be of value to ask the Committee to
visit the Centre, please do let me know.

Best wishes.

Yours sincerely

Susan Robinson
Conference Sales Director

Enc

Fig. 20.3 A letter about conference arrangements

COST INDICATION

INTERNATIONAL MICROBIOLOGY CONVENTION CONFERENCE 19--

Sunday	:	setting up registration	
	pm:	Seminar Rooms I, II and III	
Monday	am:	Opening Ceremony	Barbican Hall
	pm:	Working Sessions " " " " " "	Barbican Hall Cinema 2 Cinema 3 Seminar Room I
Tuesday) Wednesday) Thursday)	am:	Working Sessions " "	Barbican Hall Cinema 3
	pm:	Working Sessions " " " "	Cinema 2 Cinema 3 Seminar Room I
Friday	am:	Working Sessions " " " "	Cinema 2 Cinema 3 Seminar Room I
	pm:	Closing Ceremony	Barbican Hall

£10 470 + 10% service charge
+ VAT

February 19--

City of London

Barbican Centre
for Arts and Conferences

Administrator
Henry Wrong

11 Cromwell Tower
Barbican
London EC2Y 8DD

Telephone
National 01-638 4141
International + 44 1 638 4141

Telegrams
Barbicen London EC2

AW/VM/E.12.8.1   18 July 19--

The Duty Officer
City of London Police
A Department
37 Wood Street
London
EC2V 7HN

Dear Sir

Barbican Committees Chairmen's Reception

This is to notify you that the Chairmen of the Barbican
Committees will be holding their annual reception at the
Guildhall School of Music and Drama at 6.00 pm on Thursday
24 July, attended by the Lord Mayor. Access for the
approximately 600 guests will be via Silk Street. I am
sure that you already know that there is also a reception
attended by HRH Prince Charles at Whitbreads the same
evening.

I believe that it would be desirable if a degree of traffic
control could be arranged in this area to prevent undue
congestion.

Yours faithfully

Angus Watson
Head of Publicity

Fig. 20.4 A letter about a formal reception

Chewton Glen Hotel

New Milton, Hampshire, England BH25 6QS   Telephone Highcliffe (04252) 5341   Telex 41456

MS/BST   ★★★★   December 19--

Dear Member

We are very grateful to the General Secretary of your Organisation for
allowing us to contact you through the medium of your December Newsletter.

Chewton Glen is a privately owned deluxe country house hotel with fifty
bedrooms, situated on the fringe of the New Forest.   For your information,
I am enclosing our current house brochure and tariff.

For a few years now we have been specialising in providing facilities for
small meetings at director and top executive levels.   We have a purpose
built board-room which can accommodate up to forty people and we also have
eight smaller suites, accommodating up to ten people.

Over the years, we have built up a great deal of expertise in looking after
these important meetings and I would be very pleased to hear from you if you
feel that the executives in your company would like further details.

If you would like one of our special conference brochures, together with our
all-in conference rates, please feel free to contact either myself, or our
Conference and Banqueting Organiser, Mrs Susan Kimpton.

Yours sincerely

Martin Skan

Chewton Glen Hotel
owned by Skan Developments Limited

Member of HOTEL REPRESENTATIVE INC.
RELAIS ET CHATEAUX
PRESTIGE HOTELS

Registration No. 864881 England
Registered Office:
Chewton Glen Hotel, New Milton, Hants BH25 6QS
Directors:
R.N. SKAN   Martin SKAN   S.E.M. SKAN

Fig. 20.5 A circular for distribution through a magazine of a professional organisation

The Institute of Hydrology

Benta Sebrang, Pahang, Malaysia

27 April 19--

Our Ref: ST/DC/1
Your Ref:

Dr P G Weisskopf
2048 Grahame Close
Blewbury
Oxfordshire
England

Dear Dr Weisskopf

Seminars on Water Quality: Chewton Glen Hotel, New Milton, Hampshire

I believe you are already aware that a group of scientists interested in water quality, with particular reference to pollution by agricultural fertilisers, is meeting in England from 24-28 July 19-- at the Chewton Glen Hotel, New Milton, Hampshire, BH25 6QS.

We should like to invite you to conduct two of these seminars, and to speak on the research you have recently undertaken with regard to the pollution of United Kingdom rivers by chemical run-off. Naturally we can offer you a fee on the scales usually paid to Principal Scientific Officers, and a per diem maintenance allowance for the five days of the conference, on the usual scale.

I understand the hotel has a wide variety of facilities for illustrating lectures, and will be pleased to discuss your requirements well in advance so that you are quite happy about the arrangements.

Would you please indicate as soon as possible by air mail whether you are willing to accept this invitation, and your preferred titles for the two lectures. A brief outline would assist the committee in preparing the conference brochure. Lecture notes are being prepared in the United Kingdom under the supervision of Dr Kaufmann, whom I believe you know personally. Would you please contact him directly about the preparation of this conference material, in good time.

Yours very sincerely

T Mersing
Conference Secretary

University of Thurrock

Woodview Road, Grays, Essex, England.   *Tel:* (0375) 46910

Our Ref: Health and Safety 1

25 April 19--

Heads of Department
Health and Safety Departments
All European Ports

Dear Sirs/Mesdames

CONFERENCE ON HEALTH AND SAFETY IN THE PORT TRANSPORT INDUSTRY

Developments in the port transport industry have brought many changes
in the conduct of port operations, which present new hazards to port
employees. They have also placed heavy responsibilities on management,
and led to substantial payments in compensation by insurers. In these
circumstances all ports are seeking ways to reduce the dangers, and
ensure adequate medical and health facilities. This University has
always had a particular interest in port activities, and our students
regularly visit continental ports. These visits have revealed the
patchy nature of the improvements being effected, and the need for a
mutual exchange of ideas.

To this end we have arranged a two-day conference on these problems at
the University. The details are as follows:

Venue: The College of Sea Law, University of Thurrock
Dates: Thursday and Friday, 24 and 25 July 19--
Cost: £240 including three nights at the Thamesview Hotel, Thurrock
        with full board, attendance at all conference functions and
        cars and coaches as required.
        Delegates must arrange their own transport to Thurrock by air
        or sea.

A brochure giving full details of the conference agenda, the names of
speakers and their curriculum vitae and the social functions arranged
is enclosed, together with an application form. Seating is available
for 500 delegates and early booking is recommended.

Yours faithfully

T S Concord
Course Organiser
College of Sea Law

University of Thurrock

Woodview Road, Grays, Essex, England.   *Tel:* (0375) 46910

Our Ref: Health and Safety 3/107

24 May 19--

J T Confreres
Avenue Charles de Gaulle 2021
Port de Ste Marie
France

Dear Sir

CONFERENCE ON HEALTH AND SAFETY IN THE PORT TRANSPORT INDUSTRY

Thank you for your completed application form and your deposit. I
now enclose the following documents

(a) Letter of acceptance as a delegate to the conference
(b) Details of accommodation made available for you and your wife,
and the separate booking for your daughter, who will be in an adjacent
room
(c) Current literature on London entertainments etc and details of
West End daytime excursions for visitors not attending the conference
(d) Receipt for your deposit. An official invoice will be issued for
the balance, and a personal invoice for your wife's and daughter's
accommodation.

We look forward to meeting you at the conference. Our representative,
Jill Seymour, will host a special function for non-conference visitors
on Wednesday 23 July at 6.00 pm at which the special excursion
arrangements will be explained. This will be followed by a sherry
party for all visitors at 6.45 pm, and dinner in the main dining hall.

Yours faithfully

T S Concord
Course Organiser
College of Sea Law

SL20.10

```
Memo from:  Head of Department
To:         Roger Walters                    Date:  6 July 19--
```

Message: At the meeting of the Health and Safety Sub-Committee it was
agreed that our department would provide and supervise the public relations equipment, display materials etc at the Conference on Health and
Safety in the Port Transport Industry on 24-25 July. I am therefore
appointing you to take personal charge of these aspects at the Conference. Would you please make yourself available tomorrow at 10 am for a
discussion of the requirements already passed to me by staff and visiting lecturers. At that meeting I will also discuss with you a small
budget for extra payments to technicians appointed to do overtime, and
also for payment to a limited group of students who can assist with the
fetching and carrying inevitable on these occasions on the two days of
the conference. It is better to have a few extra staff on these occasions, rather than too few. It will be necessary to cover these assistants by an insurance policy so please think about names and let me
have your suggestions - not necessarily tomorrow - but in good time for
cover to be arranged.

```
Reply required:  No                     Signed:  R Tweedsmuir
```

SL20.11

```
Memo from:  Head of Department
To:         All members of staff               Date:  20 July 19--
```

Message: I must remind all staff that the utmost cooperation is needed
if the two-day conference on Health and Safety in the Port Transport
Industry is to be successful next Thursday and Friday. We shall have
some 500 delegates from all the major ports in Europe present, and it
is essential that they are dealt with efficiently and courteously.
Please make yourselves thoroughly familiar with the individual parts
you are to play, referring to your head of division if you are in any
difficulty. Please attend punctually on both days, and be prepared to
stay as late as is necessary to ensure that the building is clear and
every guest has been transported to the hotel accommodation reserved
for him/her. The University will be on public display for two days at
this time, and your active participation in portraying the quality and
extent of our work will be appreciated.

```
Reply required:  No                     Signed:  R Tweedsmuir
```

Memo from: The Chancellor
To: All members of staff   **Date:** 28 July 19--

Message: I should like to convey my warmest thanks to all those who played a part in the Conference on Health and Safety in the Port Transport Industry last week. It was one of the most interesting conferences held in the University, and particularly appropriate for the port area we seek to serve. Several top-ranking officials from major European ports spoke to me in appreciation of the organisation, and expressed the view that it had made a major contribution to the harmonisation of port safety procedures.

The social arrangements made also called forth high praise for the consideration shown to wives, husbands and children who were non-conference visitors.

May I particularly praise the work of all those who carried out routine activities so willingly and unobtrusively. The presence of 500 delegates and 300 visitors was managed without any disturbance of normal timetables and with a universal good-humour which is much appreciated by the Governing Body.

Reply required: No   Signed: Westley

20.4   Exercises on conferences and functions

1 The management of the Association of Road Hauliers decide to run a conference on the carriage of dangerous goods by road. They propose to invite members to attend the one-day conference for a fee of £25. Value Added Tax at 15 per cent must be added to this charge. Make it clear that the fee includes a buffet lunch. The conference will hear talks on the following topics: (i) the European Convention on the Carriage of Dangerous Goods; (ii) precautions to be taken and warnings to be displayed; (iii) health and safety of employees; and (iv) insurance aspects of the carriage of dangerous goods. Write:

a A letter to be sent to all members inviting them to attend.

b An application form with instructions for payment.

2 Write the copy for an advertisement to be placed in *Road Transport,* the weekly magazine of the road haulage industry, about the conference mentioned above.

3 Mary Hampshire has been appointed organiser of a one-day seminar on Exporting to Zimbabwe. It will be held on 9 March 19-- at Mary's workplace, the Free Trade Hall, Liverpool. It will be sponsored by the local Chamber of Trade. Write the following letter and memo:

    a One from Mary to Mark Hewitt, a local audio-visual aids supplier, asking him to inspect the hall and consider what public equipment will be required. Outline some imaginary requirements.

    b One from Mary to chief groundsman, Liverpool Parks and Gardens, giving him the date of the seminar and requesting floral decorations for the hall, foyer and dining room at the Free Trade Hall. Ask him not to exceed a budget of £100.

4 Write a circular to be sent to all members of the Chamber of Trade who are exporters drawing their attention to the seminar referred to in Question 3. Ask them to support the Chamber of Trade by appointing one individual from each firm to assist on the day of the conference. It will be necessary to attend a briefing meeting at 2 pm on 8 March 19-- and to be in attendance from 8.45 am until 6 pm on the actual day. Design a tear-off slip at the bottom of the letter which can be used to notify Mary of the individual concerned. She needs to know the firm's name, address and telephone number, the name of the helper and his/her extension number, and the type of work normally performed by the individual named.

5 Write to the duty officer of your local police station requesting police cover for traffic and crowd control outside the Abbey Stadium on the occasion of an inter-town sports meeting on Saturday 16 July 19--. The athletic events start at 2.30 pm, but teams will be arriving by coach from noon onwards, and it is expected that 15 000 spectators will arrive by coach and car between 1.30 and 2.30 pm. The programme is estimated to be completed by 5.30 pm and considerable congestion may occur between 5.30 and 7 pm.

6 An exhibition of computer and word-processing equipment for business use is to be held at the Commercial Hotel, in Airport Approaches, at your local airport on Friday 27 October 19--. You have been appointed to make the detailed arrangements for the event. Accordingly write the following letters and memos:

    a A letter to Josiah Brown Ltd, West Gate, Long Eaton, Nottingham, NG10 1EG. They specialise in business gifts for advertising purposes. Ask them for a price list and catalogue containing suggestions for end-of-conference gifts to be presented to delegates on departure. Mention that some 500 business visitors are expected, of both sexes.

b Write copy for a newspaper advertisement to be inserted in your local newspaper advertising the event and referring to the revolution that has come over business correspondence as a result of the word processing facilities available.

c Write a letter to a leading personality of your choice as if you intended to invite him/her to open the exhibition and asking: (i) Will they be free — the opening ceremony would take place at 10.30 am? (ii) What fee would be payable? (iii) Who acts for him/her in the signing of contracts, etc?

d Write an internal memo to the head of caretaking staff asking him to nominate a team of six strong and helpful people to act as assistants on the two days before the exhibition and on the day itself, so that help is available to exhibitors when required. Ask him to be available on all three days as well, to supervise any arrangements. Assure him that the event will call for extra pay for all members of the caretaking staff required to attend.

7 You have just organised a convention on 'Passenger handling at major air terminals'. Write the following follow-up letters and memos:

a A letter to be sent to a major speaker at the convention, Miss Mary Brent, who spoke on the subject 'The problem of security'. She is the chief security officer of Mid-West Aviation Corporation, 2724 Lakeway Drive, Chicago, Illinois, USA. Her speech had attracted widespread interest, and had been highly praised by delegates.

b A letter to the chairman of the convention. He is Dr Mark Thyssen of Goethe Airport, West Germany. Not only did he make an amusing and original contribution to the debate in a paper entitled 'Handling the over-booked passenger', but his chairmanship during a final 'Brains Trust' session which concentrated rather too heavily on the problems posed by terrorist passengers, had been widely acknowledged as fair to all those involved, even the most forthright speakers having an opportunity to put their points of view.

c A letter to the Convention Centre, 2735 Airport Approaches in your own home area, thanking them for the arrangements made. Refer to the success of the convention, and in particular to the cooperation of the audio-visual team at the Centre who handled every mini-crisis speedily and efficiently. Express your willingness to use the Centre on a future occasion.

d A memo to all internal staff expressing your personal thanks for their assistance during the convention. Refer to its success, the credit it brought on the airport generally, and the high standard of cooperation of staff which had been commented on by visitors.

20.5 Appendix on the English language: the organisation of ideas

If your business letters and reports are to be as clear as possible you must take special care to organise your ideas and information into a sensible order. A report or consultative document which is not organised will lose much of its value as the reader has to waste his time trying to interpret the report instead of considering the value of its recommendations.

Often in business you may have to write an account of a certain event or sequence of events; for example, it may be necessary to give the details of an accident for an insurance claim or the circumstances surrounding an industrial dispute for a tribunal. In such a case, especially if your account is likely to have legal implications, it is essential to describe the events in the order in which they happened. A rough draft of your report should be sufficient planning to ensure that your communication is well organised and therefore clear to any reader.

Just as it is important to list a sequence of events in a logical order, so you must think carefully about the organisation of your ideas if you are putting forward an argument. Business clients are unlikely to buy your goods or services if you cannot persuade them of the advantages you have to offer, and you will never do that if the argument in favour of your product is weakened by disorganised thinking. Once again, the best way to overcome any weakness of this kind is to plan thoroughly what you wish to say, arranging your ideas into the most suitable order. This is a skill which only comes with practice, but it is a facility which can greatly improve your ability to communicate effectively, once it has been learnt.

20.6 Exercises on the organisation of ideas

1 The following sentences describing a fire in a warehouse and its consequences, have been written down in the wrong order. Rewrite the report, putting the sentences in a logical order:

Residents living in West Street, Town Avenue and Hilton Road were evacuated to local schools and community centres.

He contacted the other emergency services.

After three hours the fire brigade managed to bring the fire under control, preventing the fire from spreading beyond the work area to the storage tanks.

When they arrived, the chief fire officer recognised the danger of the fire spreading to the chemical tanks in the warehouse.

The local people were allowed to return to their homes next morning.

The fire was first detected by the night watch man, who saw smoke coming from a store room.

Following consultations between the three emergency services and the management, who had been alerted, it was decided to evacuate the surrounding neighbourhood.

The fire brigade were notified immediately.

2 Write a letter to a newspaper on one of the following topics, remembering to convey your ideas clearly by organising your thoughts on the subject chosen:

a Industrial development versus the environment.

b Small businesses are as important as large ones.

c Machines will never replace man in the business world.

d Investment in research and development is an essential aspect of business and industry.

21 Organising a business correspondence department

21.1 The nature of the problem

Every business is unique, with its own pattern of products, projects, departments, personnel, suppliers and customers. Every external business relationship, and every internal link between staff in different areas and at different levels, calls for some form of business communication. Much of this will be in written form, as memos, documents, letters and reports. In every piece of written communication one person (we will call him/her the *author*) tries to communicate effectively with another person (the *addressee*). Usually, between the author and the addressee, there is a third party whose function is to produce the memo, letter, report, etc., in reasonable style. To use a modern term, we will call this person the *word processor*. Pharaoh in Ancient Egypt had his scribe; medieval rulers had powerful administrators called secretaries; today every manager has his/her secretary or typist, who processes the words en route from author to addressee.

The problem in organising a correspondence department is to provide as economically as possible a system of work in which every author (who is entitled to initiate communications of one sort or another) has available a secretary, typist or other 'word processor' who will produce the necessary memo, letter, report, etc. We cannot, for example, appoint an export manager unless we also ensure that export documents can be produced; we cannot appoint a team to investigate an incident like a burglary, or a fire, unless its report can be printed and circulated. Economy requires that the department shall only be as big as necessary, and some degree of priority will have to be devised to take account of peaks and troughs of activity. The managing director's urgent letter will take precedence over the junior clerk's request for a review of salary, but everything must eventually be processed in a proper manner.

To devise such a system of work we must answer the following questions:

a Who are the 'authors', and what types of communication are they likely to initiate?
b Who are the 'addressees', and what types of communication are likely to be the most effective in rousing them to action on the firm's behalf?
c What types of equipment are needed to produce the necessary memos, letters and reports?
d What grades and numbers of 'word processing' personnel are required to ensure an adequate service to the authors?

A fifth point, which is often the greatest consideration of all, is:

e What do we do at present?

Unless a firm is just starting it will already have certain machines and certain staff who will be working to a reasonable degree of efficiency. Any reorganisation will at best produce a temporary disturbance; at worst it may cause staff to leave, or organise opposition to the proposed changes, or demand new wage structures, etc.

Frequently the work of producing business correspondence is kept under constant review, with a periodical major analysis of changes in requirements.

The specimen memos and letters which follow illustrate the types of situation which lead to reorganisation of the correspondence department.

21.2   Memos and letters about a review of activities

SL21.1

Memo from: Managing Director   27.11.19--
To: Head of General Administration Department

I see from my diary that the next Board meeting, 8 January, is the one where we examine the whole question of the provision of secretarial services throughout the firm, and pinpoint weaknesses or waste of resources. It is usual for you to collect and summarise opinions on these matters before the meeting, and generally act as a clearing house for suggestions. My own observations which are relevant are as follows:

a I wish we could replace the photocopier in use in the Buying Department - when I call for a copy of a document it is almost illegible. The machine should be replaced by a modern type of plain paper copier.

b Morale seems to be very low in the typing pool. I wonder whether the purchase of a new word processing system with fewer employees doing the same amount of work in a more interesting way would not be an improvement. The labour turnover is high, which would make it relatively easy to implement a change-over.

I think I should have your report in by 2 January to give me time to think over any points before the meeting. I will therefore mark it in my diary as receivable on or before that date.

SL21.2

Memo from: Head of General Adminstration   14 July 19--
To: Head of Typing Services

I know Mr Reynolds has warned you that he proposed to raise the question of the priority given to his correspondence. I feel somewhat at fault myself for not realising the extent to which his export department is subject to deadlines imposed by the banking system through letters of credit and by the changes in Customs procedure implemented last October. For example he has had to send some correspondence to banks with hand-written covering letters to ensure that documents were lodged before the expiry of letters of credit worth thousands of pounds. This cannot be good for our image with the banks, while Mr Johnson in accounts department would be very annoyed if these funds were lost even for a matter of weeks due to typing delays. They are all part of his cash flow system which in the present economic climate is vital for the firm's survival.

Would you therefore give Mr Reynolds' letters top priority from now on, until the annual review of secretarial services comes round in October. We may then decide to give him a personal secretary to remove this type of priority work from the general pool. I am sure you appreciate that this complaint bears no reflection on you or your department - indeed Mr Reynolds spoke very highly of your cooperation with him.

Organic Petroleum (Canvey) Ltd

Refinery Way, Thameswharf, Canvey Island

Telephone 037 43 51108

Your ref: -
Our ref: JT/BD

1 October, 19--

Adams Consultants Ltd.,
3024 Park View Lane,
London,
SW1 2DC.

Dear Sirs,

Time and Motion Study - Secretarial Services

We have reason to believe that our present system of operations in the clerical field is out-of-date and expensive. We are considering a full scale review of clerical activities and the purchase of a modern and comprehensive range of equipment to meet our needs.

Your firm has been recommended to us as being an experienced organisation with a wide knowledge of the range of facilities available and their appropriateness to particular fields of activity. Would it be possible please to meet someone from your organisation, preferably here in our offices, to discuss our problems and describe the types of correspondence we initiate and process?

If this introductory activity could be regarded as separate from any eventual contract between us, and invoiced accordingly, we should appreciate it. The fact is that we are not quite ready to go ahead with a full-scale enquiry, which is subject to approval by our Head Office in Texas, but we are authorised to open preliminary enquiries with a reputable firm of consultants.

Yours faithfully,

J. Thompson
Manager

SL21.4 (Response to SL21.3)

ADAMS CONSULTANTS LTD

3024 PARK VIEW LANE, LONDON SW1 2DC.   Tel: 01 450 2600

```
Your Ref:  JT/BD
Our Ref:   MC/AT
```

3 October 19--

```
Organic Petroleum (Canvey) Ltd
Refinery Way
Thameswharf
Canvey Island
```

Dear Mr Thompson

Time and Motion Study - Secretarial Services

Thank you for your letter dated 1 October 19--. As explained in my
telephone call today we shall be happy to conduct such an investigation for you, and as a preliminary stage to visit your offices on 11
October as arranged, at 9.30 am.

My colleague Peter Daimler has an encyclopaedic knowledge of equipment, and will accompany me. It will be very helpful if he could see
the various rooms and the equipment in use at present.

May I make one further point. It is in our experience not advisable
to apply the term 'Time and Motion Study' to office activities,
although such considerations inevitably form part of any evaluation
we might carry out for you. The greatest economies are to be secured
in other ways. For example, in evaluating which types of correspondence are suitable to each of your problems we shall automatically
consider machines and operators in their most time-effective and
labour-effective situations. Success in clerical and secretarial
activities depends on people, organisation and technology - in that
order. 'Time and Motion Study' has had an unfortunate press over the
years, and we should like to avoid any overtones from a bygone era.

I shall look forward to meeting you at 9.30 on 11 October.

Yours sincerely

Michael Crawford
Clerical Consultant

21.3 Analysing an existing department

A modern word processing system is described later in this chapter, but first we must consider what is being done already in an existing correspondence department. The questions to ask are 'What is being done now?' and 'How can we do it better?' Sometimes the answer to the second of these questions is 'Let's not do it at all.' One world-famous company which was requiring counter-staff to put in written memos of stock they required to re-stock their counters, and to sign a receipt for it when it arrived, saved six million internal memos a year by discarding the system altogether. Counter-staff were released in rotation from their counters, took what they wanted from shelves in the warehouse and returned with their trolleys loaded to capacity.

We have to decide who is doing typing, and for whom. A convenient way, which produces a massive pile of evidence, is to require every typist, audio-typist and secretary to take an extra copy of every letter or memo typed in a particular fortnight. Each piece of work is coded with some essential data. Examples might be:

a Author's name.
b Typist's name.
c Method used; was it typed from shorthand, composed by the secretary from a mere note, transcribed by an audio-typist, etc.
d Retypings should also be submitted, so that the extent of waste can be assessed.

The resulting mass of correspondence will need to be carefully analysed to discover:

a The various types of input.
b Author-typist analysis. (Who does what for whom, and why?).
c Author-input analysis. (Which authors use which type of input, and why? It may be necessary to interview them to find out).
d Document analysis. (What documents are in use, and why?)
e Typist/secretary analysis. (Who is overloaded; who is free-wheeling and why?)
f Turn-round time analysis. (How long does it take for letters to return to the author in typed condition ready for dispatch?)
g Work-elimination analysis. (Can we eliminate any of the work-load? Are some records, copy letters, etc. unnecessary?)

The result of this analysis should be a clear pattern of activity, on which a report about the work of the existing correspondence department can be based. We should then be able to see whether some work can be eliminated, and how the remainder may best be processed. For example some systems may call for the preparation of standard letters, or at least standard paragraphs. Reports which need to be redrafted and reissued might merit the use of a sophisticated word processing system to save tedious copying of material, etc.

21.4 Memos about a reappraisal of correspondence

SL21.5

```
Memo to:  All Staff                    Date: 27 June 19--

From:     Managing Director
_____

     It is proposed to conduct a complete re-appraisal of methods in
use for business correspondence in the company.  The aim is to intro-
duce a modern word-processing system for a wide range of staff.  This
will eliminate a great deal of the tedious re-typing work in some
departments, and should make life more interesting in many clerical
and secretarial fields.

     As part of the re-appraisal a 'Suggestions Box' is being placed
in the main foyer.  It is hoped that all staff will place comments in
this box, criticising their present systems of work (or perhaps prais-
ing aspects they do not wish to see disappear).  Comments may be
anonymous if preferred, but prizes will be awarded which will reflect
the cost savings achieved by adopting suggestions.  Prizes awarded to
anonymous suggestions will be donated to charity.

     No redundancies are expected from this exercise, but re-training
may be needed for staff who have not used word-processors before.  It
is an opportunity to acquire additional skills, and to promote the
general efficiency of our organisation.




                              Signed:  K. Hughes
                                       Managing Director
```

```
Memo to:  All clerical staff                    Date:  1 July 19--
From:     Organisation and Methods Department
```

Following the memo from Mr Hughes earlier this week, the word processing
investigation will start on Monday next. All clerical staff are
required to take an extra copy of all memos, letters, reports etc produced in the two weeks commencing 4 July and 11 July. These should be
placed in a file cover labelled WP Investigation and showing your own
name. On each piece of work please add the following coding, as near
to the top right hand corner as possible.

```
A.................. This is the author's name i.e. who sent you the work.
P.................. This is the process used to produce the work - i.e.
                   copy typing, audio-typing, word processor, original
                   composition by yourself from notes etc
Rec............... Received at .......... time received
Ret............... Returned at .......... time returned
```

Any comments or notes may be added if you wish.

Please include all rejected or re-typed letters so that the full extent
of your work is appreciated.

Thank you for your cooperation.

                                        Rita Griffiths
                                        WP Project Teamleader

21.5 Some elements in improving the work of the business correspondence department

A business correspondence department can only work smoothly if
everyone is clear how their correspondence is to be presented and to
whom it should be given for transcription. How should complaints be
made, and to whom? There must be an adequate system of control,
with supervisors in particular areas who have the knowledge and the
authority to ensure that the work proceeds smoothly. There must be
an adequate range of modern facilities, so that work is interesting
and rewarding. Thus a young copy typist, with an efficient machine,
may achieve great satisfaction from producing a thick wad of neatly
typed correspondence which is accurate enough to deserve a word of
praise from the supervisor. Ten years later the same person would
not achieve complete satisfaction from the same output, but might

realise his/her full potential as the supervisor of a group doing this sort of work.

Some of the elements in improving the work of a business correspondence department are described below.

Correspondence improvement programmes

Periodically a company should institute a correspondence improvement programme which will look at the correspondence currently being produced at all levels and take steps to raise the general standard. Some salient points are as follows:

(a) House style

House style should be prescribed by management, taking advice from senior supervisory staff where necessary. A manual (or leaflet) on house style should be drawn up and made available to all staff. In the case of revised versions a short explanation of the changes made, and the reason for them, should be given. This manual should also be part of the induction programme for all new staff, who should be required to attend a talk by the head of the correspondence department where the whole procedure is explained and discussed.

(b) Training in letter-writing

Not everyone writes well. Managers frequently reach managerial level because of proven technical or practical ability and find the paperwork a tedious and difficult task. Their handwriting may be poor, so that writing a letter in manuscript is not easy and wastes time, yet dictation is difficult to correct and leaves no written record which can be considered, before sending to the typist. For this reason it should be a policy of top management to provide training where necessary, and for as long as necessary, to all those promoted to a level where they are expected to act as 'authors'. Individual counselling should be available, and an allocation of time for staff improvement should be made. Teaching should if possible be professional in nature, with an outside teacher from a local technical college giving individual consultations.

(c) Dictating techniques

If dictation machines are used, it is essential that staff should be properly trained in the use of the particular system chosen. A *Manual of Dictation Techniques* should be prepared by the manager in consultation with the supervisor of the transcription department, who will know most of the problems. Particular care should be given to:

i *Preparation for dictation.* The dictator cannot begin until all the details needed — names, addresses, references, etc. — are available and arranged in correct order, where they can be found easily at the moment of dictation. A note of the points to be mentioned should be made, in the correct sequence, so that a series of paragraphs can be dictated in correct order. Letters should be dictated in groups of four or five. This gives the supervisor an opportunity to allocate work to typists as they become available. The dictator must disconnect from the system and reconnect later. It is wrong to hold on to the connection until all correspondence is complete.

ii The dictators must introduce themselves and give the names of their departments so that finished correspondence can be returned.

iii The dictation must then proceed with some details of the work required, particularly some indication of the length of the letter, to assist the typists to select the right size paper, the correct number of carbons, etc. A typical instruction might be 'This is a short letter, A5 paper will do on Mills and Wright letterhead 1 + 2 copies. Please date the letter 27 April 19--. The references are: Your Ref AB/CD, Our Ref TS/followed by your own initials please. There is to be an enclosure at the end — our current price list.'

iv The letter should then be dictated in a clear, even voice at a steady pace, and without mumbling, or running words together. If punctuation can be given, this is an advantage. It helps both author and transcriber. Give instructions for new paragraphs, and bear in mind the rules about opening, main and closing paragraphs.

v Give a clear complimentary close, a signature and if necessary the position you wish to appear on your letter, e.g. manager, credit controller, chief buyer, etc. Finally repeat the instruction about enclosures.

Typewriting

A modern correspondence department should be equipped with modern machines, either electronic typewriters or word processors. The basic features of an electronic machine are as follows:

a The merest touch on a key completes a circuit to type the character.

b A variable-touch control enables the power behind the key to be adjusted according to the number of carbons being used.

c Certain keys often have repeat actions, particularly the dot, dash and underlining keys, the space bar and the back spacer.

d Some sort of visual display is provided, either a single line visual display or a complete page display on a visual display unit (VDU).

e A variable-impression key enables the impression achieved to be adjusted to give an even appearance to the letter, which is no longer subject to changes of pressure as with the manual machine.

A major development in the field of typewriters has been the fixed-carriage machine. Instead of a heavy carriage carrying the paper across the machine, the paper is held in a fixed carriage, and the typing element moves across the face of the paper. This element may be a vertical pillar, with a golf-ball or print-wheel daisy unit which turns to bring the characters opposite the paper as required. These typing units are interchangeable so that different typestyles can be used, giving a pleasing appearance to the typed output. Reports can be typed with distinctive sub-headings, for example, simply by disconnecting one print unit and replacing it by another.

The next development was the automatic typewriter. It enables a permanent record in the form of punched paper tape to be made of any document as it is typed. Subsequent copies can be produced simply by inserting the punched paper tape in the machine. It then reads the paper tape with a paper tape reader, and prints it out at 145 words per minute, stopping at appropriate points where a particular addressee needs information of interest to him/her only.

Word processing

Word processing is a system which is developing very rapidly. Almost all companies are beginning to invest in some type of word processing system, and to realise the potential of this type of equipment. If we consider the relatively simple use of the word processor as a replacement for a typewriter, what are its special features and what benefits does it bring? They may be listed as follows:

a The keyboard of a word processing typewriter is similar to an ordinary typewriter, with a range of special-function keys to instruct the machine to perform a variety of tasks.

b The machine records automatically all keyboard operations, so that a letter or report is stored in a memory. This magnetic memory may be recalled at any time by a 'search' facility. Thus a standard paragraph can be recalled for future use, and the typewriter will type it out automatically faster than any typist, and error-free.

c Before any line of a letter or report passes into the memory it is held in a buffer memory and displayed for the typist to see. If there is an error it can be erased by moving the cursor to the mistake and correcting it. All the copy after the corrected error will automatically re-space if necessary.

d When re-fed into the machine the memory unit, a recall card, cassette or floppy disk, will reprint the letter or report at a very high speed, after any corrections or alterations have been made. Thus a report where words have been changed, paragraphs deleted, new paragraphs inserted, etc., need not be retyped. The word processor can be stopped at the first mistake, and a correction made, even of a single letter. The processor will then adjust the following passage, moving words up to make room for any extra words or letters inserted, and if necessary into the next line until the end of a paragraph is reached. The machine can recognise the end of paragraphs, with a 'mandatory' carriage return (one which must be obeyed). It can recognise underlinings, and will return to underline them, etc. In fact, as its name implies it can 'process' the words according to the pattern of instructions it has received.

e These instructions include automatic line-length adjustment, automatic centring, automatic underscoring, automatic tabulation and numerous other instructions which make life easier for the typist.

The most straightfoward uses for word processing are in the use of standard paragraphs, standard letters, repetitive typewriting of contracts, leases and similar documents, revision typing for such things as price lists, reports and even whole textbooks, and all high-volume typing of any sort.

Its wider applications involve the processor being given the chance to assume not only the secretary's burden, but also the work of filing clerks, ledger clerks, addressing machine operators, etc. With each floppy disk holding about forty A4 pages of information, and any number of disks available, the memory is almost limitless and the use of the machine can be made very economic. This may require links to be established between the correspondence department and other departments such as the accounts department.

Updating personnel
It has been said that an efficient correspondence department requires people, organisation and technology — in that order. While much is

written about the latest equipment available, and the contribution it can make to the work of the correspondence department, little is said about the need to secure the correct number and types of employees. Today we cannot rely on staff staying with us indefinitely unless we offer them an opportunity to develop their skills, experience a variety of work, achieve a suitable measure of job satisfaction and also adequate monetary rewards. Labour turnover tends to be high, and the expenses of securing and retraining staff are considerable. In general, offices should aim at 'growing their own' as far as secretarial staff are concerned. This means that young and inexperienced staff who appear to be of the right quality should be developed into the future supervisors and managers of the company. This requires periodical 'career evaluation' sessions with the personnel officer; encouragement to attend general educational courses on a part-time or evening basis; sponsoring for in-house and other specialist training courses; movement around departments to broaden experience and understanding of the company's work, etc.

21.6 Specimen letters about the work of the correspondence department

SL21.7

M E M O R A N D U M

FROM: J Russell   27 July 19--
TO: Head of Business Correspondence Department

You asked me in my capacity as office equipment supervisor to remind you when the next International Business Show came round at the National Exhibition Centre in Birmingham. I see they have advertised it for the last week in October and invite applications for tickets. You will remember that the managing director and the purchasing officer both expressed the wish to attend this year in connection with the proposals to install a small word processing section in your department.

Would you please let me know how many tickets to order. I do hope I shall be allowed to attend, although I could go in a personal capacity if you prefer it. When we go together I usually act as general factotum collecting advertising brochures etc which are invaluable in our work later in the year. I could still do this if we go as a general party, leaving you to deal with the managing director and other members of the group. Perhaps we could discuss this when you are free.

World-Wide-Distributors (Tilbury) Ltd

Estuary View, Tilbury, Essex
Telephone: Tilbury 76452

Our Reference RTJ/SD

26 May 19--

Head of Department of Business Studies
College of Sea Studies
Woodview
Grays
Essex

Dear Sir

After attending the prize giving last week I feel I should write to
make you a proposition which has been under consideration in this firm
for some time. It is that we should offer your department a suitable
word processing system for use in training staff in the latest techniques. In return we would hope that any member of our staff designated to attend a short course on word processing would be accepted,
on payment of the usual course fees.

The alternative to this suggestion is that we should set up some sort
of in-house training facility, which quite frankly we do not have the
expertise to do. It seems clear that you must have secretarial studies
lecturers who would be pleased to add such a facility to the range of
courses on offer. The benefit would accrue to business firms in the
area in general, which we would not mind at all.

Would it be possible for you to come to see us, with a suitably
qualified lecturer to undertake the course, to discuss the types of
equipment and the software programmes available?

Yours faithfully

R T Jones
Managing Director

Workington-Matthews (Thanet) Ltd

1284 Channel View, Margate, Kent, CT9 1HX.   Tel: 674764

```
The Circulation Manager                          Our Ref:  RTM/JCD
Business Systems and Equipment
MacLean-Hunter Ltd                               27 September 19--
76 Oxford Street
London W1


Dear Sir

I have recently been appointed in this large company to the post of
Purchasing Officer: Equipment, with particular reference to office
equipment.

Please add my name to your circulation list for 'Business Systems
and Equipment' and any other magazines which cover this general field.

Yours faithfully



R T Matthews
Purchasing Officer: Equipment
```

21.7 Exercises on the organisation of a business correspondence department

1 You are the managing director of Martin Tyler (Singapore) Ltd, 2047 Harbour View, Bedok, Singapore, a small but expanding company. Part of the expansion envisages the establishment of a business correspondence department which will be able to undertake the majority of secretarial work for the five main departments. These are the factory, the transport department, the export department, the general administration department and the accounts department. Draft the text of an advertisement to attract applications from people with the necessary experience.

2 The Board of Multinational Ltd are proposing to conduct a review of secretarial procedures, and ask you to submit plans to discover:
a Who does what secretarial work for whom at present?

b Whether any of this work could be eliminated.

c How the rest of it could be more economically achieved than at present.

They have particularly emphasised that staff goodwill is to be maintained. What suggestions would you make to achieve these aims? Write a short report for distribution to Board members.

3 You are about to purchase new equipment for the secretarial department of a large firm, and wish to know exactly what work is being done at present, by whom, for whom. Devise a questionnaire to be sent to every member of staff which asks suitable questions under the following main headings:

a Who are the 'authors' of correspondence, etc., in the firm; how much do they do in a week; who does it for them and what sort of time delay is there?

b Do they have duplicating, photocopying or printing work done? How is it done and are they satisfied with it?

c What method do they use to pass material for typing to the person who types it for them? Do they think the system is a good one, or would they prefer some other system? If so, which system do they approve of?

Remember that a questionnaire should have a place for the name, position and department of each individual (unless it is to be a secret and confidential one).

4 Write to the managing director of Office Productivity (Zimbabwe) Ltd, 2124 Freedom Way, Harare City, Zimbabwe asking their help in reorganising your business correspondence department in the Tobacco Growers Cooperative of Lilongwe, Malawi. Express the opinion that you wish to achieve a more complete coverage of certain areas, particularly export documentation and home sales, and reduce the amount of repetitive retyping involved with reports prepared quarterly for Government control purposes. Invite them to visit you at Lilongwe as soon as possible.

5 Reply to the correspondent in Question 4, expressing your willingness to visit Lilongwe with a colleague who is a specialist in export documentation. Point out in your letter that a Rank Xerox Automatic Overlay Device would probably meet their entire export and home sales documentation needs, and could also be used for routine

duplicating. Clearly you could not bring such a large machine with you, but could demonstrate it in Salisbury at a later date if a return visit could be arranged. Suggest three possible dates next month when you would be free for a 48 hour visit to Lilongwe.

6 A debate has developed in your office between Mr Informal and Mr Pernickety about the best way to write the many letters required. Mr Informal always replies to his correspondence at once, using his wide knowledge of the business. Any detailed points which are not immediately to hand he discovers by quick phone calls to departmental chiefs. He uses the familiar style of address, which he calls the 'you-attitude', and keeps the tone of the letter friendly, informal and natural.

Mr Pernickety bases his style of correspondence on the Seven Cs mnemonic, which goes:

> A business letter must be neat,
> Clear, concise, correct, complete,
> Consistent, courteous, cautious — these
> The correspondent's seven Cs.

He generally delays replying to letters for 48 hours, and chooses a formal, official style which observes the rules in the mnemonic.

Give your opinion of these two approaches. Which do you personally favour, and what are the likely problems to arise from the style you have selected?

21.8 Appendix on the English language: making notes

The active businessman will be subjected to a constant flow of data and information, some of which he may reject as of no use to him, but much of it containing valuable ideas and details which he may wish to remember for future reference. The sources of any important new information are diverse: technical reports, journals, radio, television and newspaper articles, business lectures and seminars; therefore you must be equipped, physically and mentally, to take useful notes at any time. It is a good idea to carry a notebook ready to jot down any details, for notes made on the back of an envelope or any other scrap of paper are likely to be lost or sent to the cleaners.

When making notes you should aim to select only the most important information and to reproduce it in a way which makes the content immediately comprehensible. Devise a clear title, and then the information under a series of headings, sub-headings and numbered points. Try to create a logical order in these skeletal notes as they will lose their value as brief reminders if they are poorly arranged and confusing. Clarity may be improved if you devise a system of notation which informs you at a glance of the relative importance of a particular section. For example, always write your title in capital letters, underline your main headings with a double line and your sub-headings with a single line. Your main headings could be noted in block capitals, and your sub-headings with initial capital letters. Pieces of information under the sub-headings could be listed with small roman numerals. For example:

TRAINING STAFF FOR WORD PROCESSING

(a) Staff Selection
  (i) Select those interested in a change of routine.
  (ii) Warn those who do shorthand that there will be only limited opportunities to keep up this skill.
  (iii) Emphasise that the only justification for the expense is higher productivity on a slightly higher rate of pay.
  (iv) Emphasise that an innovative approach is helpful — can the word processing operative suggest new uses for the machine?

Notes made from a lecture or a programme on the radio and television are probably the most difficult to perfect; if only because the spoken word is heard only once and then is gone for ever. Ideally, the note-taker should learn some form of shorthand if notes are frequently made from the spoken word, but if not you must develop a quick style of writing. Remember, however, that notes are of no use if you cannot read them later on.

The skill in all note-taking is to distinguish between the important and the trivial. When taking notes from a speaker, this clearly is difficult, as we do not know what is to come. You must listen closely to the speaker's tone of voice. A good lecturer should emphasise the most important points, perhaps by repeating them, or by speaking more slowly or more loudly.

When you have finished listening to the talk it is advisable to rewrite your notes, turning your hastily made draft into a final version presenting all the information clearly and effectively.

21.9   Exercises on taking notes

1 Listen to a radio or television programme on a subject in which you are interested, taking notes at the same time. When the programme has finished, check back over your notes to see if they are clear and well-organised. It is a good idea to do this exercise with someone else, comparing notes at the end to see if you agree on what was important in the talk.

2 Prepare a set of notes on the following topics, based on passages in this book:
   a Bills of exchange (see pages 171-84)
   b Letters of credit (see pages 204-10)
   c Agents and principals (see pages 227-44).

22 The correspondence department and claimants on the business

22.1 The concept of the claimant

Every business, and every department within a business, operates within an environment in which various individuals and institutions are making demands upon it. It is useful to regard them as claimants upon the organisation, and to draw up a 'claimants' chart' to discover exactly who they are, and the extent of the pressure they can exert. The degree of success in meeting these claims can then be estimated.

Every correspondence department has a unique environment, so that any discussion must necessarily be in general terms only. If readers who are in employment in such a department apply the general principles to their own situation they will soon see the implications in practical terms. The chart may be drawn up in loose-leaf style, with a slip of paper to each claimant. The slips can then be arranged in order of priority, with the dominant claims at the top of the chart. The framework of the chart should be as shown in Table 22.1.

TABLE 22.1

Name of claimant	Nature of claim	Requirements to satisfy claim	Special responsibilities
1. Managing director	Routine letters only	Standard letters or standard paragraphs. Word processing equipment	Shirley Clarke

The implications of the first entry are that the managing director has a personal assistant or executive secretary so that only routine letters are passed to the correspondence department. These routine letters will probably be of a repetitive nature so that it will be possible to use standard letters, or standard paragraphs on a word processing system. An individual, Shirley Clarke, has been designated to attend to these letters, and deal with any queries that arise. Obviously as the work will come from the managing director's secretary a sound link will be established between Shirley Clarke and this secretary.

In order to give clear guidance on the preparation of a claimants' chart it is proposed to use the example of a small college to illustrate the claim that will be made on a correspondence department. We will assume that the department is a central bureau to which most lecturers can turn for correspondence to be prepared, and also for lesson notes, conference material, etc. as and when required.

22.2 A claimants' chart for the correspondence department of a small college

In preparing Table 22.2 we will assume that the college has the following staff:

a A principal, who has a personal secretary

b A vice-principal, who has a personal secretary

c A head of general education department, with his departmental secretary. There are eight lecturers in the department and thirty-two part-time lecturers.

d A head of business studies, with a departmental secretary. There are fifteen full-time lecturers and twenty-four part-time lecturers.

e A head of catering and domestic arts, with a departmental secretary, six full-time staff and eighteen part-time staff.

f A college administration officer with seven full-time clerical and secretarial staff and eighteen porters, caretakers, cleaners and canteen employees.

The claimants' chart might be as shown in Table 22.2.

Such a group of claimants will present many problems to the correspondence department, particularly with regard to questions of priority and timing. The work of a college frequently has the most important impact at the lecturer-student interface, where the real work of the college is carried out, often by relatively junior lecturers who cannot expect high priority to be accorded to them. Such lecturers who do not get their lesson notes in time for lectures will have their work programmes interrupted and the adequacy of their teaching reduced, to the detriment of students. Heads of departments exerting excessive pressure on the correspondence department for priority attention may have to be restrained in the interests of the lecturer-

335

TABLE 22.2 A claimants chart for a correspondence department in a college

Name of claimant	Nature of claim	Requirements to satisfy claim	Special responsibilities
1. Head of governors	None — except right to inspect department from time to time.	None — any correspondence done by principal's private secretary	Not applicable
2. Principal	Principal's secretary may require help on special occasions, in particular a With duplication of minutes and agenda for governors' meetings b Duplication of minutes, for all college committees c Special functions — prizegiving, Founders' Day, Sports Day, conferences, etc.	a Electrostatic copiers b Stencil duplicators c Clerical assistants d Addressing systems for mailing lists of various sorts e Internal mail distribution system f Mail outwards facilities	a All arrangements made via head of correspondence department b Reprographics supervisor c Address system supervisor d Petty cashier and postal clerk
3. Vice-principal	As above	As above	As above
4. Heads of department	In general the departmental secretary should do all the head of department's correspondence, but occasionally for major conferences, etc. may call on the services of the correspondence department	As above	As above

5. Departmental lecturers	a Claim to have routine correspondence typed b Claim to have priority correspondence typed c Claim to have lesson notes duplicated d Claim to have assistance with submissions to examining bodies e Claim to have assistance with work connected with governing body or college committees	a System for handling manuscript letters, including standard paragraphs b System for handling dictated materials c Copy typists d Audio-typists e Full reprographic facilities including electronic copiers, stencil duplicators, etc. f Collators, punches, binding facilities, etc., for presentation of reports, conference materials, etc.	a Lecturers' correspondence supervisor b Reprographics supervisor c Graphics and audio-visual aids supervisor
6. Students' representatives	a Claim to have assistance with submissions to governing body b Claim to have assistance with submissions to college committees c Claim to have advertising material for student functions duplicated	As for (5) above, but use controlled by lecturer in charge of student liaison	As for (5) above
7. College administration officer	No major claim, since clerical and secretarial staff are available, but access to all specialist machines by arrangement	As for (1) above	Close liaison with all specialist staff listed above

student body. The lecturers' correspondence supervisor must be an important member of the administrative staff who can represent them adequately.

22.3 Specimen letters based on standard paragraphs

In the specimen letters below, lecturers have indicated their replies to the students applying for entry to the College of International Trade, 2024 Regent Street, London, W1, by indicating the appropriate standard paragraphs taken from the list of standard paragraphs, as follows:

Paragraph A   Thank you for your letter dated . . .

Paragraph B   I regret that it is quite impossible to offer you a place at the college next session as your qualifications for entry are inadequate. It is essential for you to have achieved four 'O' level passes or their equivalent, and two 'A' level passes or their equivalent. These passes should include at least one subject which has a business orientation. You should therefore secure these qualifications as soon as practicable.

Paragraph C   I regret that it is impossible to offer you a place at the college next session because the qualifications you offer are inadequate for entry. For a course in International Trade it is considered essential to have at least some business orientation in earlier studies, and your 'A' levels in . . . and . . . are therefore not appropriate. We suggest you try to secure at least one (preferably two) 'A' level qualifications (or equivalent) in subjects chosen from Economics, Economic History, Accounting, Business Studies, Communication Studies, General Principles of Law, Statistics, French, German, Spanish, Arabic, Russian or Chinese.

Paragraph D   I enclose the brochures and course material you require, together with an application form. The person and department to whom the completed application should be sent are printed in the bottom right-hand corner. They are . . . of the . . . Department.

Paragraph E   I am delighted to offer you a course at the college since your application details meet our requirements.

Paragraph F   It remains for you to satisfy the college bursar that you are able to meet the course fees, and will have adequate funds to support yourself for the duration of your studies, which will, of course, be . . . year(s). I have passed your application form to the bursar's department. They will write to you shortly.

Paragraph G   We look forward to receiving your completed application form in due course.

Paragraph H   Once you have attained the necessary qualifications we shall be happy to consider a renewed application.

Paragraph I   Your joining papers will reach you from the college bursar in due course. I look forward to meeting you at the start of next session.

SL22.1

```
To: Miss Mary Green, 3174 High Street, Billericay, Essex.

        Paragraphs A (17 October 19--)
                   D (Mr G Robarts, Business Studies)
                   G
```

SL22.2

```
To: Isaac Nakanda, 3814 Lafia Road, Shendam, Nigeria

        Paragraphs A (23 June 19--)
                   B
                   H
```

SL22.3

```
To: Gordon Frazier, 2741 Castle Street, Edinburgh 2

        Paragraphs A (24 July 19--)
                   C (Photography, History of Art)
                   H
```

SL22.4

```
To: Peter Shelagh, 715 Ayr Road, Townsville, Queensland, Australia

        Paragraphs A (15 May 19--)
                   E
                   F (two years)
                   I
```

To: Margaret Wakamba, 725 Kilifi Road, Mombasa, Kenya

     Paragraphs A (27 February 19--)
             E

Your sponsorship by the East African Community Scholarship Board means that your fees and support while in this country will be provided, and your return fare home will be guaranteed. There are accordingly no financial difficulties.

        I

22.4   Letters in manuscript

Letters are frequently dictated to a secretary, or to a recording machine, before typing, but there are many situations where it is more economical for the author to write out the letter by hand. This is called 'manuscript'. Junior members of staff may be expected to write their letters in this way, and even senior staff will frequently do so when away from the office, or when the letter is particularly difficult and needs careful phrasing. Naturally they will save time where they can – for example they may leave the typist to pick up the internal address from a previous letter clipped on the manuscript reply. Frequently words like 'would' and 'should' are abbreviated to 'wd' and 'shd', 'possible' is written 'poss.' and 'Yours sincerely' as 'Yrs sin.' All such abbreviations should be typed in full.

A number of correction signs are in common use in correcting manuscripts, and it is essential to be familiar with their meanings. They are also in use to correct typescript, and printers' proofs. The more common ones are illustrated in specimen letter 22.6 below.

Those who wish to obtain a complete list of such corrections should order the pamphlet called *Marks for copy preparation and proof correction,* from the British Standards Institution, 2 Park Street, London W1A 2BS. It is quite inexpensive. The reference number is ISBN: 0 580 09057 4.

22.5 Specimen letters in manuscript

SL22.6

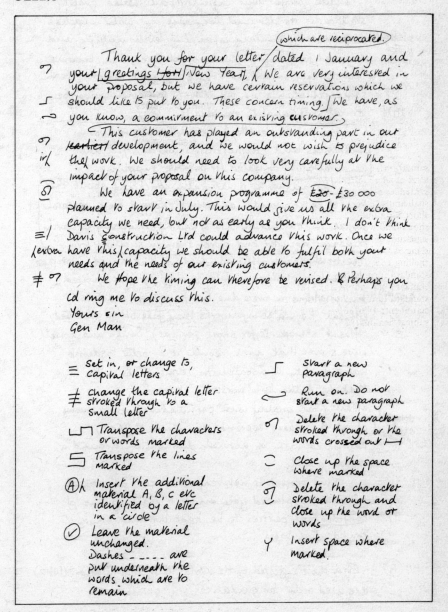

Fig. 22.1 A manuscript letter with marks for copy preparation

Thank you for your inquiry about water quality standards. As demand presses on our water supplies the problems of maintaining satisfactory quality levels multiply and the need for ~~adequate~~ water quality criteria become increasingly important. There appears to have been some reluctance in the U.K. to ~~lay down~~ prescribe formal water quality standards. Ⓐλ

The World Health Authority standards list substances and characteristics which affect the acceptability of water for potable supply.

The authority is naturally concerned about this lack of criteria and is at present engaged on a research project in conjunction with a leading University to clarify standards required and express them in scientific form. The trouble with WHO standards is that they do not take account of changes in water supply systems caused by temporary variations in rivers due to inflows (for example effluent from a sewage works may fall below permitted effluent standards for short periods). Smith and Howell have shown that as a result it is better to define water quality in probabalistic terms. This is the line that the Authority is pursuing at present, giving a mean river quality with permitted variations ~~from~~ about the mean expressed in terms of biological oxygen demand (BOD) associated with a normal distribution around a mean quality.

This project is not very advanced at present but I have placed you on our mailing list of ~~confidential~~ parties to be kept informed, on a confidential basis.

Ⓐ   Even those suggested by the World Health Organisation (WHO) are used only for guidance.

Fig. 22.2 A manuscript letter on a scientific topic

22.6 Exercises on meeting the claims of claimants

1 A junior editor in a publishing house specialises in manuscripts which are in 'picture strip' form for comics and children's annuals. In the course of her work she receives many manuscripts from aspiring authors, many of which are quite unsuitable but some are useful and can be turned into finished material. Prepare a standard paragraph for each of the following topics:

a A paragraph thanking an author for his/her letter, dated . . . and the manuscript received.

b A paragraph rejecting the manuscript on the grounds that it is quite unsuitable and contains serious errors of English, including spelling and punctuation.

c A paragraph rejecting the manuscript on the grounds that it is not pitched at the correct age group, which is the 9-13 age group.

d A paragraph rejecting the manuscript on the grounds that it is not quite polished enough. Suggest it is revised and the story line made more vigorous, but encourage the author and recommend that he/she keeps writing.

e A paragraph accepting the manuscript, which will become the subject of a contract from the contracts department very shortly. Express an interest in seeing further work when available, but express the hope that it will be as lively and interesting as the present material.

f A paragraph regretting that you cannot be more helpful.

g A paragraph expressing your hopes that you will receive the revised material fairly soon.

h A paragraph expressing your good wishes for the future and your interest in seeing the work in print in due course.

2 Write out in manuscript form a letter to John Hillier, of 2472 Downs Way, Royston, Herts. Thank him for his letter of 21 October, which complains about the poor quality of the photographs taken with a film purchased from a market trader in Cambridge. Point out to him that the packet purchased on 1 September 19-- bore a clear statement that it was not guaranteed for quality after 31 May. Ask him to seek redress from the stallholder who must have known that the film was time-expired. Mark the letter asking the typist to do an extra copy for the sales manager, East Anglia.

3 Write in manuscript form for typing a letter to the principal of your local technical college expressing your interest in a course for apprentices in the electronics field. Ask if someone from the college who organises such courses would telephone you and arrange an appointment to discuss them. Ask the typist to do 1 plus 2 copies.

4 Allbrights (Workington) Ltd make glassware. Draw up a list of claimants on the correspondence department, bearing in mind that only the managing director and factory manager have personal secretaries. There are five departments besides the factory. They are general administration, sales, export, research and development, and the company secretary's office. Bear in mind that 50 per cent of output is sold abroad, and that a major problem for the company is keeping ahead of their competitors.

5 You are in charge of a correspondence department in a major firm. Lay down priorities for your staff for dealing with the work that comes to them. The following types of problem arise:

a Senior staff are given priority on any work they mark with a letter P. It is, however, expected that they will get as much correspondence as possible to the department in good time, and this should not be marked P. It is suspected that some senior staff abuse this.

b Junior staff letters do not have any priority, but the occasional letter is urgent. How can this be arranged?

c Advertising copy is often urgent, but the advertising department is a new department and does not have a senior member of staff. How shall this problem be resolved?

d A peak of work occurs at the end of each month when the accounts department sends out statements of account, and a monthly circular is mailed to all customers by the sales department. The reprographic machine operator, who also works the addressograph machines, is under pressure at this time. How might this problem be resolved? Suggest *several* alternatives.

22.7 Appendix on the English language: summarising information

Much of the English work in this book has emphasised the need for clear presentation of ideas and data. Of equal importance in the business and industrial world is the correct selection of information contained in reports and business documents. In our daily lives we often practise the skill of summary, giving an account of a film, play or book. In business there are frequent occasions when we need to perform the same process of selecting the main ideas in a piece of writing and expressing them briefly for a third party. For example a junior executive may be required to report to the Board of a company on the competitiveness of a rival firm's products. This may require summaries of a number of reports made by various departments on the technical, scientific and commercial aspects of the products under consideration. Similarly a scientific adviser's final report may only contain the important details selected from a mass of statistical and research data.

In order to summarise effectively you must understand all the information which has been given you; have the judgment to select that which is important and be able to re-express it in a lucid manner.

First read through the reports or documents carefully, several times if necessary, trying to grasp the important points and to follow the line of thought. Earlier in this book you were introduced to the idea of **key sentences** in a paragraph (see section 2.20). A useful skill is the ability to recognise the key sentence in someone else's writing, as this will give an important clue to the main idea in each paragraph.

When you feel you understand the document, make a brief note of the content of each paragraph, remembering to keep your notes in the logical order followed by the original. Avoid repetition and only use examples and illustrations where they are essential. Having gone through all the material, extracting only that which is important, check back through to make sure that nothing vital has been omitted, and that nothing trivial has been included. If you are finally satisfied, rewrite your notes in fluent, economical English, bearing in mind that someone else has to read or listen to your summary, and that he/she will assume it contains everything important and essential from the original reports, documents or statistical data.

22.8 Exercises on summarising information

1 Summarise the passage on 'Offer, acceptance and valuable consideration' (section 3.2 of this volume).

2 Summarise the section on 'Checking an order' (section 6.5 of this volume).

3 Summarise the passage on 'The legal consequences of carriage' (section 17.2 of this volume).

23 Examinations in business correspondence

23.1 Why take examinations?

Examinations, it has been said, are very much like life. We are presented with a series of problems, none of which we have met before, though we have been doing our best to prepare for them. We use the skills we have acquired, and the natural talents with which we have been endowed, to solve the problems and demonstrate that we are competent to deal with whatever situation may present itself. There is a great deal of nonsense talked about the stresses and strains of examinations, and it is important to put these in perspective. Of course the first time we do anything it is an emotional moment, and we must expect to be a little nervous. In pursuing a business career we shall have to jump many hurdles, and gradually we shall become used to examinations. The actual day of the examination is the least important time, really. The vital thing is to attend classes regularly in the preparation period before the examination; take plenty of notes at lectures and discussions; work through the exercises systematically and relate them to the syllabus which has to be covered. As the examination approaches you should begin to find that every detail of the syllabus has been covered, and that you are familiar with the whole range of subject-matter on which you are to be tested. The actual examination will be a simple hurdle to jump if the preparatory work has been well done.

We take examinations purely to present to our families, our friends and our future employers some small testimonial of our ability in the field we have studied. They equip us to take our first few steps into the business world, or on to the new level to which we have been climbing. From that time on life itself will present us with the problems of the business world. If we continue to pass life's endless succession of examinations we shall successfully earn our bread and butter; we may perhaps grow rich; we shall certainly help our families, our nations and humanity itself towards a more prosperous future.

23.2 Pitman Examinations Institute

There are many examining bodies throughout the world, but as this book is called *Pitman Business Correspondence* the reader will perhaps excuse a reference to the Pitman Examinations Institute. The greatest merit, perhaps, of the Pitman Examinations Institute is its worldwide organisation. Almost any major school, college or education authority may complete a proposal form for registration as a centre for the conduct of Pitman examinations. Naturally the conduct of the examinations must conform to Pitman's high standards; invigilators must be of the highest calibre and absolute integrity must be observed in the safeguarding of question papers, the dispatch of the worked scripts, etc.

The second great advantage of Pitman examinations is that they are not tied to the calendar, like some examinations, but may be taken whenever a group of students has made enough progress to warrant their entry to the examination. This means that the greatest worry about some examinations — 'Will I be well on the day and do justice to my entry?' — is much reduced. The centre which has candidates who were ill on the day may apply for a further examination a few weeks later, and will not need to wait a whole year. Nervous candidates are also made less nervous, for they know that this is not a single examination which has to be passed at the first attempt. They may try two or three times if necessary (at a small expense), and this means that almost everyone in a class who has prepared conscientiously will be able to pass the examination.

23.3 Examinations in business correspondence and report writing

This book is about business correspondence and it will be of greatest use to students taking courses in English for business communication, business correspondence, communication studies and secretarial studies. These subjects range from elementary to advanced levels. For example, the Pitman Examinations Institute has the following examinations:

English for Business Communications (EBC)
These examinations at Elementary, Intermediate and Advanced levels are intended to test the candidate's skill in using the English language in business correspondence.

Overseas candidates are advised that they should have reached the Elementary or Intermediate standard of the English as a Foreign Language examination before attempting the English for Business Communications examinations at the corresponding levels.

At all levels correct layout, tone, spelling and punctuation are of prime importance, as is the ability to use words appropriate to the situation to convey the writer's meaning.

Candidates will be expected to have a background knowledge of office practice; a knowledge of basic office organisations and personnel, a background appreciation of modern office equipment, and staff working conditions.

Exact copying of the questions will be heavily penalised.

Elementary (time allowed — 2 hours)
The examination will be in two parts:
Part I — ten objective test questions on the correct choice of medium of communication and layout.
Part II — four questions from a choice of six, one of which, a letter, is compulsory.

Candidates will be expected to:

a Compose draft letters from notes given dealing with business transactions, including letters of inquiry, complaint and sales.
b Compose personal letters and formal invitations and replies.
c Compose memoranda.
d Write telegrams or telex messages on general business matters.

Intermediate (time allowed — 2½ hours)
At this stage candidates will be required to answer five questions from a choice of seven; two of the questions will be compulsory, one a letter and one a report.

Candidates will be required to:

a Compose letters from brief notes dealing with general business matters, such as letters of complaint, inquiry, acceptances, sales and travel arrangements.
b Write personal letters for business employers, including letters of introduction and recommendation; letters of welcome, congratulations and seasonal greeting; formal replies to invitations.

c Compose memoranda.

d Write telegrams or telex messages with confirmatory letters; telephone messages, advertisements.

e Write draft reports from information given.

Candidates should have the ability to read and analyse correspondence received by a firm and assess the type of reply needed.

Advanced (time allowed – 3 hours)

At this stage candidates will be required to answer five questions from a choice of seven, three of which will be compulsory: a letter, a report, and an exercise in composing a concise text, e.g. telegram, notice or advertisement.

Candidates for the Advanced examination will be expected to compose correspondence from a minimum of given information. They must have a knowledge of the Intermediate syllabus and be able to deal with other similar matters coming within the scope of general business. A higher standard of composition will be expected, however, and the matters dealt with will be of a more advanced nature and relate to a wider range of business undertakings.

They will require a fluent command of English, and sufficient office knowledge to enable them to expand notes into clear concise language, adding all necessary details to provide authentic and realistic answers.

Secretarial Practice, Intermediate

(A knowledge of the elementary Office Practice syllabus will be assumed.)

Time allowed – 2½ hours.

The paper will be in two parts:

Part I – in which there will be 25 objective questions, of which 20 must be answered.

Part II – will contain one compulsory question of a practical nature and a further four questions from a choice of six to be answered in detail.

Some areas will be examined in greater depth and new topics will be introduced, as follows:

The office

The office as a centre of information analysis, decision-making and co-ordination; organisation and line charts; the place and responsibilities of the office supervisor or manager; deployment of staff.

The secretary

Personal relationships in the office; working as part of a team; office etiquette and reception duties; the business diary; external visits; travel and currency arrangements and itineraries; initiative; problem-solving.

Communications

The use of shorthand and audio systems for the dictation and transcription of communications; the drafting and writing of letters; memoranda, reports; correct forms of address; sources of reference; telephone technique; message-taking; the word processing centre — its function.

Meetings

Notice of meetings, preparation and circulation of agenda.

Post Office services

Business reply service, Freepost, Express services, Railex, special delivery; poste restante, cash on delivery, photo-telegraph services, Datel; cost-effective use of surface and airmail services; international calls and time zones.

Stationery and control of stock

Use of requisitions for stock; stationery cupboard and control; security; supervision of junior staff.

Accounting procedures

Petty cash (imprest); bank loans and overdrafts; bank reconciliation statements; bank clearing systems.

Storage of documents

Uses of different methods of filing; indexing; cross-reference, follow-up systems; centralised and departmental filing; microfilm and microfiche records; security.

Personnel department

Staff records, gradings, promotions, welfare, recruitment; job advertisements; confidentiality; job descriptions; job specifications.

Statistical/financial records

Extracting information; interpreting and representing material in suitable form, e.g. tables, graphs, charts.

Machinery and equipment
The place of the computer, microprocessor and word processor in the modern office; reasons for installation; possible effects on personnel.

Secretarial Practice — Advanced

The aim of this examination is to test the knowledge and aptitude of those candidates aspiring to posts in the secretarial field that carry an executive responsibility.

Time allowed — 3 hours

The paper will be in two parts:
Part I — in which there will be 10 objective questions all of which must be answered.
Part II — will consist of five questions from a total of seven.

In addition to the topics covered at the Secretarial Practice Intermediate stage, questions will be set on the following:

The management function
Different styles of management in the business structure — their purpose and how they work; the secretary as part of the management team.

Assisting management
Planning the smooth running of the office; dealing with clients; staff liaison at all levels; leadership and delegation; selection, induction and training of junior staff; decision-making; problem-solving; deductive and lateral thinking.

Office furniture and equipment
Design, layout and equipment of an office; understanding new technology and its place in the office and effect on personnel; benefits and problems of the various types of equipment and machinery, including computer, microprocessor, and data processor.

Communications
Communicating with individuals and groups; oral, written and mechanical methods — choosing the right one; writing letters, reports, memoranda, telegrams, advertisements; form design; interviewing techniques; job descriptions and specifications; expansion of notes into letter, report or summary form.

Meetings

Differences between formal and informal; procedures adopted before, during and after; conduct of meetings; documents and records; taking, writing and distributing minutes; action plans, terminology.

Industrial relations and employment law

Legislation affecting office workers; role of trade unions; role of management in consultation and negotiation; safety regulations and accident prevention.

Business and property finance

Basic principles of financial management; outline knowledge and simple interpretation of: long-term financial plans; budgets; management accounts; management forecasts; financial targets; cash flow and debtor/creditor information; knowledge of long-term and short-term freehold/leasehold premises; maintenance agreements and work services.

Secretarial Group Certificate
See below.

Higher-level Secretarial Group Certificate
Both these certificates are awarded to students who achieve passes at an appropriate level in a range of secretarial examinations, shorthand, typewriting, secretarial practice, English and one other subject (from a range of optional subjects). Full details of these examinations are provided in the *Handbook of Regulations and Syllabuses.*

23.4 Registration as a Pitman examinations centre

The principal, head teacher, area organiser, training officer or other responsible person of an educational establishment (from now on called the proposer) wishing to conduct Pitman examinations must first complete a proposal card obtainable from the Institute, giving details of the proposed centre. If the proposer does not wish to organise and arrange the examinations, the name and official position of an authorised deputy who is willing to undertake this responsibility should be submitted. The organising official, whether the proposer or not, will be referred to as the local examinations secretary.

Full details of the procedure and a proposal card may be obtained from the Examinations Director, Pitman Examinations Institute, Godalming, Surrey, GU7 1UU, England.

23.5 Specimen letters about examinations

SL23.1

PITMAN EXAMINATIONS INSTITUTE

GODALMING . SURREY GU7 1UU   **Telephone:** Godalming (STD Code 04868) 2348

Company Number 381335 England   Telegrams: Pitex Godalming

Examinations Director: G A Alexander MA Dip Ed

JB/ER/R
Your ref: JB/NB

2 March 19--

Mr J Bootah
Principal
Candeo Business College
290 Dharamtolla Street
BOMBAY 401 026
India

Dear Mr Bootah

Registration as a Centre for Pitman's Examinations

Thank you for returning the completed application forms in connection with
your request to register your College as a Pitman Examination Centre.

We have considered your application very carefully and are pleased to tell
you that it has been approved. I have pleasure therefore in enclosing the
official acceptance letter, together with a further copy of our Regulations
and Syllabuses, a Requisition Form and a Specimen Order Form for you to
purchase past examination papers. I should like to draw to your attention
Regulations 11 to 16 on pages 4 and 5 of the booklet, which give in detail
the full duties and responsibilities of the Invigilators at all examinations.
I cannot stress too strongly that these instructions must be carried out to
the letter, and any infringement will result in your registration becoming
void. I am sure you will appreciate the need to choose Invigilators of the
highest calibre who will not only do justice to your College, but also
uphold the good name of Pitman which is known world-wide.

I should like to wish you every success with your new venture; if at any
time you experience problems with your examinations please let me know.

Yours sincerely

F Rowbotham

Mrs J Rowbotham
EXAMINATIONS SECRETARY & REGISTRAR

Encs

Sir Isaac Pitman Ltd (Training Division of Pitman Ltd)
41 Southampton Place, London WC2B 3BW Registered Office

Fig. 23.1 Registration as an examinations centre

PITMAN EXAMINATIONS INSTITUTE

GODALMING . SURREY GU7 1UU   **Telephone:** Godalming (STD Code 04868) 2348

Company Number 381335 England   Telegrams: Pitex Godalming

Examinations Director: G A Alexander MA Dip Ed

GG/IP/3000/734

23 July 19--

The Examinations Secretary
Coulidge High Street
33 Middle Road
SINGAPORE 7

Dear Sir

Proposed New Invigilator

Thank you for your letter of 5 July and I was very sorry to learn that
Mr Kang Ngo Wing is no longer able to act as one of your Invigilators.

From the description you give of Mrs Kam Poh Song she would appear to be
absolutely the right kind of person to fill Mr Kang Ngo Wing's place, but
you will of course appreciate that she will have to complete the enclosed
Invigilators Form in order that we may assess her suitability for this
important position.

Whilst writing I should like to take the opportunity of reminding you that
your re-registration becomes due on 31 August next, and I am therefore taking
the liberty of enclosing with this letter the relevant documents for you to
complete and return.

Yours faithfully

G Gavin

G Gavin
ASSISTANT REGISTRAR

Encs

Sir Isaac Pitman Ltd (Training Division of Pitman Ltd)
41 Southampton Place, London WC2B 3BW Registered Office

Fig. 23.2 Registration of invigilators

PITMAN EXAMINATIONS INSTITUTE

GODALMING . SURREY GU7 1UU   **Telephone: Godalming (STD Code 04868)** 2348

Company Number 381335 England   Telegrams: Pitex Godalming

Examinations Director: G A Alexander MA Dip Ed

PJ/LLN/1556

30 March 19--

Mr J Bartlett
Goldthorpe Business College
135 London Road
BRIGHTON
Sussex
BN1 3BW

Dear Mr Bartlett

Elementary Typewriting Examination - 4 April

I enclose the 20 examination papers for the above date as requested by your Requisition, received only yesterday. I am sure you will appreciate the need to give at least three weeks' notice of your intention to hold such an examination, as stated in the Regulations. At this time of the year particularly when schools and colleges all over the world are sending in their Requisitions, it places a very heavy extra burden on our staff if they are asked to produce the papers at such short notice. However, in view of the special circumstances set out in your letter, the staff have very kindly made an extra effort to ensure that the papers arrive with you in good time for the examination. They all join me in wishing your students every success.

Yours sincerely

Penelope Jameson

Mrs Penelope Jameson
EXAMINATIONS OFFICER

Encs

Sir Isaac Pitman Ltd (Training Division of Pitman Ltd)
41 Southampton Place, London WC2B 3BW Registered Office

Fig. 23.3 A letter enclosing examination papers

PITMAN EXAMINATIONS INSTITUTE

GODALMING . SURREY GU7 1UU   **Telephone: Godalming (STD Code 04868)** 2348

Company Number 381335 England   Telegrams: Pitex Godalming

Examinations Director: G A Alexander MA Dip Ed

GAA/GH/PEI/4

15 July 19--

Mr J Burberry
Millhampton Comprehensive School
MILLHAMPTON
Hants
ML2 3BW

Dear Mr Burberry

Elementary Typewriting Examination - 14 July

Thank you for your letter of 14 July, and I have noted with interest your
remarks on the above examination which your students sat yesterday.

We are always very pleased to receive comments such as yours, as not only
does this help us to maintain an efficient examination service, but it
confirms us in our view that the examinations we offer are what teachers and
students alike are looking for. We aim to keep all our Elementary examinations as simple as possible, not only in their content but also in the
instructions which are given to candidates. At this stage we do not feel
that students should be struggling with the finer points of language, layout
or style, but should be showing how much progress they have made in their
initial lessons in the subject. Success at this stage gives them the
necessary confidence and motivation to carry on with their studies to the
Intermediate and Advanced levels.

I am very pleased that your students have fared so well in this your first
Pitman examination, and I am sure that with the expert guidance and help
your teachers are obviously giving, they will continue to do well.

Yours sincerely

G A Alexander
EXAMINATIONS DIRECTOR

Sir Isaac Pitman Ltd (Training Division of Pitman Ltd)
41 Southampton Place, London WC2B 3BW Registered Office

Fig. 23.4 A letter concerning the content of examinations

PITMAN EXAMINATIONS INSTITUTE

GODALMING . SURREY GU7 1UU **Telephone:** Godalming (STD Code 04868) 2348

Company Number 381335 England   Telegrams: Pitex Godalming

Examinations Director: G A Alexander   MA Dip Ed

JR/EW/CA 989

19 March 19--

Mrs E Robinson
Clandon Secretarial College
54 Ladywell Crescent
SALISBURY
Zimbabwe

Dear Mrs Robinson

Intermediate Book-Keeping Examination - Enock Zindasa Nyakudya

I enclose the result slips for the above examination, and in particular I would like to congratulate your student, Enock Zindasa Nyakudya, on the splendid result he has achieved.

The Examiner writes: "Please give my warmest congratulations to this student. In all my 15 years as an Examiner for the Institute I have never marked a script which was so well presented, thought out, and showed such a complete knowledge of the subject. He gained 100% of the marks."

Not only is your student to be congratulated, but his teacher also, and perhaps you would please convey to everyone concerned the pleasure we all feel at your student's success.

With best wishes.

Yours sincerely

Mrs J Rowbotham
EXAMINATIONS SECRETARY

Enc

Sir Isaac Pitman Ltd (Training Division of Pitman Ltd)
41 Southampton Place, London WC2B 3BW   Registered Office

Fig. 23.5 Congratulations on an exceptional result

PITMAN EXAMINATIONS INSTITUTE

GODALMING . SURREY GU7 1UU   **Telephone: Godalming (STD Code 04868)** 2348

Company Number 381335 England   Telegrams: Pitex Godalming

Examinations Director: G A Alexander MA Dip Ed

JR/EW

5 June 19--

Mrs E M Robinson
1 Larkswood Rise
STROUD
Glos
ST1 2LN

Dear Mrs Robinson

Thank you for your letter of 14 June enquiring about the possibility of
sitting for your 120 words per minute Shorthand Speed, and Advanced
Typewriting examinations.

I am pleased to give on the attached sheet the names and addresses of two
establishments near to your home which are Pitman registered centres, and I
suggest that you apply to the Examinations Secretaries direct to make
arrangements for you to sit the examinations as an external candidate.

You are right in thinking that the Civil Service accepts these Certificates
on the following basis:

Shorthand Speed Test   - Shorthand allowance
Typewriting Advanced Pass   - Trainee Typist
Typewriting Advanced First Class - Typist, Specialist Typist and Personal
                                   Secretary

May I wish you every success in your examinations.

Mrs J Rowbotham

Mrs J Rowbotham
EXAMINATIONS SECRETARY

Enc

Sir Isaac Pitman Ltd (Training Division of Pitman Ltd)
41 Southampton Place, London WC2B 3BW Registered Office

Fig. 23.6 A letter to a prospective external candidate

```
REG/24


Thank you for your interest in sitting Pitman examinations.  We would
inform you that these can be taken only at educational establishments
which are registered with us and we have no power to place external
candidates at any of these Centres.

The Centres given below have intimated that they may be willing to
accept external candidates.  Will you please contact the Examinations
Secretary at the Centre, sending a stamped addressed envelope, and ask
whether you can be accommodated for the Pitman examination you wish to
sit.  Dates and times of examinations are decided by the Centres which
are entirely responsible for making all the necessary arrangements.
In addition,you may make enquiries at any evening centre in your
locality, or at your local education office.

If you wish to sit shorthand and typewriting examinations, you may
find you can be accommodated at Pitman Central College, 154 Southampton
Row, London WC1 upon application to the Executive Principal there.


CENTRES THAT MAY ACCEPT EXTERNAL CANDIDATES

Centre Name:  Stroud College of Further Education
Address:      Cirencester Road
              STROUD
              Glos  ST2 5LY
_____

Centre Name:  The Lansdowne Secretarial College
Address:      41 Mead Road
              STROUD
              Glos  ST1 7RZ
```

23.6   Conclusions about examinations

The chief conclusion to be drawn from this chapter on examinations is that success in examinations can only be achieved by students who have given a reasonable degree of attention to their studies over a sufficiently lengthy time. Passes cannot be achieved by taking short cuts, cramming preparation into a few hectic weeks before the actual examination date. One needs time to assimilate and digest ideas, to acquire manual dexterity where necessary, and to prepare fully for the theoretical and practical tests to be undertaken.

Confidence in examinations comes from the knowledge that one has studied the syllabus in great detail, so that every aspect of it has been considered and investigated fully. This study has then been applied in practical and written work not once, or twice, but countless times. For such a student the day of the examination holds few terrors, for he/she has already anticipated all the likely questions and has thought seriously about every likely problem. The only embarrassment on the day will be which of the questions to answer, for they are all within the student's competence, all equally attractive and all offering the same prospect of success.

23.7 Questions about examinations in business studies

1 You are the principal of an evening institute in your own home town. You wish to register your institute as an examination centre for Pitman Examinations. Write to the Examinations Director, at the address given in section 23.4 above, asking for a proposal card, current handbook and specimen examination papers in the range of subjects offered by your institute.

2 Reply to the letter outlined in Question 1, from the Pitman Examinations Institute, expressing your willingness to consider the proposal when it is submitted, and referring to three enclosures: the proposal card, the current handbooks (two copies) and a selection of specimen examination papers. Refer in your answer to the necessity for strict control of all examination procedures, and absolute security for both examination question papers and worked scripts waiting to be dispatched to examiners.

3 You are a lecturer in a college of business studies and have recently submitted students for an examination in commerce. One of the questions appeared to be outside the terms of the syllabus, and none of your students has received any instruction on the matter concerned, which was about the law relating to multi-modal transport operators. Write a letter to the examination body expressing your concern at the difficulty of this question, and asking whether the examiner was justified in including it.

4 You have been notified, as the local examination secretary, by the Pitman Examinations Institute that one of your candidates has been awarded a First Class pass at Intermediate Level, with an exceptionally high mark of 98 per cent. You are to do the following things:

a Send a memo to the principal of your college notifying him of the result and suggesting it might be a suitable item for mention in the college news sheet, or in his annual report to the governors. Invent a suitable name for the successful candidate.

b Write a letter to the candidate's parents offering your congratulations to the student, and quoting the actual words used in the letter, which were:

> 'We would like to offer our hearty congratulations to this candidate on an outstanding result; one of the best papers in this subject ever submitted to the Institute.'

5 Write a letter as the chief examinations officer of the Motor Transport Technicians Association, 2785 High Street, Pontianak, Borneo to a student, L V Nagpur, 1284 Main Street, Kota Kinabalu, Borneo. He complains that his examination results do not conform either with the amount of work he put into preparation for the examinations or with the results of the monthly tests he did while his course was proceeding. Point out to him that the regulations make it quite clear that the Examining Board cannot enter into any correspondence on the results of the examinations, and a review of his papers has revealed that the examiner was quite right to fail him in three out of five subjects. Point out also that an initial failure on the part of young candidates is not at all uncommon, and if he works hard for a further year and re-sits in the next series he may well find that he is successful.

6 Write a letter in your capacity as examinations officer to the Institute of Personal Secretaries, to a student who complains that her certificates have been stolen from her wall during a burglary. Refer in your answer to a form you are enclosing for her to complete. This requires in particular that she obtains a certificate from her local police that the crime was in fact reported to them. If this is obtained you will issue a replacement set of certificates in six months' time if the certificates have not been recovered – but a charge of one unit of local currency will be made for each certificate issued.

7 Write as the newly appointed local examinations secretary of your college to the Institute of Hotel Managers, 2142 Seagrave Way, Kendal, Cumbria, to explain that due to the sudden death of your

predecessor the college's entries for the Institute's examinations were not posted as expected. The packet was in his car when he was involved in a collision and killed. The police did not appreciate its importance, and it was handed to the next-of-kin as personal property. Although the final date of entry has now passed, express your hopes that they will exercise this special dispensation in view of the unusual circumstances.

8 Reply to the letter in Question 7 expressing the Institute's willingness to overlook late entry in the circumstances, and expressing their condolences at the death of a colleague they have dealt with over many years.

Appendix: Glossary of terms

Acceptance: The act of the acceptor of a bill of exchange when signifying assent to the order made in the bill. By writing 'accepted' and signing the front of the bill (just the signature will also do) the acceptor agrees to honour the bill on the due date.

Acceptor: The person accepting a bill of exchange (see above).

Act of God: A concept in English law which relieves the common carrier of liability for losses suffered as a result of extraordinary events so unusual as to seem to be the result of a supernatural power. Thus to be struck by lightning, or a tidal wave, would be an Act of God.

Air waybill: A document made out in the carriage of goods by air, in at least three copies; one for the consignor, one for the carrier and one for the consignee. These days it may also be in electronic form — i.e. present in a computer system in a memory bank somewhere (see Montreal version, 1975, of the Warsaw Rules).

Appointment: The process of nominating someone as agent to act on your behalf.

Bill of exchange: A method of payment in both inland and foreign trade. A definition (which should be learned by heart) is given on page 173. The essence of the system is that the debtor will honour the bill on the due date, and dishonour is a serious matter, amounting to an act from which bankruptcy may follow.

Bill of lading: A document made out in the carriage of goods by sea. It has three functions. It is a receipt for the goods shipped; it is evidence of the terms of the contract of carriage; and it is a quasi-negotiable instrument (q.v.). This means it can be used to transfer ownership of the goods listed in it while they are still on the high seas. The one who holds the bill of lading can claim the goods from the master of the vessel at destination.

Block discounting: A process by which a finance company buys blocks of invoices (evidencing unpaid debts) from a supplier, paying a large proportion of their value at once. After collecting the debts the finance company deducts its charges and settles with the supplier for any outstanding balance. It enables the supplier to ease the cash-flow problems of the business.

Breach of warranty of authority: An agent should only act within the authority granted on appointment. If the agent exceeds this authority, and the principal refuses to ratify the unauthorised act, the disappointed party to the abortive contract may sue the agent for breach of warranty of authority, and secure damages for the disappointment suffered.

C and F (See CFR)

Carriage forward: A situation where goods are supplied on the understanding that the carriage charges will be paid by the buyer to the carrier on arrival at their destination.

Carriage paid: Goods are supplied at a price which includes delivery to the buyer's premises.

Cash with order: A method of payment requiring the buyer to pay the price when placing the order.

Certificate of incorporation: A certificate issued by the Registrar of Companies to signify that a company has been registered under the Companies Acts. It confers full legal status on the company, which may now own property, employ staff, supply goods and services, sue and be sued in the courts, etc.

CFR (cost and freight): One of the standard 'terms of trade'. The price charged to the foreign customer includes the cost of the goods, delivery to the ship or airport, loading costs and freight charges. Insurance costs are not included and must be paid by the buyer. (Under the old terminology of Incoterms this was coded as C & F, not CFR.)

CIF (cost, insurance freight): Another of the standard 'terms of trade'. The price charged to the customer includes the cost of the goods, loading charges, insurance and freight. The buyer must pay the charges for unloading at destination and onward delivery.

CIM: The Convention on International Merchandise, drawn up in 1914 and renewed from time to time, is about international carriage of goods by rail. The United Kingdom is not a party to the convention, but incorporates it into all railway documents contractually, so that all goods travelling on a CIM waybill are covered by the rules of the convention. It makes the railways liable for many things such as loss, damage, and delay. Before 1914 many railway companies excluded liability for such losses.

CMR: The Convention on Merchandise carried by Road Hauliers is a similar convention to the CIM (see above). Goods travel under a CMR waybill and the rules of the convention as to damage, loss, delay, legal action, etc. apply.

Code of practice: An agreed set of rules, usually drawn up by a trade association, often in agreement with the Director General of Fair Trading, to ensure that members of the association, in their dealings with the general public, behave in a proper manner.

Combined transport operator: A transport operator who uses multi-modal transport for international carriage (e.g. road-sea-road; road-sea-rail-road) to deliver goods door-to-door. By undertaking responsibility for the entire journey legal problems are reduced. The customer whose goods are lost or damaged is compensated by the CTO, who then discovers where the actual trouble arose and seeks indemnity from the carrier actually at fault.

Common carrier: A carrier who holds himself out as ready to carry for the public at large. He is liable in law, as an insurer of the goods, for every loss that occurs except the five common law exceptions. These are Act of God, Act of the Queen's enemies, inherent vice, fraud of the consignor, and fault of the consignor.

Condition: A provision in a contract stating terms that must be met.

Conditions of carriage: Most carriers by road exempt themselves from liability under the 'Standard Conditions of Carriage' of the Road Haulage Association.

Confirmed credit: A sum of money (the credit) has been made available in his own home country by an importer of goods. A bank in the exporter's country (the correspondent bank) notifies the exporter of this in a letter of credit, and undertakes to pay the full amount due on receipt of documents (named in the letter of credit) proving that the goods have been shipped or forwarded by air and in compliance with any other terms mentioned in the letter of credit. The bank thus confirms the credit, which is payable in full on delivery of the documents to the bank.

Confirming house: An export house which buys goods for foreign customers, guaranteeing payment to the exporter at once, and thus 'confirming' that the order is from a reputable customer.

Contract: A legally binding agreement between two persons, or more than two persons, which confers rights upon each party in return for some supply of goods, payment of money, act of service to the other party, or perhaps for some forbearance shown by him/her.

Correspondent bank: See **Confirmed credit,** above.

Creditor: One who is owed money by a debtor.

Credit reference agency: An agency which keeps records on those who borrow money, or buy good on hire purchase, which it is prepared to reveal to businessmen who consult it, on payment of a small fee. A potential borrower is now entitled to know whose records have prevented him/her from borrowing money, and to correct the records if they are incorrect in any particular.

CTO: See **Combined transport operator.**

D/A: See **Documents against acceptance.**

D/P: See **Documents against payment.**

DDP: Delivered duty paid (see **Franco domicile**).

Del credere (in the belief that): A name given to the extra commission earned by an agent who agrees to bear the risk of bad debts. The agent has sold to the customer *in the belief that* the customer is solvent, and will pay for the goods in due course. In return for his extra commission the agent will bear the loss if his belief that the customer is solvent proves to be ill-founded.

Documents against acceptance: A system of payment for goods whereby documents of title to goods (bills of lading) are released to the consignee when he/she accepts a bill of exchange, so that the goods may be claimed from the ship on arrival at destination.

Documents against payment: Similar to the system mentioned above, but this time the consignee must pay for the goods before the bills of lading are released.

Drawee: The person drawn upon in a bill of exchange (the debtor) who is ordered to pay a sum of money on demand, or on a given, or determinable, future date.

Drawer: The person who writes out (draws) the bill of exchange (the creditor). The drawer calls upon the drawee (see above) to pay the sum due on demand, or at some fixed, or determinable, future date.

Endorsement: Written instructions, including a signature on the back of a cheque or other negotiable instrument to transfer the document to another person.

Exclusionary clause: Any clause inserted in a contract which seeks to exclude liability on the part of one party to the contract for any breach of a statutory duty, or to evade compliance with the common law.

Export house: A commercial house which specialises in making purchases for foreign customers and in exporting the goods thus obtained. It may 'confirm' the order, which means it undertakes to pay for the goods, and collect the debt from the foreign customer in its own name.

FAS (free alongside ship): One of the standard 'terms of trade'. The seller must deliver the goods to the quayside. The charges for hoisting the goods over the ship's rail, and the freight and insurance costs, are payable by the buyer.

FOB (free on board): One of the standard 'terms of trade', as defined by the International Chamber of Commerce. The seller undertakes to deliver the goods over the ship's rail free of charge. The freight and insurance charges and all other expenses after this point are payable by the buyer.

Franco domicile: One of the (now obsolete) official 'terms of trade' defined by the International Chamber of Commerce). The seller undertakes to deliver the goods free (*franco*) to the buyer's premises, wherever they may be. (Under the Incoterms 1980 nomenclature this has been renamed **DDP** – delivered duty paid.)

Frustration: The failure of a contract because of some major event which prevents fulfilment. Frequently a government declares contracts of certain kinds to be illegal, and thus frustrates them. A ship which has been chartered may sink on its way to load cargo, and the contract clearly cannot be fulfilled, etc.

Holder in due course: A holder in due course is a person who takes a bill of exchange before it is overdue, in good faith, for value, without knowledge of any previous dishonour and without notice of any defect of title of the person who negotiated it to him/her. Such a holder has the right to sue on the bill in his/her own name, and to hold it free of any defect in the title of previous holders, and to require payment of it by anyone who is a party to the bill.

Inherent vice: Any defect in goods which is a natural consequence of their nature, and cannot be blamed on a carrier. Thus fruit tends to rot, powders tend to blow away, cattle can be violent at times, etc. Inherent vice is one of the five common law exceptions for which a carrier is excused liability.

Instalment credit: A system of credit whereby a loan to purchase goods is repaid in regular instalments, covering both the original capital sum and interest.

Insurable interest: The interest that an insured person has in the thing that is insured. I may insure my own life, and property, but usually I may not insure any other person's life or property unless I can show that I shall suffer a loss if he/she dies, or his/her property is lost or damaged.

Invoice: A business document which is made out whenever one party sells goods or supplies services to another. It is written evidence of a contract, and may be produced as evidence in the courts.

Irrevocable credit: A credit established by an importer with a bank which places a sum of money at the disposal of an exporter so long as he/she performs exactly what is required in the 'letter of credit' which notifies the importer's requirements. The word 'irrevocable' means that the credit cannot be withdrawn without the exporter's consent.

Laydays: The days agreed between a charterer and a shipowner when a ship must lie alongside a wharf for the purpose of loading or discharge of cargo. If the laydays are exceeded a payment called **demurrage** may become payable, to compensate the shipowner for the fact that the ship is out of action. Where no laydays are specified the goods must be loaded or unloaded in a reasonable time.

Liquidated damages: In many contracts where failure to complete a process or supply goods on time is likely to cause serious loss to the customer, it is usual to insert a 'liquidated damages' clause. Liquidated damages means 'money damages'. It is an attempt to place a value upon the likely damages which will follow from breach of contract for each day's delay. This sum is payable each day until completion. However, if the sum is not a true estimate of the loss, but is much larger (put in to frighten the supplier) it is said to be a penalty clause, and is not valid in law. Liquidated damages must be a reasonable estimate of the loss that will follow from the breach of contract.

Management by exceptions: A system of control whereby management sets certain limits on performance, and results achieved within these limits are not subject to investigation. Management only needs to investigate the exceptional results, either to discover why they are so bad or to see what can be learned from very good results.

Management feedback: A control system built into any business whereby management is made aware of results achieved. The results may be fed back into the system at various levels, for example to influence immediate output (failure of components to pass inspection by the inspection department), or to redesign or replan, or at the very highest level to enable top management to redirect the efforts of the company or firm in a new direction.

Multi-modal transport: A system whereby goods are moved by the most economical transport system available from door to door. Thus road-sea-road, road-barge-road, rail-barge-road systems are in use. Easy transfer from one mode to another is essential, and containerisation of cargo is very helpful in this respect.

Negotiable instrument: Any document which may be passed from one person to another either by mere delivery, or by endorsement and delivery which transfers a perfect title of ownership to the one taking it in good faith and for value, even though the transferer had no right to it. It transfers a better title to it than the giver of it had. Examples are banknotes, bills of exchange, promissory notes, certificates of deposit, etc.

Notary public: A lawyer appointed to note and protest bills of exchange and thus formally bear witness to the failure of one party to honour these documents.

Noting: The act of noting on a bill of exchange the failure of a party to accept the bill on presentation for acceptance, or to pay the bill on presentation for payment on the due date.

Offer: A proposal by one potential party to a contract which is susceptible of acceptance by the other potential party to make a binding contract between them.

Power of attorney: A special type of agent. When given power of attorney an agent may sign legal deeds on behalf of his principal — a power not conferred on ordinary agents.

Premium: A sum payable in advance on an insurance policy so that cover can commence. It is a contribution to the pool from which compensation will be provided. The word is used in several other ways, and a dictionary should be consulted for these.

Private carrier: A carrier who does not hold himself out as willing to carry for the public at large, but only carries under a private contract with those who wish goods to be moved.

Progress-chaser: An individual employed to prevent bottlenecks in production, and distribution, by ensuring that components and materials are available to complete particular orders and that delays in transfers from department to department do not occur.

Proposal form: A standard form to be completed by a person wishing to be insured, so that the insurer knows the full facts needed to assess a fair premium. It must be completed with the utmost good faith.

Protest: A process applied to foreign bills which are dishonoured by non-acceptance or non-payment. The notary public makes out an official document, the protest, including a copy of the bill, and formally declares that it has been dishonoured. The protest may then be used as evidence in an action to recover the money.

Quasi-negotiable instrument: The bill of lading is usually called a quasi-negotiable instrument. The word quasi (*kwah-zee*) is Italian for 'almost'. While a bill of lading can be assigned to a third party by endorsement it is not fully negotiable since it does not pass a better title to it than the giver of it has, but only the same title as the giver of it has. Thus a person taking it in good faith for value is liable to lose it if the true owner proves title, and the transferor's title is shown to be defective.

Recovery agent: A specialist who attempts to recover from the one liable for the damage, loss or delay any sums paid by an insurer to the insured.

Remittance advice note: A document, frequently a copy of a statement, or a tear-off portion of a statement, which the debtor may use to accompany the remittance sent to the creditor.

Revocation of agency: The act of withdrawing from the agent the power conferred upon him earlier.

Short-form bill of lading: A simplified bill of lading which does not contain the detailed terms of the contract of carriage but only refers to a standard set of conditions of carriage available on request. It combines a simplified procedure for the carrier with safeguards to the consignor and owner of the goods, to the mutual advantage of all parties.

Statement: A document sent out at regular intervals, or when requested by the customer, to show the state of his/her account with a bank or a supplier.

Subsequent ratification: The consent of a principal to an agent's unauthorised act which brings that particular act within the agent's authority. It makes a valid contract between the principal and the other party with whom the agent has been negotiating.

Trade association: An organisation formed to represent the members of a particular trade, and act as a pressure group on their behalf.

Uberrima fides: The Latin for 'utmost good faith' (see below).

Uniform Rules for Collections: A body of rules drawn up by the International Chamber of Commerce for controlling the collection of money by means of cheques, bills of exchange and other commercial documents.

Utmost good faith: One of the principles of insurance: the insured must show the utmost good faith in providing the information on which risk is to be assessed and premiums calculated.

Valuable consideration: An essential element in a contract. It is taken for granted that a contract must be beneficial to both parties, and some valuable thing or some worthwhile service must pass between them. Money payment is a common form of valuable consideration.

Word processing: A recent development in communication equipment which offers a variety of automatic devices to the secretary, such as automatic centring, automatic justification of the right-hand margin, correction of errors and subsequent realignment of text.

Index